A Mother's Promise

Also by Kate Thompson

A Spoonful of Sugar
Tuppence for Paper & String
Aprons and Silver Spoons
The Refuge
Secrets of the Singer Girls
Secrets of the Sewing Bee
The Wedding Girls
The Allotment Girls
The Stepney Doorstep Society
Secrets of the Homefront Girls
Secrets of the Lavender Girls
The Little Wartime Library
The Wartime Book Club

Renee Salt, BEM, is a 95-year-old Holocaust survivor and educator. Born Rywka Ruchla Berkowicz in Poland in 1929, she was just ten years old when the Second World War brought horror to her doorstep. Having survived Auschwitz-Birkenau, Renee was liberated from Bergen-Belsen in 1945. After moving to Paris, Renee met her husband, Charles, a military policeman in the British Army, and part of the liberating forces at Bergen-Belsen. They married in 1949 and lived in north London, having two children and five grandchildren.

Kate Thompson is a journalist and bestselling writer. As well as being passionate about capturing lost voices and untold social histories, Kate's also a library campaigner. Her 100 libraries project celebrates the richness and complexity of librarians' work and the vital role of libraries in our communities. Alongside her journalism and writing, Kate is also a podcaster and recently launched her own podcast, *From the Library with Love*.

You can find Kate at her website: www.katethompsonmedia.co.uk, on Facebook @KateThompsonAuthor, on X @katethompson380 and on Instagram @katethompsonauthor.

A Mother's Promise

My true story of surviving Auschwitz and the horrors of the Holocaust

RENEE SALT

WITH KATE THOMPSON

SEVEN DIALS

First published in Great Britain in 2025 by Seven Dials,
an imprint of The Orion Publishing Group Ltd
Carmelite House, 50 Victoria Embankment
London EC4Y 0DZ

An Hachette UK Company

The authorised representative in the EEA is Hachette Ireland,
8 Castlecourt Centre, Dublin 15, D15 XTP3, Ireland (email: info@hbgi.ie)

1 3 5 7 9 10 8 6 4 2

Copyright © Renee Salt and Kate Thompson 2025

The moral right of Renee Salt and Kate Thompson to be identified as the authors of this work has been asserted in accordance with the Copyright, Designs and Patents Act of 1988.

All rights reserved. No part of this publication may be reproduced, stored in a retrieval system, or transmitted in any form or by any means, electronic, mechanical, photocopying, recording, or otherwise, without the prior permission of both the copyright owner and the above publisher of this book.

A CIP catalogue record for this book is
available from the British Library.

ISBN (Hardback) 978 1 3996 2540 1
ISBN (Export Trade Paperback) 978 1 3996 2541 8
ISBN (Ebook) 978 1 3996 2543 2
ISBN (Audio) 978 1 3996 2544 9

Printed in Great Britain by Clays Ltd, Elcograf S.p.A

www.orionbooks.co.uk

To my lost family

Contents

Author's Note ... xi

Chapter One: Home ... 1

Chapter Two: The Beginning ... 13

Chapter Three: Gallows and Prayers ... 23

Chapter Four: Stenia ... 35

Chapter Five: Łódź ... 49

Chapter Six: Hunger ... 63

Chapter Seven: Auschwitz-Birkenau ... 77

Chapter Eight: Lost Hope ... 89

Chapter Nine: Germany ... 102

Chapter Ten: Mama ... 111

Chapter Eleven: Bergen-Belsen ... 118

Chapter Twelve: Liberation ... 127

Chapter Thirteen: Do Not Cry When I Die ... 140

Chapter Fourteen: Learning to Live ... 153

Chapter Fifteen: Paris ... 163

Chapter Sixteen: Charles	174
Chapter Seventeen: Surviving	185
Chapter Eighteen: New Beginnings	193
Chapter Nineteen: Revisiting the Past	203
Chapter Twenty: Testimony	213
Chapter Twenty-One: Laying the Ghosts to Rest	224
Chapter Twenty-Two: Now	231
Epilogue: Answers	239
In Search of Renee's Past by Kate Thompson	249
The Archive of Lost Lives	267
Acknowledgements	271
Sources and Bibliography	276
Picture Credits	289

Author's Note

My name is Renee Salt. I am ninety-five years old, at the time of writing, and I am a witness to history. I am a survivor of the Holocaust and this book is my attempt to make sense of a story which, at times, I can scarcely believe happened to me. But it did.

I have relived it all with the help of author and journalist Kate Thompson, who traced my footsteps: first to Poland, and then to Germany and on to London. There are times when the past is vividly bright and clear for me, almost as if events happened yesterday, instead of eighty years ago. Sometimes, I close my eyes and I see everything so clearly. It plays in my mind like a film.

Trauma is complicated, though, and Kate has stepped in to help me find out the parts of my story I don't know so well and commit them to the page. She has found out things that I, as a ten-year-old prisoner of the Nazis, could never have known. I was a child at the time and couldn't have been aware of everything going on around me. Our words flow around each other to create my story in full, Kate's historical research adding to the telling of my very personal story.

Indulge an old woman as I share my story. Some of the pages that follow are drenched in horror, but, every so often, a little light of hope and humanity shines out. There is love, too, believe me, so much love.

This book is timed to come out eighty years on from my liberation from Bergen-Belsen, a place that even in your worst nightmares you could never imagine. On this significant anniversary of the liberation of the Third Reich's camps, we should learn to live in peace. I think the world would be a better place.

Renee Salt
November 2024

The last act of genocide is always denial and silence. For the witnesses to have the final word, inscribed in history and memory, is to overcome the attempt to silence truth.

> Stephen Smith, co-founder of the National Holocaust Centre & Museum

Learning about Auschwitz and the Holocaust became a challenge for many. But with the help of survivors like Renee Salt, and her story, everything that happened over eighty years ago is so close and personal. This publication will be part of the legacy so graciously left for the next generation to come.

> Dr Teresa Wontor-Cichy, historian at the Research Center of Auschwitz-Birkenau Memorial and Museum

Chapter One

Home

I was born Rywka Ruchla Berkowicz on 8 August 1929, in a city in the middle of Poland called Zduńska Wola. Growing up in Poland, I was known as Renia (only many years later did I become known as Renee). And what a happy childhood it was.

April 1939

Steam. Chatter. Fragrant smells of roasting chicken and bitter herbs. Every so often the kitchen door would open, releasing its secrets. The preparations for Passover (Pesach) had begun and, to the Berkowicz family, like all religious Jewish families, it was a time of glorious celebration. As one of three major festivals in the Jewish calendar, Passover symbolised their liberation from slavery. For Renia, it's a perfect, untainted memory.

Pesach was my favourite holiday. All my family would gather at my maternal grandmother and grandfather's house, or Bubbe and Zayde's, as we called them. They lived in a beautiful, historic city not far from ours called Kalisz.

My mother, Sala (Sura Bajla), her younger sister, my Auntie Gitel, and Bubbe would begin by cleaning and scrubbing every corner of the house, replacing all the cutlery, crockery, pots and pans with others used only during these eight days of the year, and get rid of any food that contained leaven such as bread, pasta, cakes or biscuits.

For Renia and her family, it was a timely metaphor, a call to remove the parts of themselves that might become overly important, to remember humility, love and the worth of everyone else. So, her mother and bubbe bought matzah to remind themselves that when their ancestors left Egypt, they had no time to allow their bread to rise.

My family observed the Seder, eating symbolic foods to relive the experience of liberation from Egypt. Charoset, a sweet mixture of apples, dates, nuts and wine, stands for the mortar the slaves used to build the Egyptian pharaohs' buildings. Maror, a bitter herb like horseradish, represents the bitterness of slavery. Karpas, usually parsley, is dipped twice in salt water to remind us of the tears shed during our years as slaves in Egypt.

On the first and second evening, the whole family sat around the table and retold the story of our escape from slavery to freedom. The adults stayed up until late talking and my little sister Stenia and I would beg to stay up too, until our eyes were too heavy to stay open. What a time that was. Pesach was family, it was love, it was togetherness.

My father, Szaja, (sometimes spelt Schaja) was one of eight children and my mother was one of four. There was a non-stop flow of aunts and uncles, cousins and two sets of grandparents coming and going. We spent every Jewish holiday and festival together, as well as the long summer months. Bubbe and I were very close. I loved her so much. She was incredibly elegant and wore beautiful tailored coats and, like a lot of married orthodox women, a sheitel (wig).

HOME

Whenever we got together, the women cooked all the time. How those women could cook! They were the best cooks in the whole world. To me, my bubbe's yeast cake, rich and buttery, was the best in all of Poland. She would cut me off a big slice whenever I stayed with her. A stream of beautiful food cooked with love poured out of her kitchen. Beetroot borscht, dill pickles, pickled herring and rye bread. It was her puddings and desserts I loved the best, though. Lokshen kugel, poppy seed cake, marinated melon and light-as-air sponge cake always served with a little glass of cherry juice.

Food was more than fuel to these women. It was family, symbolism and nostalgia, an expression of love. In Bubbe's kitchen, there was always a jam pot to lick or a pudding basin to scrape.

Renia longed to learn the secrets of this kitchen, watching intently as her mother's long, graceful fingers kneaded dough for challah bread for Shabbos. She was, her mother felt, too young to learn to cook, at only ten. Education, prayers and play should occupy her time. There was plenty of time to become familiar with the stove. Besides, her parents had greater ambitions for her beyond being a *balabusta*, a good homemaker.

My father was Chief Accountant for Rosen-Wiślicki, one of the largest textile firms in Europe, its grand offices and factory taking up a whole street over the road from our home. Over 600 people worked there. There were floors filled with spinning workshops and drying rooms, and even its own shtiebel, a small synagogue. To me, it seemed like a very important place, its red-brick chimney soaring over the city rooftops.

Mama and Tatuś (Polish for Daddy) were modern orthodox, speaking Yiddish in the home but Polish outside. They were cultured people, interested in world politics, history and literature.

Tatuś had lots of books in French and English. He had set his sights for us not on marriage when we finished school, but further education in Paris. He wanted his girls to go on to get good jobs. He set great store on the value of education as a means of a better life.

Opposite our block of flats, there was a small school which taught Jewish boys carpentry skills. Tatuś would take me over there. I loved to watch them carve the wood, creating things, and the lovely scent of wood shavings.

Tatuś was well regarded, a man of influence and status. People would bow their heads to him in the street or knock on our door and ask for work in the factory.

And what of Mama? Mama was an elegant, well-dressed lady. I close my eyes and I can see her now. Lovely skin. Beautiful thick, dark hair. She was my whole life. She was such a loving, kind mother. Tatuś was the strict one, but my mama was more indulgent and there would be lots of hugs and kisses. She would sit and read with me and my sister, or take us for walks in the park to play with other children.

Like nearby Łódź, where Renia's paternal grandparents lived, Zduńska Wola, situated in the broad, low-lying plains of central Poland, was one of the largest cloth, linen and cotton weaving centres in Poland between the wars, with a population of over 27,000. Most of the cobbled streets that spooled out like thread from their home at 42 Piłsudskiego Street were involved in the textile trade. Clustered around the factories were hundreds of smaller workshops crammed with cobblers, weavers, yarn merchants and tailors.

It wasn't one of the famed, historic cities of Polish Jewry like Kraków or Warsaw but for the approximately 9,300 Jews who lived there, who were hard-working, prosperous people, it was a spiritual place with a big beating heart. The remaining inhabitants were Poles and ethnic Germans. Yiddish, Polish and German were all spoken on the streets.

My parents were one of the most respected Jewish families in Zduńska Wola – elegant, cultured people.

On Tuesday and Friday mornings, a peasant woman came from the villages nearby with freshly churned cream, big blocks of crumbly white cheese, and geese and chickens, still alive, which Mama would take to the shochet, a man officially certified as competent to slaughter cattle and poultry in the manner set out by Jewish law.

On Friday, before dark, the table was laid with our best white linen tablecloth. The apartment was spotlessly clean, the silver candlesticks polished until they gleamed.

Mama lit the white Sabbath candles before sunset, then Tatuś would say the special Kiddush prayer, drink from the silver cup of kosher wine and then pass the cup around the table for the family to share.

Mama then served the Shabbat feast she'd prepared the previous day, and on Friday morning. Poached gefilte fish first, making sure to serve my father the head of the fish, then chicken soup with matzo balls, followed by chicken or duck with roasted potatoes or vegetables. I was a picky eater so I used to hide little pieces of food on a ledge that ran under the table. How I wish I'd known then how precious food is. How, in the years to follow, I would torture myself with memories of that hidden food.

After dinner, I loved strolling with my parents, holding Mama's hand. What a time. So many sights and sounds – people stopping to chat in Yiddish, horses clopping over the cobbles and pulling carts known as dorożki.

Renia was a Zduńska Woler. It was more than a city; it was an identity, and to take a stroll with Renia and her family through the pretty cobbled streets after dinner on the Sabbath is to glimpse a bygone world.

Sala, always elegantly dressed, turned heads in a powder-blue dress made of the finest wool, cinched in at her slim waist, matching gloves, silk stockings, high-heeled shoes and a fashionable little hat, perched just so. Szaja, in a tailored suit and natty trilby, matched his wife in the sartorial stakes. They might have stepped straight off the silver screen.

Renia's mother and father

HOME

Renia and her little sister Stenia, younger by two years, walked behind in royal-blue velvet dresses embroidered at the collars with little bees.

There were few cars on the road and electricity only came in the early 1930s, shortly after Renia's birth. Children played out on the streets, running hoops or playing hopscotch. On Shabbat, the air was thick with the smell of cholent, a rich stew cooked at the Jewish bakers and eaten on the Sabbath.

If we were lucky, on a Sunday, Mama would take us to watch a picture starring our favourite actresses, Deanna Durbin or Shirley Temple, at one of the town's two picture houses. That reminds me of the only row I had with Stenia, when I was nine years old, such a silly row. In those days, they sold little bars of chocolate for children, with pictures of Shirley Temple on the wrapper. Both Stenia and I wanted the wrapper and as I grabbed it, I accidentally scratched her on the cheek! Poor little thing.

Sometimes, we went to the park, which had a beautiful lake with rowing boats and ducks. School was something to endure. Stenia was so clever, brilliant even, but learning didn't come so naturally to me. I always felt behind, though I did enjoy geography and maths. We went to the only Jewish school in Zduńska Wola. The only thing I really liked was the uniform, a smart black dress with detachable white collars and cuffs, which my mother changed every day so that they were always snowy white. 'My daughters aren't going to school with dirty nails, hair or ears,' Mama always used to say.

Like so many women, she was a house-proud balabusta, *always polishing, peeling, kneading or baking. Whenever I got home from school, Mama was waiting.*

Mama was the centre of everything.

At the end of our street was an orchard with apple trees where

I loved to play. When I was ten, I remember reading a book that everybody seemed to be reading, Gone with the Wind. *At that age, I dare say, I was probably too young for it. It took me a long while to read each chapter, but I loved reading books. I've always loved stories and being transported into imaginary worlds.*

Life was very smooth then, and I thought that it was always going to be like that.

Within Renia's world, everything had a place, and life played out with a comforting, familiar rhythm. It was a time of innocence, as timeless as the 600-year-old tree that grew in the park.

Until it wasn't.

Sala and Szaja had done a good job protecting their daughters from the hatred and antisemitism spreading like gangrene through the guts of Europe. Were it not for local boys, whose minds were conditioned to hate, it might have passed Renia by altogether at this time.

When I came out of school, there were local boys who used to demand money and frighten us. I had to give them a few groszy, *which was small money, and which I had to have ready for them. I was scared that they would beat me up if I didn't give it to them. They had such nasty, spiteful tongues. It wasn't just me. All Jewish children were targeted, but we got used to it.*

Other than their cruel taunts, Renia was oblivious to the dark clouds brewing on the horizon. Since Hitler had become chancellor of Germany in 1933, a barrage of vicious antisemitic propaganda had begun, echoed in Poland by the Endecja (Polish right-wing National Democratic Movement) spreading poison and hatred into the once-harmonious city.

HOME

An aerial photograph of Zduńska Wola, believed to have been taken by the Germans after the invasion of the city, in September 1939

Jews, Poles and ethnic Germans had integrated well in Zduńska Wola and by and large had lived peaceably together until Hitler's rise to power. By 1935, that changed.

One spring day, two weeks before Passover and Easter, three eight-year-old Christian boys went missing. They were last seen playing in sand dunes at the edge of a beautiful pine forest near the city. Wild rumours soon started to fly. *They had been kidnapped by Roma people. They had been killed by Jewish people, sacrificed for Passover.*

The National Democrats' newspaper, *Orędownik,* stirred unrest and blamed the Jewish community, calling for a boycott of Jewish stores and for limiting Jewish access to trades, professions and universities. Tensions reached fever pitch. The Jewish community feared a pogrom.

In January 1936, the truth was revealed. The dunes had collapsed on the three boys while they were digging tunnels in the sand and suffocated them. Overshadowed by events that followed, it symbolised the start of change in Renia's life.

After that incident, many in Zduńska Wola saw darkness ahead. But few could have imagined how unspeakably tragic that future would be. Some managed to leave Poland, travelling over the border to Russia, or emigrating to the United States, Palestine and Great Britain if they had money, family connections or influence.

Most people, though, went about their business, hoping and praying for the best.

In August 1939, we went on holiday with Bubbe and Zayde. Each year, we all went away together for the month of August to escape the hot Polish summers. They would rent a villa outside Kalisz on the edge of a deep forest, where the air was so clean you could drink it. After the smoky air of Zduńska Wola, everything smelt so fresh. I looked forward to these holidays all year round. Tatuś always joined us for two weeks at the end of summer and then we all went home together.

Mama, Bubbe and my Auntie Gitel, who had just married and had a little baby boy called Rywus, would take their deckchairs into the forest and play cards or backgammon. Stenia and I took baskets and picked wild blueberries, raspberries, herbs and mushrooms. We played games of hide and seek and dominoes, or sat in the shade of a tree and read books. Apart from Pesach, these holidays were the happiest times of my life. No school, just the chance to feel free, play in the forest and be a child with no cares or worries.

Stenia and I enjoyed each other's company greatly. We weren't just sisters; we were best friends. She was the other half of me.

HOME

Stenia, around six years old

Cushioned in that cool and fragrant forest, Renia could almost imagine that the fear was not real, that there weren't conversations that trailed off when she walked near the adults. Oh, they tried very hard to keep it from her, Bubbe and Zayde, her mama and tatuś, but Renia was observant. *War.* A whispered word that came laced with a dark edge of fear.

The word 'Hitler' hung in the late summer air that year like a ripe odour, frightening Renia and silencing the once garrulous adults. What she didn't wholly understand, she felt. And she felt that war must be a very bad thing indeed to steal smiles off her mother's face.

It was a Friday evening in August 1939, at the end of the holiday. Tatuś had joined us by then. Mama, Tatuś and her two younger brothers, Szachna and Szlomi, went out for a stroll after Friday night dinner. It was a lovely warm evening. Stenia and I stayed home with Bubbe and Zayde.

While out strolling, they were all beaten up by a gang of young men. Poor Mama got it the worst. Her back and shoulders were covered in bruises. They didn't know who these men were, but it was clear they were attacked because they were Jewish.

Bubbe had to put cold compresses on her injuries all night long. She was in pain. I was so terribly frightened for her. Everyone was so upset and scared. We knew something bad was going to happen, but we just couldn't imagine what lay ahead.

That night, Renia buried her face in her mother's thick, perfumed hair and hugged her tight, fearful, but unable to articulate exactly what she feared. A few days later, the Berkowicz family returned to Zduńska Wola and the long summer holidays came to an abrupt end. There would be no more *Gone with the Wind*, no more of Bubbe's yeast cakes, no more Passover celebrations.

On the cusp of war, real life was about to snatch Renia from her quiet, ordered childhood.

Chapter Two

The Beginning

As soon as they got home from holiday on Thursday, 31 August 1939, Sala, still bruised and tender, urgently started buying provisions.

Mama bought extra food and stocked up the cellar with enough coal to last for a war. My parents hoped we would have enough for as long as the war might last, not knowing it would last for nearly six years.
   That evening, a lorry load of material turned up at our home. Zayde owned a textile business in Kalisz and he started sending out all his material to different family members for safekeeping. I can see it all now, rolls of material stacked up to the ceiling. We could hardly get in through the front door. Then, we waited . . .

The next morning, Friday, 1 September 1939, while Renia's mother was polishing her silver candlesticks and preparing for Shabbos, German warplanes and tanks invaded Poland.

It happened so quickly. No one could believe it. The bombs, the bombs, the bombs. We all ran outside to shelter under the trees in the apple orchard at the end of the courtyard, along with other families from our street. The air was filled with the deafening sound of explosions and wave after wave of German planes flying so low, I could see the outline of the pilot. We all huddled together in the orchard, trembling and crying. Apple trees didn't offer any protection from the bombs, but where else could we go?

The bombing seemed to last a long time. All weekend long, they were throwing bombs. On Sunday, 3 September 1939, as Great Britain declared war on Nazi Germany, the factory where my father worked was destroyed by a bomb. You could see the flames billowing up into the blue sky. Just like that, no more factory, no more work for my father. It's all a terrifying blur. There was smoke and flames, the sounds of people crying. To a ten-year-old child, it was very frightening.

As soon as there was a break in the bombing, we fled Zduńska Wola, with only what we had on our backs and a little food and water. I don't really know why we fled, other than my father thought maybe we would be safer with his parents in Łódź, over 50 kilometres away.

But as Szaja was about to find out, nowhere in Poland was safe. Hitler's *Blitzkrieg* offensive was launched with astonishing speed and ferocity.

Nazi Germany possessed overwhelming military superiority over Poland. Germany launched the unprovoked attack at dawn on 1 September 1939, with an advance force consisting of more than 2,000 tanks, supported by nearly 900 bombers and over 400 fighter planes.

The world watched as Poland burnt. Infernos raged. Museums, libraries, ancient buildings, synagogues, churches and thousands of years of culture burnt to the ground.

Villages, towns and cities like Zduńska Wola were deliberately bombed to create a fleeing mass of terror-stricken civilians. There was little military significance to these attacks. To the Germans, it was a show of power and dominance, as well as a chance to weaken civilian morale.

Roads and fields were jammed with people carrying bundles. Children cried. Dogs howled. And over it all, the roar of German Heinkel and Dornier bombers and the screaming howl of Ju 87 Stuka dive-bombers.

It was chaos. Many people from Zduńska Wola left too, along with others from surrounding towns and villages, and as we began our long trek we were soon joined by others. Columns of men, women and children, with bundles of bedding and clothes tied to their backs, many of them bewildered and sobbing. Everyone thought that we would be safer in Łódź, because it was a larger city.

We stuck to the small country lanes and fields and by night we slept in stables. By first light we were on the move again. We survived on the rye bread and cheese and whatever else Mama had brought for us to eat on the journey. We drank water and milk provided by the farmers.

For three days, we trudged through the countryside. Everywhere was so silent. Everybody was hiding inside their homes, waiting to see what would happen. Stenia was only eight years old, but she was very brave, holding on to my hand and not crying or moaning.

By the time they reached the home of Renia's paternal grandparents, Chaim Wolf and Brana Berkowicz, the Germans were close behind. Poland's second largest city, the industrial Łódź, was officially occupied on 8 September 1939. Escape from the Nazi regime was seemingly impossible.

The following morning, the sun rose over the defeated city. German tanks rumbled down the streets and Nazi flags festooned the buildings. Łódź's smartest hotel, the Grand Hotel, was bedecked with garlands of flowers. Some 60,000 German nationals had lived in Łódź pre-war and some, feeling safe to do so, took to the streets to greet the invaders with happy cries of *Heil Hitler*.

I don't remember much about that time. We stayed with my grandparents for about a week and my parents kept me inside while they tried to work out what to do.

Hidden inside her grandparents' home at 30 Zakątna Street in Łódź, Renia was spared the sight of the Nazis in the city streets. Jewish inhabitants were seized for forced labour, beaten and robbed. Jewish leaders were forced to clean lavatories with their prayer shawls, laughing soldiers shaved the beards off Jewish men and threw their holy books in the mud. Ancient synagogues were torched.

Back in Zduńska Wola, the first three Jewish men in the city were murdered. Reb Mendel, Abraham Ozorowicz and Avrum Yiedel Hirschberg had been praying at home when the Germans burst in and accused them of conducting secret meetings and planning to overthrow the German Reich. The men denied the ludicrous accusations, but the Germans lined them up in front of the town hall and shot them.

Exhausted and terrified, the Berkowiczs returned to their home in Zduńska Wola. In their absence, the once vibrant city had changed completely. No more people chatting outside cafes, sharing platters of pierogi (Polish dumplings) and lemon tea in a glass. Just blank-faced disbelief and piles of rubble.

We got a coach back from Łódź and walked up Piłsudskiego Street, desperate to get home. We found a strange sight. In the courtyard

THE BEGINNING

outside our home were dozens of foot-operated sewing machines. Women sat behind them, pumping the treadles, feeding through long strips of material. It looked like an open-air factory.

Our landlord, Mr Kornatowski, spotted us and rushed out to meet us on the street.

'You've got nothing to go back to,' he told us. 'I tried to save your place, I told them you were poor and there was nothing for them, but they didn't listen. If I hadn't been German-born, I'd have been shot.'

He was a kind man; at least he had tried. But the most shocking thing was that all the material that the women were machining was my grandfather's, left by the door when we had fled. The Germans had taken it from our home and were using it to make blankets for the German Army. And just like that, we'd lost everything. Our home. Our belongings. My mother's beautiful dresses, her white damask tablecloth and silver candlesticks, paintings, her best china and silver. My father's books and records. All the coal and food we'd stockpiled. My copy of Gone with the Wind. *Everything they took from our home was loaded on to a lorry and taken to Germany, for their families. We had nothing but the clothes we stood up in. Not even a change of underwear.*

When the Nazis invaded, most Jewish families were ordered to be out of their homes in ten minutes, or else be shot. Families were forced at gunpoint to calculate what to take and what to leave. *Ten minutes.* Just enough time to try to calm their hammering hearts and examine the contents of their life.

What to take and what to leave behind? The wedding photo above the bed. Candlesticks. A few pots and pans. Boots and warm coats. A whole domestic life had to be abandoned. The little things, hard earned and much cherished. In the case of the Berkowiczs, they weren't even given so much as one minute. They had lost everything.

It must have been so hard for my father. He'd lost his job, his home, his dreams of a Paris education for my sister and me. He had no means of supporting his family. Mama was a resourceful, strong woman and immediately set about trying to scrounge a few bits and pieces from friends, some clothes for Stenia and me, pots and pans, a blanket.

I felt an ache in the pit of my stomach. I felt lost. It was all too much to take in.

Sala managed to find them one room, a few streets away in Złotnickiego Street, a far cry from their old comfortable apartment that backed on to an apple orchard. Renia doesn't remember their reduced circumstances, save to say it was frightening enough for Sala to want to send her elder daughter to her mother's house.

Mama told me, 'I'm sending you to stay with Bubbe and Zayde in Kalisz; you'll be safer there. You have a home there.' I was sad to leave my parents and Stenia, but I always felt safe with Bubbe. Mama took me. I don't remember how we got there, leaving Stenia behind to be cared for by Tatuś.

On Renia's arrival in Kalisz, she craned her neck to look up at the elegant old buildings now swathed in swastika flags. Ancient monuments, churches, theatres and museums were smothered in the Nazi emblem.

Kalisz was considered by many to have the oldest Jewish community in Poland. By 1939 there were about 15,000 Jews living in the city. Many, like Renia's grandparents, worked in the textile industry.

THE BEGINNING

It was always such a beautiful place. My grandparents' elegant apartment took up the whole top floor of its block. Its balconies had views over the park. Previously, I had loved sitting on the balcony on the Sabbath looking out across to the park, watching people go by in their beautiful Sabbath clothes. Believe me, I can see it now.

What a change the war had brought. My mother told me to be a good girl and delivered me into the safety of her mother's arms.

'My bubbala is always a good girl,' said my bubbe, giving me hugs and kisses. I felt very relieved to be with her, and I felt safe.

There were so many Jewish shops, but suddenly my grandparents couldn't buy anything. Bubbe stood in queues for hours to buy bread, sometimes coming home empty-handed. Bubbe worked hard to keep the dangers from me and to try to keep things normal. Her friends donated their grandchildren's clothes, which she adapted to fit me.

The price of everything soared. Meat was an unheard-of luxury. More and more rules were brought in, banning Jews from public life. A curfew was introduced. Jewish bakers were only allowed to bake bread. We were no longer allowed to take public transport, trams, trains or buses. I wasn't allowed through the doors of a public library, and I would never watch Shirley Temple at the cinema again.

The synagogues were closed or destroyed. Jews were forbidden to have more than 1,000 Reichsmark or 2,000 Polish złotys, and forbidden from trading in manufactured goods, which meant Renia's grandparents had to close their business and had no means of making money. Jews were being stripped of their rights, their livelihoods, their dignity. The Nazis tossed books from Polish and Jewish libraries into the River Prosna.

A MOTHER'S PROMISE

News filtered back to Renia's family that Warsaw had been heavily bombed.

∼

Autumn blew in, trailing dead leaves and sweeping changes. On 8 October 1939, five weeks after the German Army invaded Poland, Adolf Hitler issued a decree by which Poland's western territories, including Renia's home of Zduńska Wola and her grandparents' cities of Łódź and Kalisz, were incorporated into the German Reich. He renamed it Reichsgau Wartheland and it was decided in Berlin that these areas should be Germanised as soon as possible. Eastern districts were annexed to the Soviet Union and Lithuania, in accordance with the agreement signed in the Molotov–Ribbentrop Pact, and an enclave in central Poland was converted into the General Government, to be ruled as a Nazi colony of Germany.

For the 400,000 Jews, including the Berkowiczs, now trapped inside the *Reichsgau*, terrifying changes beckoned.

Wednesday, 6 December 1939, Chanukah, the Jewish Festival of Lights, was darker than Renia could ever remember.

I used to love Chanukah. It's the Jewish eight-day Festival of Lights, celebrated with a nightly menorah lighting, special prayers and presents.

The melodies, the light of the candles illuminating the darkness, the story of the oil that miraculously burnt for eight days. Back in Zduńska Wola, we celebrated it with gifts and special foods.

Bubbe and Zayde had no more candles and so we couldn't celebrate.

THE BEGINNING

Some Jewish families managed to scrape together wax from old candles and made wicks from cotton wool, but in Renia's home, it was impossible to observe the rituals and holidays.

The world became smaller and darker every day, as all the small joys of life were rubbed out, replaced with only long, hungry, repetitive days.

I'd been with my grandparents about three months when suddenly, at the beginning of December 1939, the city was made judenfrei, *free of Jews, and we all had to assemble in the market hall. I remember sitting on the cold, stone floor. There was so much noise and a thick, nasty smell like toilets.*

The snow fell thickly, the temperature plunging to minus 12 degrees, when Sala appeared in the market hall and managed somehow to get her daughter back to Zduńska Wola. The city was unrecognisable.

Renia's school had been closed down. The synagogue had been destroyed, with only its scorched exterior walls still standing. The old name had been taken down and replaced with its new German name, *Freihaus*. Other new signs appeared too. *Psom i Żydom wstęp wzbroniony*. Dogs and Jews are not allowed.

The German Army were everywhere. All you could hear were loud German voices. Jewish homes had been plundered. At least it was good to be back, reunited with Mama, Tatuś and Stenia. She was so pleased to see me. Somehow, Bubbe and Zayde were able to join us from Kalisz and soon we were all together.

Also living in Zduńska Wola was my Aunt Gitel, her husband Mordechai and toddler son Rywus, and Mama's two younger brothers, my uncles Szachna and Szlomi.

Not long after came yet more change. It was the beginning of the end, the death of Renia's childhood.

We were forced into the ghetto.

Chapter Three

Gallows and Prayers

March 1942

Ten corpses hung, rotating slowly in the brisk March breeze. They had been there some time so were already growing stiff, their mouths slack and eyes bulging. On the executed men's jackets, clearly visible to all, was the yellow Star of David. Twelve-year-old Renia put her head down and kept on walking, eyes fixed firmly on the grimy street.

Two years on, her childhood was barely a memory. Seeing ten bodies hanging from the gallows on the way to an eight-hour night shift in a factory was a sight that summed up the brutality and horror of the ghetto. How quickly a childhood can be dismantled. How rapidly dreams diminish, until all that is left is the will to survive.

For the estimated 10,000 to 12,000 prisoners of the Zduńska Wola ghetto, life was a daily litany of horror, hunger and overcrowding. When the Berkowiczs were first herded into the ghetto at the beginning of 1940, there were 7,500 local Jews, but by March 1942, thousands more from neighbouring towns and villages had been pressed into a small area sealed off from the rest of the city by fences and barbed wire. The chronic overcrowding meant that, on average, seven people occupied one room.

Pillars marked with a Star of David indicated the borders of the ghetto. The five entrance gates were guarded by Jewish Police from inside and by German Order Police, known as Schupos, from the outside. Renia and her family lived at 21 Juliusza Street, a dark, dingy block that fell under the brooding shadow of the Gestapo HQ.

There were eight of us living in one room. Me, my sister and our parents, Bubbe, Zayde and my two uncles – we all lived, slept, ate and washed in that one room. Auntie Gitel, her husband and toddler son lived over the road. Everything had to happen in that room. How did we live like that?

Mama, Stenia and I slept on the only bed together, covered with a blanket, or old clothes. Of course, we had no sheets or pillows. We had a few chairs, and I think my uncles and Tatuś slept on them, or on a straw mattress on the floor. At night, Bubbe and Zayde went over the road to sleep in Aunt Gitel's room.

We had a tin bath which we would take to the tap in the courtyard outside and fill half-full, before hauling it in and taking it in turns to bathe in the cold water. We didn't have the fuel to warm it.

The toilet was also outside; we didn't even have newspaper to use as toilet paper. We tried to do whatever we could to keep our privacy. As for things like soap or toothpaste, we had none. No one did, unless you had the money and connections to buy on the black market. It was so terribly hard to keep clean. In winter, we froze, the cold going right into our bones. In summer, Mama waged war against bugs and blowflies.

Poor Mama did what she could to try and keep the place clean, always washing floors, but it was a losing battle because we had no soap or detergent. She was the greatest housewife that ever lived. Mama wasn't strong in the physical sense, but she was tough in her mind. I followed her example. I knew if Mama kept going, I had to as well. Mama never cried in front of us but she must have wanted to, she must have. She was helpless to prevent our suffering, which only got worse when I was sent to work in the factory.

The exploitation of Jewish labour had started in 1939 but intensified in 1941, the year after Renia and her family were forced into the ghetto. In factories and workshops, Jews were forced to work for the German Army. Renia doesn't know the name of the factory she worked in, but it was likely to have been one of the cluster of unheated old workshops and factories huddled around the burnt synagogue. The largest factory, managed by a company called Striegel & Wagner, used the labour of 2,000 Jewish people to manufacture fur clothing, leather jackets and work in knitting and weaving. There were also workshops for dressmaking, hosiery, gloves and straw shoes for German civilians. Childhoods dripped away.

I was eleven years old when I started work in early 1941. I went from being a schoolgirl, learning arithmetic in a smart uniform, to working eight-hour shifts in a factory making socks on a production line for the German Army. Sometimes I worked the night shift, sometimes the day.

The machine was twice as tall as I was so I had to stand on a stool all day long just to reach it. What did I know about making socks? I was taught for two weeks and then I had to teach someone else.

Mama worked in a fur factory, sewing pieces of it together to make clothes. Tatuś worked in administration for the Jewish police station in the ghetto, probably because of his previous work as an accountant. Stenia was eight when we went into the ghetto, so I think she must have been looked after by Bubbe. Gitel helped her husband in a workshop where they made clothes, taking their little boy with them.

Apart from the work and the constant hunger, the cold was our enemy. Winters in Poland are very cold, believe me, and we had no coats and hats, or thick socks and scarves to help keep us warm. Eventually, we got so desperate we had to burn furniture as we had no fuel.

On winter days, the water pump froze over; ice covered the inside of the window pane and you could wake up to find your clothes stuck to your skin with ice. Temperatures would go down to minus 12 degrees, or worse. But I came to know far greater cold than this as the war went on.

By 1942, conditions in the ghetto were dire, as they were in the estimated 1,143 ghettos in the occupied eastern territories. Starvation and cold led to outbreaks of disease like typhus and in March of that year, ninety Jews died in the ghetto in one month, as many as had died in Zduńska Wola each year before the war. The head of the Judenrat, or Jewish Council, was the physician Dr Jakub Lemberg, who spoke fluent German.

Some hoped that the Judenrat might be a voice in dealing with the Germans. In reality, the Nazis saw them only as a means of relating and implementing their orders. Despite the impossible position Dr Lemberg found himself in, having to liaise between the Germans and the ghetto prisoners, he was a popular and well-respected man.

Behind Ogrodowa Street, within the ghetto, Dr Lemberg and the Council of Elders established a small farm that produced milk and vegetables. In this precious patch of green, fifty young people aged between seventeen and twenty-one, all members of Zionist youth groups, worked there, learning Hebrew and studying Jewish history while tending to the farm. Despite their efforts, there was never enough to go round. At times, the calorie intake in the ghetto could be as little as 200 calories a day.

We were starving the entire time. We lived off our rations which you could only get if you worked for the Germans. Believe me, it was starvation rations. We worked all day long for a bit of bread and old vegetables, which we made into a soup.

I remember my two uncles, both young men in their twenties, begging and pleading with Bubbe before work.

'Please, Mama, can we have some bread? We're starving.'

And poor Bubbe being so upset because she could not give it to them. She was in charge of managing the rations.

'I'm sorry, but I can't. If I give you some now, we'll have nothing for this evening when we'll need it more,' she would reply, with tears running down her face at having to say no to her two sons.

Even today, aged ninety-five, each time I eat a piece of bread, I think of that conversation with great sadness, especially because now I know what lay ahead for those lovely young men and my bubbe.

We often went to work with no food in our bellies. When I think about it now, it hurts me so much. Some people think they know hunger, but they don't. Not real hunger, where your stomach is empty all the time. You can't describe it. Please God, you should never know it. It's so terribly frightening to be starving.

I don't remember them giving us food in the factories. Stenia would bring me up a flask with a little bit of soup at dinner time. I was always so happy to see her, and she me. Before the war, we were like two peas in a pod, always together. In the ghetto we missed each other as I was always working.

When I think of the ghetto, I just think of people, so many people, all pressed together into every nook and cranny. Every room in the ghetto was like ours, housing six to eight people in one room.

The room we lived in was part of a flat. We had the living room. An elderly woman lived in the kitchen. That was her home, just the kitchen. Next to the kitchen was another small room where her son and his wife and baby lived. They were nice people I think, but it was so hard living on top of each other like that, listening to the hungry baby crying all the time.

We were so hungry, cold and tired that we were mostly numb. Talking took too much energy. I don't remember much but it was like going through the motions every day, just existing, not living. Everything was grey, shabby and run-down. The people, the buildings.

If we talked about anything, it was food, torturing ourselves with memories of Bubbe's yeast cake and roast chicken.

What could Mama and Tatuś give us except their love? We had nothing but our love for each other.

And to the Germans, we were nothing.

Life was distilled to one urgent need – survival. The ghetto prisoners were deliberately cut off from the world outside its perimeter. An enforced curfew meant no leaving home after dark, unless you were on a night shift. Blacked-out windows were compulsory.

In wartime Britain, showing the tiniest chink of light meant a ticking-off from an ARP warden in a tin hat. In the ghetto, it came with the death penalty.

There were no wirelesses or newspapers in the ghetto in Zduńska Wola, so the Berkowiczs knew nothing of the world at war. They had no idea of the blood-soaked beaches at Dunkirk, the fall of Paris, bombs raining down nightly on blacked-out British cities and towns, nor the attack on Pearl Harbor, bringing the United States into the war. All they knew was starvation, brutality and slave labour, month after month, year after year. They might as well have been in a soundproof cage.

One thing, though, kept the Berkowiczs' souls nourished when all else had run out.

GALLOWS AND PRAYERS

My family never stopped believing in God Almighty, especially Mama. Without the synagogue, Jews prayed at home. Every single night without fail, in the ghetto, Mama said her prayers. I can picture her now. She would cover her head with a scarf, then gently cover her eyes with the palms of her hands and murmur these words . . .

> Shema Yisrael Hashem Elokeinu Hashem Echad.
> *Hear O' Israel, the Lord is our God, the Lord is One.*
> *Blessed be the name of His glorious kingdom for ever and ever.*
> *You shall love the Lord your God with all your heart and with all your soul and with all your might.*
> *And these words which I command you today shall be upon your heart.*
> *You shall teach them thoroughly to your children.*
> *And you shall speak of them when you sit in your house and when you walk on the road, when you lie down and when you rise.*
> *You shall bind them as a sign upon your hand and they shall be a reminder between your eyes.*
> *And you shall write them upon the doorposts of your house and upon your gates.*

Her prayers left a huge impression on me. Now, eighty-five years on, it's the same prayer I recite every night in Hebrew. That's how I continue to feel connected to my mother.

I would watch her praying and take comfort from her faith. It's what gave her the hope to survive when everything else had been taken from us. The Nazis could never steal her faith, her commitment to God, or her prayers. When we drifted off to sleep in that cold, damp room in the ghetto, Mama's prayers wrapped us in a spiritual hug. We had no idea how long the war was going to last, we just hoped that it would end, and we would be liberated.

But liberation was to be a long way off. Hitler's chilling plans for the Jews were evolving, the culmination of the Nazi Party's long-held belief that Germany's destiny relied on the Aryan blood that ran through the veins of its people. To them, Jews were a polluting counter race, not really human at all, but rather subhuman, or *Untermensch*.

What differentiated Nazi antisemitism from other forms of Nazi racism was their belief that Jews were an existential threat to the survival of Germany, and to humanity itself. The Nazis believed in the existence of a worldwide Jewish conspiracy, which aimed to subjugate mankind.

In 1939, an idea was formulated to exile all Jews living within the Reich to a reservation in the Lublin district of the General Government in Poland. By the spring of 1940, it was clear Poland did not have enough territory to spare for the Jews.

By May 1940, the Nazis came up with the Madagascar Plan, a plan to deport all Europe's Jews to the island of Madagascar, a French colony off the east coast of Africa. The plan was abandoned in September 1940 after Hitler failed to defeat Great Britain, necessary in order to sail across the British Navy-controlled Indian Ocean in order to reach the island.

In January 1942, as Renia was slaving in a factory making socks for the German Army, her future was again being discussed. At the Wannsee Conference, German government and SS leaders met to coordinate the extermination of every Jew in Europe. From this time, until the end of the war, the Final Solution became the code name for the Nazis' plans to solve the 'Jewish question'.

GALLOWS AND PRAYERS

Renia and her family's lives were in peril, and a sharp reminder of this came in March and May of 1942.

They erected wooden gallows in the centre of the ghetto and held two public executions. They hanged men they accused of smuggling food. My poor father had to watch.

Dr Lemberg had been ordered by the Gestapo to choose Jews for two public hangings, ten on 3 March and ten more on 21 May. He refused and attempted to bargain for their lives, offering to increase the work output of the ghetto. The Germans denied his request.

The first public hanging was at 11am on the morning of Purim, usually a joyous holiday marking the saving of Jews from a massacre in ancient Persia.

Renia's mother shielded her from the actual executions, keeping her inside their room, an act of resistance as all Jews, including children, had been ordered out of their homes and forced to spectate.

Often, acts of public violence and deportations were carried out on, or very close to, a major Jewish holiday, in a practice which would later be called, with bitter irony, Goebbels' Jewish calendar.

Eichard Helmrich, Deputy Chief of the Schupo (German police), insisted that Dr Lemberg be forced up a stepladder to read out the death sentences to the stunned and silent crowd. Helmrich gave the order and, within minutes, the men were rotating in the breeze, the wooden gallows creaking. Their bodies were left there all day before being cut down and buried in a mass grave.

The next came on the day of Shavuos, and the crowd swelled with German officers who had brought their mistresses along,

A MOTHER'S PROMISE

as if it were a fun spring outing. A hush fell over the crowd as the men walked to the gallows with their hands tied behind their backs.

According to eyewitnesses, one of the condemned, a gentle and deeply religious man called Shlomo Zelichowski, lifted his face to the sky and began to sing a song from the *Neilah* service, the climax of the closing of the Yom Kippur (Day of Atonement) service, offering repentance and acceptance of God's sealing of one's fate.

Soon, the entire crowd of several thousand Jews joined in, including the other condemned men. The Germans were furious.

After the hangings, the Jews in the square refused to go home, standing in silent homage, until the ghetto police set on them with whips and dogs. Shlomo's act of spiritual resistance became legend.

These events were also significant for Renia, because this was the first time she had seen dead bodies, and it left a profound mark on the twelve-year-old.

I'd never seen a dead man before then, never mind ten. I must have seen them on my way to and back from work, when their bodies were left hanging there for all the ghetto to see. I knew I couldn't look. When I saw their legs dangling from the gallows, I had to look away and keep walking. It was so frightening to see. It was something that you could never forget, and it has stayed with me for the rest of my life.

It would not be the last time Renia would witness such atrocities.

Three months later, on 8 August 1942, Renia turned thirteen. They had long ago stopped marking birthdays in the ghetto. It was a day like any other, characterised by pain, perpetual hunger and hard work.

No cake. No presents. No parties.

Unlike other girls her age, Renia's physical development was paralysed too, trapping her in a skinny child's body.

I didn't grow breasts, nor did I get my periods. Starvation meant I didn't go through puberty like I was supposed to. I didn't know any different.

Stolen too were all rites of passage that Polish girls her age once took for granted. Parties. Shoeless summers. Friendships that feel like they'll last a lifetime. Giggling over boys. Teenage angst. All were sloughed away as life was distilled to one urgent and elemental purpose. Survival.

The story of Renia's persecution was etched on to her face and body. There were no mirrors in the ghetto, but she could trace the angular planes of her cheekbones with her fingers, or look down to see her protruding ribs. Her hair, once so silky and thick, came out in fistfuls.

Ghetto life had etched deep lines into Sala's skin too, bracketing her mouth and turning her once flawless skin into dried yellow parchment.

What else can I tell you about that ghetto? I got up hungry and cold. I went to work and then came home, with barely the energy to climb into bed and fall asleep. Mama's love was the only thing that made life worth living and she kept us going. We all drew our strength from her. When she wasn't working or trying to keep our room clean, she would make tea from whatever she could find, and sell it in little glass bottles. She never stopped working. Everything she did, she did for us. She was an important and respected person in the ghetto. I idolised her.

Boring, humiliating, bitter days rolled out with the same flat, grey inevitability. Until one morning, when the sleepy still of dawn was shattered.

Chapter Four

Stenia

Renia woke up with a start. A clenched fist battered the front door.

'*Alle Juden raus!*' All Jews out.

The shouts tore up and down the street. At once the room was charged with electricity. It was three months after the public hangings, in the early hours of 24 August 1942 – sixteen days after Renia's thirteenth birthday.

Her mother pulled aside the blackout material and peered out of the window. Through the darkness, she could see the ghetto street filling up with confused and bleary-eyed people, some still in their nightclothes.

'*Alle Juden raus! SCHNELLER!*'

The door seemed to explode, rattling the old peeling window frames.

Fear gripped her, hot and spiky.

'Quick,' gasped her father, hopping about on one foot as he frantically hauled on his trousers.

No one voiced it but the adults had just one thought. God knows the rumours had been swirling around the ghetto long enough to leave no ear untouched.

The Nazis are slaughtering children and old people.

On the other side of the street, Gitel was facing an impossible dilemma. Should she take her little boy out, or hide him and leave? She had moments to decide.

She walked out on the dark street alone and distraught.

Sala gripped her arm, her eyes wide, and Gitel gave an imperceptible nod.

Bubbe and Zayde, along with Gitel's husband and son, were hidden in the attic. Gitel had been the one to shut the attic hatch, her last image the faces of her loved ones disappearing into the gloom.

Gitel was frozen to the spot, unable to leave her parents, husband and young son behind.

'Come quick,' Sala urged, but she stumbled back, shaking her head.

'It's not safe out here,' Sala whispered, 'they are better off there.'

Further up the street, the shouts grew louder. Slamming doors. Thundering boots. Gunshots.

'We'll be back soon,' Sala pleaded with her younger sister, gripping her hand. 'Please, we'll all be shot if we stay here on the street.'

The family joined the bewildered, frightened masses. They were sucked into a stream of people being herded through the ghetto. Anyone not walking fast enough was shot. Under cover of darkness, they were marched along the narrow back streets to a square, surrounded by *Schutzpolizei*, Gestapo and SS officers, with barking, lunging dogs, all mobilised to support local forces. By 10.30 in the morning, most of the ghetto had gathered. Trembling, Renia reached for her mother's hand, confused and terrified at what was about to unfold.

The first order crackled over a loudspeaker in German. 'Everyone sit down!'

Then came the next order. 'Parents should hand over all children up to eighteen years of age.'

STENIA

It's not possible to describe this scene. I can only give you an idea about it. The children crying, and the mothers screaming, 'Almighty God, help us. Where are you?' still ring in my ears today.

It's unforgettable. You could soon see the children running towards these officers. The little ones, the bigger ones. Some of the big ones carrying their young siblings. They were all put in these closed-in lorries and taken away.

Stenia looked up at our mother. I will never forget what she said next.

'Mummy, are they going to kill us?'

'No, darling, they are going to send you to Łódź and you'll be together with your grandparents,' my mother lied. What was a mother to say? What could she tell our little girl?

She knew perfectly well what they were going to do to the children.

All around them, terrible scenes unfolded. According to the testimony of Jakob Wolf Sytner, the terror sent one young woman into labour and she gave birth right there in the square. A German officer threw the newborn baby on the ground and shot the mother.

Renia knew that she would never be able to adequately describe the abomination she was witnessing. Such cruelty and wickedness were simply beyond human comprehension. Some children toddled trustingly into the arms of SS officers, others shrank back and cried, clinging tight to their mother's legs.

Everywhere I looked, children were weeping, reaching out for their parents. Mothers were screaming.

My mother tried to hide Stenia and me by covering us with her coat, but it didn't take very long before she was spotted. The Germans got hold of Stenia and my mother got a beating. A guard was hitting her everywhere.

That little girl, my sister, turned to him and she begged him: 'Please stop. Please don't hit her. That's not my mother.' She did it to protect our mother. My little sister. Only eleven years old and trying to protect her mother. She was so brave.

Then she ran away from us with tears running down her face. We never saw her again. Can you imagine how I felt? I had a guilty feeling because they'd got hold of her and not me. Somehow, I was left. I don't know how or why.

Stenia, my brilliant and beloved little sister, who had turned eleven just three months before, was gone. We didn't know where they were taking her, but we knew she wouldn't return. From the whole of my life and all the experiences I will share with you, that hurts me most.

It felt like my heart had been cut in half.

Stenia. The other half of Renia. There one minute, gone the next. Vanished, like a stone sinking into water. Renia's mind photographed the scene, a memory too painful to process in that moment. Instead, she stored it away somewhere deep and private.

Sala watched her daughter disappear, her hand covering her mouth, before her body gave way and crumpled on to the cobbles.

'No . . . No . . . No. Please, God, no. Spare her.'

An unearthly keening howl came from somewhere deep and primal.

'My daughter . . . My daughter . . .'

Renia's father slid down beside her and took his wife in his arms, his body shaking with silent sobs.

The engines started up and the lorries began driving out of the square with their precious cargo. Sons and daughters. Boys and girls. Little children.

As the hands of the clock inched towards midday on the most

STENIA

tragic day of Renia's young life, she had lost not one but multiple members of her family since the darkness of that foul dawn.

Her sister. Her grandparents. Aunts. Uncles. Cousins.

How deep the chasm of their loss would run in the decades to come.

Stenia, along with several hundred other children, and the elderly and sick from the ghetto, were driven 75 kilometres north to the Kulmhof death camp in Chełmno on the River Ner.

Throughout 1942, Jews from the Łódź ghetto and many other towns and villages in the Warthegau were deported to their deaths at Kulmhof (Chełmno). It was the first Nazi stationary killing centre, where gassing was used to exterminate Jews on a large-scale basis, and the first place outside the Soviet Union where Jews were slaughtered en masse as part of the 'Final Solution'.

∼

At the site of an old palace, the Nazis gathered their victims in the courtyard, telling them that they were being sent to a work camp, and thus had to be washed. Groups of fifty were sent to the building's ground floor, where they were made to give up their valuables and undress – men, women and children together. Next, they were taken to the cellar, where they were reassured by signs that they were heading 'To the Washroom', but in fact were forced down a ramp into a gas van.

After the van was filled to the brim, the driver locked the doors and turned on the motor. After ten minutes, the exhaust gas fumes had suffocated all those inside.

The SS murdered 152,000 people, including Renia's little sister Stenia, at Kulmhof.

Renia, her mother, father and Aunt Gitel were lined up with the remaining Jews from the Zduńska Wola ghetto and marched in rows of five to the gates of the nineteenth-century Jewish cemetery on Kacza Street.

As Renia walked, she stole a glance at her mother. She was a ghost. Her expression was so raw that it was impossible to look upon her, the grief that swelled inside her wild and unfathomable. A black shroud seemed to have settled over her, drowning out whatever life force she had left.

At that moment, I knew. My parents wouldn't stop crying until the day they died.

I wanted to ask so badly about Bubbe and Zayde. What would happen if the SS found them hiding in the attic? Would they be safe? What would happen to my lovely little cousin Rywus?

Unbeknown to her, back in the square, German guards had selected four Jewish men and forced them to help two Volksdeutsche gendarmes in their search for people hiding in the ghetto. Those discovered hiding in attics and basements were shot on the spot.

The selection in the square was only the beginning. At the gates to the cemetery yet another selection was taking place, headed up by Hans Biebow, a 6-foot-tall Nazi in shiny black boots, whip in hand. With his golden hair and blue eyes, he could have been a poster boy for the Reich. In his previous life, Biebow had been a coffee merchant, but by August 1942 he was the forty-year-old Head of Administration for the Łódź ghetto and was never anything less than meticulous in his duties. He had travelled the 55 kilometres from Łódź to Zduńska Wola to personally oversee the selection of labour for the Łódź ghetto. Apparently he had claimed the town square selection had been 'sloppy' and so resolved to hold another at the gates to the cemetery.

As the crowds shuffled forward, they were directed *links* (left) or *rechts* (right). Life hung on the smallest of gestures. A nod to the left, a flick of the whip to the right. With ruthless precision, Biebow directed all the old people, invalids, pregnant women and people whom he deemed not fit to work to the left, *schlechte Seite*. Callously, the Nazis called them 'useless mouths', as they served no purpose to the Third Reich.

Which side offered life and which offered death? Of course, we didn't know. We were sent to the right and I was so relieved to be able to stay with my mother, father and Aunt Gitel. All the rest of my family, my two uncles, were on the unlucky side. Everybody was crying, everybody was heartbroken.

The cemetery was full of the memories of rich and fulfilled Jewish lives stretching back to 1826, the final resting place for so many who had worked hard and flourished in Zduńska Wola.

Orthodox, Reform and Hasidim were buried in the cemetery. Over 7,000 tombstones (Hebrew *matzevot*) made of sandstone, limestone and granite with inscriptions in Polish, Yiddish and Hebrew were a valuable source of historical, genealogical and sepulchral art. It was a sacred, beautiful place.

In three dark days, the SS ruptured the richness of that cultural life and its memory in the most devastating way possible, seeking not just to destroy life, but the memory of it.

As the blistering hot August sun began to creep over the high red-brick cemetery walls, Sala slumped on a verge of grass next to a gravestone, tears streaming down her face. There was nothing Renia or her father could say or do to console her or Aunt Gitel, who had left her son and husband in the attic, both trapped in a tormented world of what-ifs.

And that's how they remained for three long days and nights as the interminable selection dragged on. Not a drop of water or crumb of bread was offered to the estimated 1,200 people gathered on Renia's side of the cemetery.

The Nazis had specially erected electric lights placed round the perimeter of the graveyard to prevent people escaping. The glare lit up hundreds of dusty, frightened faces. Every so often, the ground would tremble as the SS fired a crackerjack of bullets, massacring those at the other end of the graveyard. Skeins of smoke drifted across to them, followed by the sound of sobbing cutting through the compressed air.

Renia could not see the slaughter from her side, but a huge pit had been dug in the middle of the cemetery, into which several hundred dead and, in some cases, still living, were flung and buried. The community of Zduńska Wola must have heard the screams from the other sides of the high cemetery walls.

Sitting there in that cemetery, I wondered whether anyone would believe such atrocities could happen. Only a young woman sitting not far from us seemed relieved.

'I'm so happy today,' she cried out. 'I'm so lucky.' She was going on all the time, she's so lucky, she's so happy, that people thought she had gone off her mind. Which was quite easy to do.

'What are you happy for?' my mother snapped. 'Who's happy today?'

'I am,' the woman replied. 'My little boy died a few weeks ago. He is buried here and no one can take him away from me.'

What could anyone say to such a thing?

Over the course of those three days, as more Jews were seized, the crowds around us began to thin out.

I knew that I'd slipped through the net. I was just thirteen, but I looked closer to eight. The women around me clearly also began to realise what a dangerous situation I was in and tried to make my face up to make me look older.

*'Here,' said a lady. 'Why don't you take this for your daughter?'
She found a tube of lipstick in her pocket and gave it to my mother.*

'Thank you,' my mother replied, taking the lipstick and applying it to my lips. Another woman put her scarf on my head. Someone else found a powder compact. I was even given a pair of high heels to wear.

These beautiful, strong Jewish women, whose loved ones had also been murdered, who had so little to give, offered Renia something precious – hope. That love and kindness could bloom unexpectedly in such a place of unfathomable loss gave Renia something beautiful to cling to.

'A *dank*,' her mother murmured in Yiddish, her tears slowing for the first time.

The women had tried their best to make me look older, but even so, I was spotted by an SS officer who came hurrying along. 'You. Stand up!' he ordered. 'How old are you?'

Of course, I was paralysed with fright. I couldn't stand up. I couldn't answer. My father, who was sitting next to me, said, 'She's eighteen years old. I know her.'

The SS man looked at me very hard. He could tell that I was no way near eighteen, then he said, 'Sie darf sitzen bleiben.' She can stay seated. Everyone around us was so happy for me.

My mother hugged me. No one could believe it. 'It is God's will,' I told myself. Almighty God was holding on to me. How else had I survived? In that moment, I felt God was with me. I knew I had to believe in something amongst all the darkness.

As I looked around the cemetery, I knew God wanted me to survive. To tell others the atrocities the Germans were committing.

Mama's strong faith became my own. My mama had nothing and yet she gave me the most powerful gift of all. Faith in God

Almighty. It became something to hold on to in the moments of madness that would come. Sitting in that cemetery, I had no idea the Nazis would strip me of everything, but they could never take mine or my mother's faith and I am so proud of that. Our faith was untouchable. It was the only thing the Nazis couldn't take away.

The kindling of Renia's faith during a time of utter desolation became the touchstone of her life, offering her security and love as well as a powerful connection to her mother.

When dawn rose on day three, only around 1,200 people out of an estimated 9,000 had survived the liquidation and were marched out of the cemetery, deemed fit for labour. Some 8,000 Jews were taken to the Kulmhof extermination camp. Just three children were left from the whole ghetto. One of them was Renia.

Łódź ghetto, children from the Marysin orphanage are lined up to be sent to Kulmhof

STENIA

The group, exhausted and starving, were lined up five abreast and marched along the street.

The pale fingers of dawn washed the cobblestones gold. And that's when it happened, an event so surreal that even amid the horror and bloodshed to drench Zduńska Wola, it would still be recollected and discussed decades later.

The cobblestones, all along the road from when we started until we came to the railway lines, they turned upside down as we walked on them. I could not believe my eyes. Everyone saw it. It was a bad omen. A very bad omen. The whole roadside was turned upside down.

It could have been that the cobblestones, loosened by heavy German traffic and footfall, wobbled and then were tipped over by the pressure of renewed footfall, but to Renia and many others, it was a sight which filled them with foreboding.

Soon they came to train tracks, lined with waiting freight wagons. The midday sun was sweltering. A miasma of heat and fear shimmered over the tracks. German guards walked up and down.

Bracelets, rings, money, watches. We had to give away everything we owned. My father had a ring on, a beautiful, heavy, gold ring which he couldn't get off. It was deeply embedded on his finger, but rather than tell them, he thought he'd keep it on and not say anything.

Amazingly, the SS guards overlooked it. Renia didn't know then, but that ring would come to symbolise something deeply profound to her.

Once most of the crowds had been stripped of their precious items, the survivors of the ghetto were pushed on board the freight wagons.

Further up the platform, Renia spotted Dr Jakub Lemberg with his family. The head of the Judenrat was much admired and respected by Renia's family and, from what she could tell, the majority of the ghetto. His efforts to save the condemned men from the gallows, his medical knowledge and his kindness endeared him to all.

Renia was relieved to see he had survived the selection and was about to get on the wagon alongside them.

They called out the head of the ghetto and shot him dead in front of us. Kicked his body into a corner, in front of his wife and children.

Unbeknown to Renia, Dr Lemberg had made the ultimate sacrifice. In the autumn of 1940, Lemberg had been invited to visit the Łódź ghetto and meet with its Jewish leader, Chaim Mordechai Rumkowski. He had returned dispirited at what he saw as Rumkowski's close cooperation with the Germans and Biebow's iron grip over the ghetto. He denied Biebow's demand to select ten Zduńska Wola Jews for the hanging Renia's father witnessed in March 1942, or provide lists of Jews for deportation. When Biebow ordered him again, he wrote three names on a sheet of paper. Reading the names of Dr Lemberg, his wife and their child, Biebow screamed that he would pay with his life for such insolence.

At the train tracks, Biebow seized his opportunity for revenge. It was a tragic end for a brave man and one he could so easily have avoided, had he had less of a conscience. In December 1939, Lemberg had obtained certificates for himself and his family to travel to Palestine, but at the request of the Jewish committee he had instead stayed with his people. His loyalty cost him his life.

STENIA

Before I even had a chance to collect my thoughts from the terrible thing I had just witnessed, they pushed and shoved us into the freight wagon.

More and more people were pushed in, tripping and stumbling, eyes wild with fear and disbelief, before the heavy steel doors were slid shut and bolted. Panic prickled over Renia as her eyes adjusted to the gloom and she took in her surroundings.

We were packed in so tight, like sardines in a tin, so that no one could sit down or even turn around without shoving an elbow in someone's face. There were no windows, only tiny slats in the side of the wagon that let in a puff of hot air. Apparently, in the corner was a single bucket to be used as a latrine, but I couldn't see it or get to it.

The crush of bodies. The overpowering smell. I thought we would all suffocate. We just wanted air to breathe. We were all terrified. How long could we survive without air?

I was a thirteen-year-old girl. It was so embarrassing being pressed up so close to men too.

Suffering and humiliation were built into every element of their situation, further dehumanising every person stuffed into the freight wagon. To the Third Reich, their Jewish prisoners were simply cargo, not people. The deportations ripped the deportees forever from the human world as they knew it.

As the wagon jerked from its siding and slowly transferred its human cargo north-east, in the direction of Łódź and Biebow's personal fiefdom, it didn't just transport Renia away from the city she had been born in, but crossed an invisible line of *before* and *after*.

From then on, I stopped assuming that tomorrow would come. You never knew what would happen from one moment to the next. The world we knew had been stolen from us. My heart was racing so fast and I was terrified for my life. We had no idea what lay at the end of those train tracks.

The journey had begun.

Chapter Five

Łódź

The establishment of the ghetto is only a transitional measure. I reserve for myself the decision as to when and how the city of Łódź will be cleansed of Jews. The final aim must be to burn out entirely this pestilential boil.

Friedrich Übelhör, German Governor of
the Kalisz-Łódź district, 10 December 1939

During the blisteringly hot ten-hour journey to Łódź, Renia's direst fears were realised. Many people did suffocate in the overcrowded freight wagons. Never wasting an opportunity to maximise the economy of death, the Third Reich actually charged to take Jews to their often final destination.

The Nazis relied on European rail networks for mass deportations. The Reich Security Main Office (*Reichssicherheitshauptamt*), booked trains known as *Sonderzüge* (special trains) through the German state travel bureau. Train companies billed the Reich for each 'passenger'. In some, but not all, cases, the Germans demanded reimbursement for these transport costs from the Jewish councils or else paid for the transport with money raised from the confiscated assets of the victims. Children under ten travelled at half price and those under four travelled for free. Conditions were appalling, often in wagons designed for carrying freight and livestock.

By the time Renia stumbled, parched with thirst and damp with sweat and grime from the wagon, she felt close to death. When they arrived at Radogoszcz station, renamed Radegast by the Nazis, they hadn't had a drop of water or morsel of food in four days. The date was Thursday, 27 August 1942, and the temperature topped 40 degrees Celsius.

At first, Renia was blinded by the bright sunlight after ten hours crushed in the dark, but when the feeling gradually returned to her stiff limbs and her eyes adjusted to the light, Renia could not believe what she was seeing. Her mother's fingers tightened around hers as, all around them, crowds were directed from Radegast station into the centre of the Łódź ghetto.

Before the war, Łódź, like Renia's home town, was a prosperous industrial textile city. With its sprawling factories and billowing smokestacks it had earned the nickname 'the Manchester of the East'.

On 31 October 1939, while Renia was sheltering with her bubbe, Reich Minister of Propaganda, Joseph Goebbels, had toured the Jewish quarter and observed: 'It is indescribable. These are no longer human beings, they are animals. For this reason, our task is no longer humanitarian but surgical. Steps must be taken here, and they must be radical ones, make no mistake.'

On the eve of war, the Jewish community of Łódź had numbered 235,000, the second largest in Europe. Upon occupying Łódź on 8 September 1939, the Germans unleashed a wave of anti-Jewish violence, plundering and confiscating Jewish property, and executing and deporting to concentration camps hundreds of the city's Jewish political, business and cultural elite.

In February 1940, the establishment of a ghetto in Łódź was announced, encompassing the neighbourhoods of Bałuty, the

Old Town and Marysin. Ethnic Germans and Poles had until 30 April to vacate their homes.

Chaim Mordechai Rumkowski, a 63-year-old Polish businessman and an orphanage director, was appointed Judenälteste, or Elder of the Jews, known to most as the Chairman.

On 30 April, more than 160,000 Jews were interned into an area of 4.13 square kilometres, or 1.6 square miles, sealed off from the rest of the world by wooden fencing and barbed wire.

The Germans changed Łódź's name and it became known as the Litzmannstadt ghetto. Along the 6.8-mile ghetto perimeter, the Schupo (German police) were posted at regular intervals with orders to shoot any Jews approaching the fence without warning.

A large sign at the manned sentry point exclaimed:
'WOHNGEBIET DER JUDEN BETRETEN VERBOTEN'.
'JEWISH RESIDENTIAL AREA, NO ENTRY'.

I can't remember how long it took to walk into the centre of the ghetto; we were so exhausted and thirsty. As we walked past the buildings, I remember thinking that they were very old and dilapidated and everyone looked so shabby and ill. It was a horrible, bleak place. Everything looked stained, dirty and grey.

We were so hungry by now we would have eaten a lump of wood. The ghetto was large compared to the last one. During this long walk, my mother disappeared briefly. When she came back, she was holding half a cabbage and her cardigan was missing. She had exchanged it for half a cabbage.

Even managing to find half a cabbage was an achievement. The Berkowiczs had arrived during a drought, which had had a disastrous effect on agriculture in the ghetto. A plague of caterpillars had devoured the already meagre supply of cabbages.

Ever resourceful, Sala was already adjusting to the barter economy of the ghetto, known as 'organising', in which Jews were forced to sell or swap their possessions for a paltry item of food, like half a cabbage or a small loaf of bread.

It would take longer for the family to adjust to the brutality of living in occupied Poland's second largest, but most ruthlessly isolated, ghetto.

To Renia, her arrival passed in a starvation-induced blur, so she can't remember much about how they got there, but she does know that they went to her paternal grandmother's home. Brana no longer lived in her comfortable pre-war apartment, but had been forced into a single room.

Somehow, my father had the address for his mother. She was a lovely lady, my bubbe. She opened the door and was so pleased to see us. My Aunt Miriam lived in the same block with her husband and son. There had been no means of communication in the old ghetto, so we must have discovered on arrival there that my grandfather, Chaim Wolf, had already died of starvation, or disease, as well as my father's younger sister, my favourite aunt, Esther. Can you imagine the shock for my father to discover his father and sister had died, so soon after Stenia, Bubbe and Zayde had been taken? We were all devastated to learn that yet more members of our family had gone.

The room was on the second floor. Bubbe had one room, which she gladly shared with us. There was one double bed, a sofa and a small table. In the corner there was a small stove for cooking and a bucket for fetching water from the tap on the landing. There were dark blackout curtains at the window.

We had nothing with us when we arrived, apart from the clothes on our back and that half a cabbage.

It was then that Bubbe handed me a parcel.

ŁÓDŹ

'This is from your Aunt Esther; she handed it to me before she died. She wanted you to have it. It was her dying wish.'

My aunt had left her dress for me. It was navy with white polka dots. It was the most beautiful dress. I felt so emotional to receive this gift from beyond the grave. I'd loved Esther so much. I remembered her from before the war, so young, fun and full of life. When I was growing up and we visited, she always made time to play with me. I worshipped her. I'd lost my little sister, my bubbe and zayde, now my other grandfather and my favourite aunt.

I tried the dress on, but of course it was too big as I was just a skinny girl, not a young woman with curves. It hung off me. Day to day I wore the same old schmatta – raggedy second-hand clothes. On my feet were a horrible clumpy pair of wooden clogs that rubbed my toes and made them bleed. But that dress . . .

Unbeknown to Renia, her father had granted her a second gift. Despite what must have been an indescribable grief at seeing one daughter snatched by the Nazis, he had the presence of mind to falsify his other daughter's date of birth.

On their arrival, Szaja, along with all the other arrivals into the Łódź ghetto, had to register at the Department of Vital Statistics in the administration block.

On their registration documents, he changed Renia's date of birth from 8.8.1929 to 8.8.1926, making her sixteen instead of thirteen, her real age. He had verbally falsified her age in the Jewish cemetery back in Zduńska Wola, but now he put the lie down in black and white. To the Nazis, a sixteen-year-old was not a 'useless mouth' but a potential worker. It was a fragile protection for his only surviving child, but the only tool at his disposal.

The geography of death and misery, in which the Berkowiczs found themselves incarcerated, was vice-like. Most of the housing was concentrated in a residential area known as Bałuty. The neighbourhoods were notorious slums, whose mostly 100-year-old housing lacked plumbing or sanitary facilities. The air was thick with the rancid stench of sewage. The lack of sewers deprived ghetto prisoners of a route for smuggling, escape or resistance, as existed in the Warsaw ghetto. The job of removing the excrement of 200,000 people fell to prisoners. Such a job was usually a death sentence as the prisoners would inevitably contract typhus. Some were children as young as ten.

Arnold Mostowicz, who held the position of doctor in the ghetto, whose life would later become entwined with Renia's, wrote in his book, *With a Yellow Star and a Red Cross*:

'The gloomy, grey, dirty little apartments, in gloomy, grey, dirty buildings were crammed with old furniture and children and always smelled of onions and washing.

'Bałuty before the war was a mixture of misery and crime. For a few pennies one could buy everything there: a knife, a diamond ring belonging to the czar's family, a girl, the goodwill of an official and the conscience of a policeman. For a few pennies one could also get a knife in the back, be hit with a club over the head or a fist in the eye.'

By the time of Renia's arrival in August 1942, an estimated 200,000 were living in the ghetto. The surviving residents of her old home town were absorbed into the jumble of overcrowded ghetto streets, never again to be seen by the Berkowiczs.

They were at least able to stay with Renia's grandmother in her home. New arrivals with no family were forced to present themselves at administration headquarters and be allocated a room with a total stranger.

At least we didn't have to live, sleep, eat and dress at close quarters with total strangers. Seeing the dead bodies after the public

ŁÓDŹ

hangings in my home town was shocking, but soon death was everywhere. People were dying all the time of starvation and disease in the Łódź ghetto.

Outside the block every morning there were dead bodies left on the pavement to be picked up by the dorożki, *the death cart, and taken to the Jewish cemetery in Marysin to be buried. The bodies were wrapped up, made ready in whatever material people could find, or in newspaper, and collected. Sometimes they had swollen limbs, endemic swellings they called it, caused by starvation.*

What a terrible way to leave this world, left out on the pavement and collected like a parcel.

In the Jewish faith, the care of the body immediately following death is to respect the sacredness of the deceased. From the moment of death until the burial, the deceased should not be left alone. Usually, the deceased are buried as soon as possible, often within hours of death, except on Shabbat and festivals.

It upset everyone in that ghetto so deeply to not be able to give their loved ones the respect and care they deserved with a proper burial, or to be able to observe seven days of mourning, a time we call Shiva. The pain and the loss and the despair in that ghetto was beyond anything you can imagine.

But we got used to the sight of dead bodies in the street very quickly.

Death was now a part of the landscape. The Berkowiczs were packed into a sodden heap of humanity, forced to walk around the remains of cadavers.

On the first weekend after their arrival, 105 people died in the ghetto over the course of just two days of either starvation, disease or both. This was a low figure; sometimes double that number could die over two days. It was the job of the family of the deceased to notify the administration. Once the body had been collected by the horse-drawn *dorożki*, it was taken to the Jewish cemetery in Marysin, in the northern edge of the ghetto. Once there, the body would at least be buried in an individual grave, unlike in the Warsaw ghetto where bodies were flung in a mass burial pit.

The Jewish cemetery in Łódź predated the ghetto and remains the largest Jewish cemetery in Europe, the final resting place for 230,000 Jews.

By the time of the Berkowiczs' arrival in 1942, the Germans had forbidden the erection of stone graves and so burial sites in the Ghetto Field, as it became known, were marked with metal bed frames or whatever people could find. An estimated 45,000 victims of the Nazis would go on to be buried in the Ghetto Field.

For those still living, food, or the lack of it, dominated the thoughts of every waking moment. On arrival in the ghetto, newcomers would receive bread and ration cards.

Rations were delivered into the ghetto every ten days and prisoners had to stand in line for hours on end at food distribution points to receive them. Only a fraction of what was promised usually arrived. The Germans strictly monitored anything entering or leaving the ghetto and used food supply as a further way to control the population.

Rations usually consisted of potatoes and, if you were lucky, turnips, radish greens, peas, beets, or a dark, lumpy and sticky bread that had to be carefully rationed to last until the next delivery. Very occasionally, meat of a dubious origin, like horse meat, became available.

Those in more privileged positions, or who were close to Chairman Rumkowski, had access to more food, but the majority teetered on the edge of starvation. Those in employment could

ŁÓDŹ

secure an extra ration, usually a thin, watery bowl of something purporting to be soup, in the workplace.

Rations had to be purchased with a special ghetto currency. Germans forced Jews to exchange their pre-war money, if they had managed somehow to keep or hide it, for this new currency, which Jews called Chaimki or Rumki after Chairman Rumkowski.

This currency only enabled prisoners to purchase the most meagre food and clothing and would have been useless outside the ghetto walls.

All we talked about was food. By the time we arrived in the Łódź ghetto, we'd been prisoners of the Nazis for nearly three years. We were starving, wasting away in that strange place.

We were so isolated and cut off. Two of the city's major roads – Nowomiejska-Zgierska and Limanowskiego streets – carrying non-Jewish traffic ran through the ghetto, but were sealed off from the ghetto. Barbed wire separated us from those roads, too, and if we needed to cross them we had to use newly built, wooden footbridges, 25 feet above ground. I think I only used them once soon after we arrived, I crossed over with Mama and we could see people, well fed, well dressed, going about their business in the trams below. It was so strange. We felt like animals in a zoo.

I've already told you that Mama was immediately affected by losing Stenia, but we began to realise how poorly she was in the ghetto. She had never recovered from losing my sister and now she had gallstones. She could never build her strength up. I hated to see her in pain and suffering. And my poor father. He was devoted to his father, and he missed him very much.

Still reeling from losing Stenia, Bubbe and Zayde, eight days after their arrival, the Berkowiczs, and all the other prisoners of the doomed ghetto, were to suffer another devastating blow.

On Friday, 4 September 1942, approximately 1,500 people gathered under a hot and leaden sky in Fire Brigade Square (13 Lutomierska Street) to hear the Chairman speak.

Old people leant on the frail and withered arms of their children. Mothers clutched children to their breasts. Orphaned children stood alone. An expectant hush fell at precisely 4.45pm as the Chairman appeared on a raised stage above the crowd, his head bowed, lips pinched.

'A grievous blow has struck the ghetto,' he announced, his amplified voice coming out of the loudspeakers and reverberating around the square.

'They [the Germans] are asking us to give up the best we possess – the children and the elderly. I was unworthy of having a child of my own, so I gave the best years of my life to children. I've lived and breathed with children. I never imagined I would be forced to deliver this sacrifice to the altar with my own hands. In my old age, I must stretch out my hands and beg: Brothers and sisters, hand them over to me! Fathers and mothers, Give me your children!'

A horrible, terrified wailing erupted among the assembled crowd.

The Chairman's voice rose to compete with the crowd. 'I had a suspicion something was about to befall us. I anticipated "something" and was always like a watchman on guard to prevent it. But I was unsuccessful because I did not know what was threatening us. I did not know the nature of the danger. The taking of the sick from the hospitals caught me completely by surprise. And I give you the best proof there is of this: I had my own nearest and dearest among them and I could do nothing for them.

'I thought that that would be the end of it, that after that they'd leave us in peace, the peace for which I long so much, for which I've always worked, which has been my goal. But something else, it turned out, was destined for us. Such is the fate of the Jews: always more suffering and always worse suffering, especially in times of war. Yesterday afternoon, they gave me the order to send more than 20,000 Jews out of the ghetto, and if not . . .'

On he went, his words thrusting with the sharpness of a sword through the stunned crowd, culminating in the line that unleashed a mournful wail to rise up.

'I must perform this difficult and bloody operation – I must cut off limbs in order to save the body itself! I must take children because, if not, others may be taken as well. God forbid.'

Hysterical mothers looked about wildly, already frantically pushing their way through the crowds in the direction of home. Cut off limbs to save the body? The metaphor was as blunt as some had come to expect from the controversial Chairman. These children weren't limbs, they were their hearts, their reasons for living.

News swept through the narrow ghetto streets like a sour wind, passing from lip to ear.

In the ghetto, Rumkowski's reputation teetered on a fine line between love and hate. Many professed admiration, in public at least. He was a powerful figure in the ghetto. But in private, many expressed distrust. Others had nothing but hatred at what they saw as his betrayal and branded him a narcissistic megalomaniac. Chaim Mordechai Rumkowski is a divisive figure. Renia's attitude was, and remains, pragmatic.

I don't think Mama or Tatuś went to listen to that speech that I remember. Rumkowski was a very controversial figure. If he hadn't delivered what they asked, they would have closed down the ghetto and killed everybody. What could he do for the best? I know he wasn't all that good, but for me, I see it as what choice did he have? I didn't hate him, but I didn't love him either. As I see it, he didn't have very much of an option.

The very next day it started. Notices began appearing, posted everywhere, warning the ghetto that no one must leave their home from 5pm on Saturday, 5 September 1942, until further notice.

It was called the *Sperre*, an abbreviation of German for curfew, *Gehsperre*. The enforced curfew was designed to make it easier for the Jewish police, ordered by the Germans, to pluck the children, infirm and elderly from their homes. On 7 September, the SS and Kripo (*Kriminalpolizei*, or Criminal Police) stepped in to oversee the selection, which lasted until 12 September 1942.

A thick blanket of smothering heat covered the ghetto as mothers began hiding their children in attics and other dark hidey-holes.

They came with their closed-in lorries, pouring into the courtyard of our block. The loudspeaker crackled through the air. 'Everyone, raus, outside and line up in the courtyard.'

One by one, doors opened and a stream of frightened people filed outside.

They picked out my bubbe and ordered her into the lorry. Somehow, I slipped through the net; I don't know how as I was small and very skinny. Then the SS man in charge of our selection noticed the ring on my father's finger.

'I want the ring!' the SS man ordered. My father tried to explain, 'I can't get it off.' The SS man tried, fiddling with it, backwards and forwards, but he could tell that he would never get the ring off, so he said to the guard next to him, 'Fetch an axe and chop the finger off!' Just like that! That's when I saw a miracle. You had to

see it to believe it. As he finished saying these few words, the ring slipped off my father's finger on its own without any prompting. It rolled along the ground and stopped at the SS man's feet.

'Pick it up!' the SS man ordered my father. My father did and gave it to him. In return, he got some very hard kicks. Then they left.

Something you can never forget. Only the Almighty could have arranged that.

The convoy of trucks started up and rolled out of the courtyard with all Renia's family treasures. Her falsified date of birth had worked; Szaja's quick thinking had saved his elder daughter's life. As far as the Germans were concerned, Renia was sixteen and didn't fall into their selection criteria.

All over the ghetto, similarly gut-wrenching scenes played out. Orphanages were liquidated, hospitals emptied. Some of the elderly looked resigned to their fate. The children cried out for their mothers, gripping the sides of trucks or carts, tears streaming down their faces. Others imagined they were going on an adventure.

Anyone caught running was gunned down. An elderly woman who was confused and didn't know which line to go to was shot on the spot. At 3 Zgierska Street, a thirteen-year-old boy found hiding in a dustbin was dragged out and executed.

All week long, the ghetto was filled with the sound of screams, gunshots, barking and the knock of rifle butts battering doors, always accompanied with the same order. '*Alle Juden raus!*' All Jews out.

The third anniversary of the war was drenched in tears. The children and elderly – 15,682 in total – were taken from the ghetto and sent to Kulmhof death camp, where Stenia had been murdered, leaving in their wake a congregation of the broken-hearted.

Tatuś was terribly upset about his mother. Tears ran down his face, but he couldn't do anything. No one could. Now there was just me, Tatuś, Mama and Auntie Gitel. My heart was breaking into little pieces as, one by one, my family were taken from me. That night, I fell asleep wrapped in Mama and Tatuś's arms, all of us crying because we knew we would never see Bubbe again.

And, of course, the terrible thought always playing on their minds.

Who would be next?

Chapter Six

Hunger

The soul was sucked from the ghetto. There was almost no one left over the age of sixty-five, or under ten. Emptied of young children and the elderly, the place became an even more bleak, colourless terrain. Nervous breakdowns became commonplace.

On Wednesday, 21 October 1942, a 46-year-old man, Icek Dobrzynski, from Zduńska Wola, whose two children had been taken in the selection, jumped from the fifth floor of his home. With her husband and children dead, the following day, his wife, Fraidla Ruchla, also decided her life wasn't worth living. At first, she 'went into the wire', a euphemism for running into the barbed-wire perimeter fence to deliberately catch a German bullet. When the sentry refused to shoot her, she leapt from one of the wooden footbridges on to the 'Aryan' street outside the ghetto. Her body was quickly removed.

Renia watched her parents carefully. Her father, always a slim man, lost more weight, his face etched with grief. Nervous spasms gripped her heart so that she thought it might actually break. But it carried on stubbornly beating.

From its very beginnings, Rumkowski had set the ghetto up as a so-called model ghetto, with primary and secondary schools, a police force, hospitals, fire service, and even its own cultural hall on Krawiecka Street, known as the House of Culture, where plays, concerts and poetry recitals were performed.

Prisoners set up clandestine lending libraries, some managed to read and even write between work shifts, producing vivid ghetto diaries, notebooks, journals, poems, or contributing towards *The Chronicle of the Łódź Ghetto*, an extraordinary, lasting testimony of day-to-day life in the ghetto. The writers' intention was to alert the world to what was unfolding, as well as provide a detailed account for future generations.

Despite, or because of, the isolation, hunger and despair, to say nothing of the constant fear of selections, some ghetto prisoners were able to escape briefly into another reality.

Fundamentally, the ghetto was a giant industrial labour camp. Under the motto *'Unser Einziger Weg Ist – Arbeit!'* ('Our only path is work'), Rumkowski believed that if the ghetto remained productive, then the Nazis wouldn't murder their workforce.

The Łódź ghetto was making such a significant contribution towards war production in the Reich that Hans Biebow had been able to ward off demands from the SS Chief, Heinrich Himmler, to liquidate the entire ghetto, compromising instead on the resettlement of 'non-productive' Jews.

After the maelstrom of the Great Sperre, ghetto life was transformed. Rumkowski's plans were crumbling and his influence with Biebow waning. Orphanages, some hospitals and schools were closed down. Biebow ordered all Yiddish and Hebrew signs to be replaced with German, or painted over. He suspended the rabbinate and ramped up the Nazi work machine.

By September 1942, over a hundred ghetto work departments, or *resorts*, used the labour of nearly 74,000 Jews. Ninety per cent of production was for the Wehrmacht, making Army uniforms. German department stores placed most of the rest of the remaining orders.

HUNGER

Every morning at 6am, German loudspeakers blared in the squares to tell people who needed work to assemble, then they would be directed to work and forced to slave for up to fourteen hours a day in overcrowded, poorly ventilated workshops.

We were all put to work straight away. I worked in a factory which made uniforms for the German Army. I was on a production line making part of a uniform. I was responsible for pockets and buttonholes. I was the youngest in the factory at thirteen.

We all worked on a long wooden bench. No one spoke much; no one had the energy to talk. Apparently in other factories, whispers would come down the line, 'Go slow,' in an effort to slow down production, but not in mine.

I don't remember ever being given any soup or bread in the factory. We had no idea the fortune our labour was making for the Germans.

Berlin made a net profit of 46,211,485 Reichsmark from the Łódź ghetto, derived from the productivity of the Jewish prisoners and confiscations of their property.

Mama and Tatuś were lucky, if you could call it that. Tatuś got a job working in a coal distribution depot and Mama and Auntie Gitel got a job in potato distribution. They were the best jobs in the ghetto, second to working in a baker's, as it meant from time to time, they got a precious extra potato, so we didn't starve like other people. If I'm not mistaken, my Aunt Miriam's husband was connected, and he got them the jobs. He knew lots of people.

It meant that we could have a bit of boiled potato in the evening. That was a luxury. Sometimes we could add them to our evening soup. I see that horrible thin soup now, with the odd bit of turnip, or occasionally potato.

Those extra potatoes saved our lives. There were so many who would have died for a potato peeling, never mind a potato.

Directly downstairs on our street was a shop called a gas kitchen, where people in the neighbourhood could pay to cook with gas without having to pay for expensive fuel, or buy a little hot water. Mama often sent me down with a pot of the evening soup to heat up. I sometimes used to burn my fingers taking the hot saucepan back up to our room. You would see people there boiling up a few turnips or heating soup.

Life was just one long shift. I had no friends my own age. Most of the children my age and younger had been taken. We never went out in the evening. Where could we go? Besides, there was a curfew and you could be shot if they saw you out.

At night, I was so tired from work that I slept like the dead. Occasionally, I dreamt of happier days, of Kalisz and the forest, of playing with my little sister. Then I'd wake up and the nightmare would begin again. Trudging to work past bodies, factories everywhere pumping smoke. People just dropped dead on the street. There were bodies everywhere.

Familiar sights on the street included people with yellow skin hanging off their skeletal bodies, grossly swollen limbs, or protruding bellies caused by malnutrition, so that even a twelve-year-old girl could look pregnant. Such people were usually referred to as resembling a *klepsydra*, 'hourglass', or 'walking obituaries'.

There was always something strange and terrible in that ghetto. We went to work and we came home and sat in that freezing cold, miserable room, night after night. Sunday was our day off and we spent it washing our clothes in a basin before hanging them in the courtyard, or trying to clean our room with cold water.

HUNGER

Occasionally, Mama cried. I'd sit next to her and hold her hand and try to comfort her. Her tears were for Stenia, always for Stenia. We'd all hoped that maybe after the war, we would find her, but after the last selection, when Bubbe and so many others were taken, that hope died. We had no idea where people were going, or what exactly was happening to them, but we knew they were being killed. We knew.

In my worst moments, I kept replaying that silly row with Stenia, where I accidentally scratched her over that Shirley Temple chocolate wrapper. Poor little thing. Why had I rowed with her over something so silly? Or I would torture myself with memories of the food I used to hide under the table before the war. It was so easy to have regrets in the ghetto.

In those long, dark, cold and hungry days, it was Mama who kept me going. It wasn't so much what she said. I barely remember anything of what she said, or what she even looked like, or the smell of her, or the sound of her laugh. The ghetto years have stolen my memories. That hurts me so much, losing memories of the little things. But I'll always remember her quiet, continual presence, her prayers and her love, and that's what counts. She was a source of comfort to me, as I was to her. We never left each other's side, apart from to go to work. In that place, she barely let me out of her sight if she could help it. In those days, she was everything to me. I relied on her completely.

January 1943 and the new year slithered in with plunging rations and epidemics of tuberculosis and typhus. The death cart became an increasingly familiar sight in the ghetto, rattling over the cobbles, with emaciated, naked legs dangling over the sides.

Every morning it was the same. The clop of the doctor's horse pulling the *dorożki*. The scuff and slap of disintegrating boots and clogs along the foggy streets as the factory whistles sounded at six in the morning. That winter, the rough, uneven streets seemed perpetually coated in thick snow and ice, which made crossing the footbridges a feat of endurance and led to huge 'rush hour' queues to cross.

Hunger draped over everything. Memories of past meals rose like steam in Renia's mind. Roast potatoes, brisket of beef, pickled cucumbers, borscht, soft white bread. Those memories lingered hour to hour, meal to meal.

By 1943, they were nothing but skin and bone. Life in the ghetto seemed a hopeless procession of long, endlessly drawn-out days, punctuated by sudden, radical events.

The morning of Saturday, 5 June 1943 dawned bright and clear. Larger than usual shipments of potatoes had been arriving into the ghetto for the previous month, keeping Sala busy and lighting little sparks of hope in people's eyes. Many began to hope that, perhaps, just maybe, they might survive. Then, quite suddenly, the Berkowiczs received a notice to leave their home and move to a different address in the ghetto. Renia can't remember this event, or what prompted it, but the order to leave their home at 11 Sulzfelderstrasse must have come as a blow. Sala and Szaja must have viewed it as a harbinger of the dreaded resettlement. It is not difficult to imagine their anxiety.

The day after, as thousands streamed out of their airless rooms and headed to the green grass of Marysin in the northern part of the ghetto, for the briefest respite from labour, Renia, her parents and Aunt Gitel moved their few possessions into 21 Kelmstrasse.

They trudged past the site of the long-ago-liquidated gypsy camp, at number 82–84, now the site of a shoemaker's department, which manufactured military boots, including straw shoes for German soldiers on the Eastern Front. Further up the street at number 10, a printing house churned out official Nazi orders. Then, they walked under the shadow cast by the two distinctive red towers of St Mary's Assumption's Church, where, unbeknown to them, the Nazis had stored the clothes and bedding of the Jews murdered at Kulmhof. Hundreds, if not thousands, of sacks of clothing, feather and down filled the aisles and spilled over the pulpit. White feathers floated up to the church roof and escaped under the door, drifting up the grimy streets, earning the church the nickname 'The White Factory'.

The new room was smaller, but just as squalid. To this day, I don't know the reason why we moved.

By the end of June 1943, those extra potatoes were nothing but a distant memory. Naked hunger gripped once more. As summer spread over the ghetto, those with the energy to do so embarked on a mission to nourish the brain, if not the stomach. Director of the Department of Vital Statistics, Henryk Neftalin, urged all ghetto superintendents to search the attics, basements and apartments that had been vacated after the Great Sperre for forgotten books.

Some 30,000 books, from age-old family heirlooms to holy books, were rescued and lovingly preserved and catalogued. Shelves reaching up to the ceiling were filled with books that had been handed down for generations, forming a unique, but precarious ghetto library. Yiddish bibliophiles also set up lending libraries from their homes, nailing notices to their door. *Attention: I lend out Yiddish books.* According to *The Chronicle,* the German authorities in the ghetto tolerated these libraries, provided they didn't stock books the Nazis referred to as 'degenerate art' – so-called subversive work incompatible with Nazi values.

Equally tantalising must have been the sight of small vegetable gardens in the heart of the ghetto city. Spinach, radishes and small bunches of lettuce were harvested that summer to be distributed, protected by a garden 'fence' fashioned from old iron bedsteads, fastened together with stretched-out mattress springs.

In some windows, hopeful residents who had been fortunate enough to purchase seeds, planted red beets in window boxes and leeks and radishes on the roof of a courtyard toilet. Even the occasional determined sweet pea was spotted climbing up crumbling walls.

The ghetto library and gardens testify to the Jewish prisoners' will to do more than just exist and to their desire to hold on to even the most fragile kind of beauty.

Despite the degrading conditions, some retained their dignity and humanity, seeking out intellectual and spiritual nourishment, in direct defiance of the Nazi, so-called 'master race's' attempt to destroy it.

What went on outside the walls of the ghetto was a mystery, the world beyond an alternate reality. Just beyond the barbed wire on Urzędnicza Street, an amusement park was set up on the 'Aryan' side. Every day after work, the surviving ghetto children made a pilgrimage to the spot where they could gaze longingly at the merry-go-round and listen to the strains of music and laughter.

Hundreds of miles further west, an altogether more thunderous noise sounded. Allied bombers were targeting German cities and, in the summer of 1943, Hamburg was reduced to rubble by the bombing raids of Operation Gomorrah, an event of which Renia was oblivious, but which would change the direction of her life. Inside the ghetto, it was so easy for Renia to forget there was a life outside the barbed wire. Unlike the Warsaw ghetto, which had a thriving black market with many young smugglers risking their lives every day to bring back food and news of events, in the Łódź ghetto they were utterly isolated.

We had no idea what was happening. We dreamt of liberation, but by 1943, we didn't expect it. We felt forgotten. It had been so many years, after all.

On the afternoon of Monday, 30 August 1943, Renia and her parents had other concerns to occupy their minds. By this stage, disease was rampant. Well water was often contaminated with faecal matter which, combined with non-existent sanitation, filth and lack of food, meant that thousands of Jews in the ghetto were dying of preventable diseases.

Perhaps it's not surprising that I got ill. Very ill, very quickly. I came home from work with a headache, then a fever. Mama managed to get a doctor somehow and he confirmed it was typhus.

'She has to go to the hospital,' he told Mama. I went to the hospital and when I got there the first thing they gave me, to my surprise, was a meal – a plate of sauerkraut! A luxury!

I had such a high temperature and was so terribly ill, I couldn't eat it. Then they shaved my head. They thought the hair carried diseases. I was crying bitterly and the doctor said to me, 'Don't cry, child. If you manage to keep your head, you'll have other hair.' I was very, very upset.

They took me up to the ward. There were adults and children, all with typhus. I was so ill that night, I can hardly remember it, but I do know they managed to find an injection. Where they got it from, I don't know, but I know it saved my life. I was very ill, close to death.

Renia had been admitted to one of the few remaining hospitals in the ghetto, the Hospital for Contagious Diseases at 74 Dworska Street, which had previously been a home for the elderly. After the Great Sperre had emptied the ghetto of the elderly, it was converted into a hospital in September 1942.

The doctor, Arnold Mostowicz, spent many months treating

typhus patients like Renia, heroically working through epidemic after epidemic, going on to contract the disease himself.

The next night, there was a big commotion. The Nazis had come! I heard the lorries pulling up outside. Then we heard heavy boots and screams, the sound of patients pleading and crying. I lay there in the dark, so sick, so terrified, waiting for them to come into our ward, but they didn't. The next morning, we learnt the SS had emptied out practically the whole hospital and took them away, except for my ward.

Ironically, being on the typhus ward saved Renia's life. The Germans were terrified of contracting typhus, so avoided it at all costs. In the dead of night, on Tuesday, 31 August 1943, the SS and Kripo had trawled the rest of the hospital and another hospital at Mickiewicz Street, and dragged 225 patients, many with tuberculosis, from their beds.

The news spread rapidly and people had run, some still in their tattered bedclothes, in the direction of the hospitals in the hopes of saving a loved one. The next morning, the door handle of Renia's ward turned and everyone froze, but it was no gloved SS monster.

It was Mama. She'd stood outside the hospital all night long. 'I am taking my daughter home,' she insisted to the doctor. I probably should have stayed in hospital, but after the selection she didn't want me out of her sight. Somehow, I'd survived yet again.

Sala slipped her arm around her daughter and helped her from her hospital bed. It wasn't hard. Renia was as light as a feather.

Outside, the air was charged and full of adrenalin, reverberating still with the screams of the patients. On the fourth anniversary of war, mother and daughter walked unsteadily along the putrid streets, a fine layer of sweat soaking their hollow cheeks. At home, Sala put her daughter to bed, gently kissed her bald head and prayed.

I had cheated death again. My poor mama. Her only surviving child had been at death's door when the Nazis had nearly snatched me in the night from my hospital bed. How must she have felt as she waited all night outside in the cold, watching, hoping and praying.

From Mama I learnt that faith equalled strength. 'God is looking after us. He gives us strength,' she told me. Through her I learnt that God's love never left us. He was protecting me all the time. I must have had a guardian angel looking after me.

The next day they had to go to work, Tatuś to the coal distribution centre and Mama to potato distribution. They had no choice. They would have been arrested if they didn't show up and so they had to lock me in the room all by myself.

'Whatever happens, don't answer the door,' Tatuś made me promise before he left.

I was still so ill and so terrified. Every time I heard the slightest noise, or footsteps outside, I thought it was the SS coming to take me away. I had to stay locked in the room for a few weeks at least. I've never known fear like it.

There was nothing to eat. Nothing to do. I just lay locked in a room, so sick and scared. I was very vulnerable then so Mama and Tatuś must have worked hard to feed and protect me.

As soon as I was strong enough to stand, I went back to work. I was only too pleased to not be on my own. I was so grateful to be with my parents and have part of my family with me. There were others my age in that ghetto who had lost all their family. If I had lost Mama and Tatuś in the Łódź ghetto I probably wouldn't have survived. I know that I wouldn't have been able to look after myself.

When Aunt Gitel was sent away five months later, in February 1944, it was just one more drop in a sea of hopelessness, her departure causing ripples of foreboding to her loved ones left behind.

She got notice to leave the ghetto and she had to go. Just like that. That's the way it happened. People got notice and had to go to a certain place and were never seen again. There were selections happening all the time. Mama was so unhappy about her sister.

The awful thing is, I don't even remember her leaving. Maybe I've blanked it out, but I do remember thinking afterwards that her departure was a tragedy. When someone left, we didn't expect to ever see them again. We all missed her greatly, not knowing what the future had in store for Aunt Gitel.

After that, we all became even closer, me, Mama and Tatuś. There was just the three of us. We were even more precious to one another.

And so it continued, terror alternating with tedium. A bitterly cold winter thawed into spring, but the icy bones of the ghetto remained frozen. By Renia's fifteenth birthday on 8 August 1944, her hair was growing back in tufts.

We'd long ago stopped marking birthdays, festivals or holidays in the ghettos. How could we? By then, after four and a half years of being prisoners of the Nazis, we'd stopped hoping for a future.

Being together with my parents was a gift and there wasn't a day in the ghetto I didn't realise that. Mama wouldn't talk about Stenia much, I knew it was just too painful, but there wasn't a day when that girl wasn't in our thoughts.

Each time I remembered her terrible parting in the square, the way she ran towards the trucks with tears streaming down her face, was like a fresh knife to my heart.

HUNGER

We lived with grief and fear. You never knew what was going to happen from one day to the next.

Unbeknown to the Berkowiczs, the fate of occupied Poland's last surviving ghetto had already been sealed. In May 1944, Heinrich Himmler, the second most powerful Nazi after Hitler, had ordered the liquidation of the entire ghetto. Over 7,000 Jews were deported to Kulmhof but the facilities weren't fast enough or large enough to comply with 'The Final Solution', so the authorities turned to another camp with more efficient methods of mass extermination.

In August 1944, under the blistering sun, something foul and forbidding was ripening. Notices began appearing, nailed to workshop and factory walls, ordering the ghetto population to ready themselves to move to the Reich and present themselves at assembly points.

When that didn't work, Biebow, together with the Commander of the Gestapo, stood up in Bałuty Square and personally visited workshops to deliver speeches. The lies flowed so smoothly from his mouth.

'There is enough space in the carriages. Enough engines have now been supplied. If you are going as a family, take your pots, drinking vessels and cutlery, because we do not have those in Germany, as they have been handed out to air-raid victims. Once again, I assure you that we shall look after you.'

They promised us everything. They came into our places of work and told us we'd be sent to working camps where the conditions would be much better. They promised us good food and good living accommodation and good medical care. The only thing they wanted of us was that we should come to the station voluntarily. Later, I found out that it was because they didn't want a repetition of what happened in the Warsaw ghetto uprising of 1943, when the Jews of the ghetto, fearing deportation, bravely fought back for several weeks. All they had to fight with was a few rounds of smuggled-in ammunition and rusty knives. Many people were killed, including Germans, before the uprising was quashed.

Conditions in the ghetto worsened. They closed down the factories. They stopped bringing food in and it got really bad. We were starving. In the end, my parents reasoned that we had nothing to lose.

'If we stay here, we'll die of starvation anyway,' Mama said.

So, one day, we packed up a few belongings and made our way to the station. We only took a small parcel of clothing, so I think I must have had to leave behind Aunt Esther's blue-and-white polka-dot dress. We lost everything; we didn't have anything.

All over the ghetto, people forced their raw and ulcerated feet into old clogs and shoes and packed up their scant possessions in shabby bundles and small cases for the journey.

Anyone who didn't go voluntarily, or attempted to go into hiding, was subjected to brutal round-ups. The transports started leaving Radegast on, or around, the day of Renia's fifteenth birthday and lasted for the rest of August 1944.

Drained of their strength, deprived of their dignity, cut off and systematically starved, an estimated 67,000 Jews from the Łódź ghetto were herded into railway freight wagons at Radegast station.

I was so scared as I held Mama's hand and we boarded the freight wagon and prepared ourselves for the journey ahead. And to think, we believed that wherever the wagons were going, surely it wouldn't be as bad as what we'd already lived through.

But then, we still didn't know what the Nazis were really capable of.

Chapter Seven

Auschwitz-Birkenau

The journey was as atrocious and dehumanising as the transport from Zduńska Wola to Łódź had been. More so, because two years on, people were even thinner and weaker. The freight wagon left Radegast station in the late afternoon and journeyed by night. As the wagons rumbled slowly south through the blacked-out countryside, a cloud of dread seeped through the foul-smelling interior.

Over a hundred of us were packed so tightly into one freight wagon built for animals. We had no space to move. We had no food, water or air. There were Germans with machine guns on the steps of the wagon if you tried to escape. Everyone was terrified. We heard rumours about notes found hidden in the walls of the wagon.

Some of these notes, written by victim Rachel Bohm, survived. She listed all the stations they passed and ended by stating that they had reached a place called Auschwitz at 10am, and stopped later at a place called Birkenau. No more was heard from her after that.

Some Jewish people tried in different ways to convey their situation and feelings to loved ones left behind and, like Rachel, wrote them letters on scraps of paper they found, in great haste and in many cases, in code. Some writers threw their letters out of the wagon, in the hope that someone would pick them up and send them on to their destination. By August 1944, though, the Berkowiczs had neither pen, paper nor any remaining family to write to.

We had nothing. Just a few clothes and maybe a saucepan. It was dark and I was so afraid. We travelled overnight, but you couldn't sleep. We were all sitting one on top of another. I held my mother's hand all the way and I hoped and prayed. The only comfort was that at least I was with my parents. We didn't speak. We were too distressed to talk. I could only see Mama's outline in the darkness. I tried to concentrate on the feeling of my mother's hand in mine. It was like holding on to life.

Dawn was breaking when the wagon finally slowed to a halt and the heavy doors were unbolted and slid open. Immediately, we heard dogs barking. All was chaos. Screaming. Bellowing. It seemed as if an army of heavily armed Gestapo and SS men with lunging, barking German shepherd dogs were waiting on the platform shouting orders. It was so terribly frightening; it's impossible to describe the chaos.

They shouted non-stop. Raus! . . . Raus! Get out. Get off the train. Be quick. Leave the luggage.

My father jumped off first and I jumped after him. By the time I jumped off I didn't see him any more. He disappeared into thin air, without a kiss or a goodbye.

I never saw my father again.

All around us were electrified, illuminated fences and above them stood high watchtowers. Prisoners in striped uniforms and caps moved amongst the crowds collecting the luggage.

One of them muttered as a warning, 'You are here now in

Auschwitz-Birkenau. This is the place where people are being taken straight to the gas chambers.' That was our greeting.

But what was Auschwitz-Birkenau? We didn't know what that meant. It didn't mean anything. But one word did make sense and sent a cold shiver running through us. Gas.

The guards moved in and we were forced to join a column of women, queuing five abreast. Stretching off in all directions, as far as the eye could see, were rows of wooden and brick huts.

Shuffling closer to the top of the line, Renia hovered on a knife edge between life and death. At Auschwitz-Birkenau, the average life expectancy for someone aged fourteen or under was three months or less. Renia had turned fifteen just a few days before.

The Berkowiczs had arrived in the clamorous heat of August 1944. The new unloading ramp Renia and her mother were standing on had been in use for the past two and a half months, since mid-May 1944, built especially for the arrival of over 430,000 Jewish prisoners from Hungary, enabling them to bring transports directly into the centre of Birkenau, making the process of mass murder more efficient.

Two months on from the D-Day landings of 6 June 1944, Allied boots were on the ground in occupied Europe, with the Soviets advancing from the east and American and British troops from the west, but this did little to slow down the gassings and burnings.

By August 1944, as well as transports from the Łódź ghetto, new arrivals were coming in daily from Italy and the Netherlands, as well as Polish prisoners arrested en masse after the Warsaw Uprising. The Auschwitz-Birkenau gas chambers and crematoria were working around the clock, sometimes leading to delays that meant people were forced to sit under armed guard while they waited their turn. When the crematoria couldn't keep up, gassed bodies were burnt in incineration pits and pyres.

Auschwitz-Birkenau is the Nazi concentration camp that holds the most powerful grip over the collective consciousness, but the Third Reich had over 2,500 extermination, concentration, slave labour and transit camps, including a vast network of sub-camps throughout Europe.

Auschwitz-Birkenau was unusual in that it served as both extermination and concentration camp, able to carry out systematic mass murder on an industrial scale and also kill inmates more slowly through starvation, abuse, forced labour and disease.

It had originally been established as a camp for Polish political prisoners and only later, in 1942, became a killing centre for Jews. Even after this time, Auschwitz always retained the functions of a site of slave labour and punishment, like other Nazi concentration and labour camps, meaning that some Jewish deportees were selected to be worked to death. This was in contrast to the other major extermination camps in German-occupied Poland – Kulmhof, Bełżec, Sobibór and Treblinka – which existed only for the purpose of murdering Jews; almost everyone deported to these sites was murdered on arrival. Despite this, Auschwitz eventually had the largest death toll as a result of the sheer numbers of Jews sent there from across Europe and the deadly nature of the work to which those who survived the selections were subjected.

Neither mother nor daughter had the slightest clue as to the vast complexity and scale of the camp they had just arrived at, or that on average, 70 to 75 per cent of new prisoner arrivals were sent straight to the gas chambers to be gassed, then burnt. Cut off and isolated, very few of the new arrivals from the Łódź ghetto had heard the rumours of mass gassings.

I didn't understand what any of it meant. My mother and I shuffled forward in the queue, holding hands, too scared to talk. At the head of the queue there stood an SS officer conducting a selection, spotless in his grey-green uniform, with silver skulls on the collar. He had such shiny black boots. We later learnt that this was Dr Josef Mengele, the butcher of Auschwitz. With a click of his finger he directed one person to live, another one to die. He played God. All the old people, pregnant women, invalids and children, people who didn't look fit for work, were directed to the left and joined a long queue of women trailing off into the distance.

At the front of the queue, the moment of the selection, I was so terrified I could hardly breathe. An SS officer noticed we were holding hands so he split us up. My mother was directed left and I was sent to the right. Before I had a chance to scream or cry out she came back to my side. There was NO WAY the SS man could not have seen her swap sides. He must have gone blind for a split second. I believe it was a miracle. There's no way that they wouldn't have noticed it. The relief I felt when she came back to my side! I can see it now, as though it happened yesterday.

To Renia, there was no logical answer to what had just happened. Similarly harrowing situations played out all around them as families from the Łódź ghetto were split up at the ramp selection. No one knew which line represented life and which equalled death. In those febrile selections, the balance between life and death was tissue-thin.

To Renia's intense relief, she was able to stay by her mother's side. For now. The SS officer pointed right and the newly arrived prisoners, known as *Zugang*, moved off under armed guard into the camp.

A MOTHER'S PROMISE

A selection of Hungarian Jews at Auschwitz-Birkenau, 1944. Picture from 'The Auschwitz Album'

We walked for over a mile through the barracks. We must have been a shabby sight. Years later I met a woman who was in Auschwitz-Birkenau when we arrived from the Łódź ghetto. She told me we looked worse than even the people in Auschwitz!

Our abandoned belongings were already on their way to the camp's warehouses, a place nicknamed 'Kanada', so called because it was a country that represented wealth and plenty. I didn't leave my mother's side for a second; I stuck to her like glue.

As we walked on the bumpy, dusty track through the camp, the sound of classical music floated over us. Auschwitz-Birkenau had its own camp orchestras.

Renia listened disbelievingly as the music drifted over her. The main function of the orchestra, all prisoners, was to go to the main gate every morning and afternoon, where they were forced to play upbeat marching music for the thousands of prisoners who worked outside the camp.

Unbeknown to Renia, her route took her and her mother between gas chambers and crematoria IV and V. Renia did not register the low brick buildings with the chimneys pumping thick grey smoke, or the marshy grey artificial ponds nearby where human ashes were dumped and floated. Even had she realised what they were, how was a fifteen-year-old girl ever supposed to comprehend the sinister function of such ordinary-looking buildings and ponds?

A terrible sickly-sweet foul smell filled the air. We didn't know what the strange smell was or where it was coming from.

Finally, we came to the far end of the camp and were ordered into a brick building, in front of a gravel square. We were pushed through the doors into what looked like a large hall with concrete floors, bare walls and wooden benches at the edges.

A guard ordered, 'Strip and leave your clothes on the benches.'

We did as we were told, trembling with fright. Women everywhere were shaking at the shame of being forced to be naked in front of strange men. Young officers walked up and down the room laughing and joking, demanding whatever jewellery we had. They were laughing at us. They were having the time of their lives.

As I got undressed and was forced to stand naked in front of the Nazis, I felt so humiliated and scared. It was terrible, just terrible. I tried to cover myself. I was only fifteen, and of course I'd never been naked in front of anyone before. Even in the overcrowded ghettos I'd managed to have some privacy. Can you imagine how I felt?

For the first time I was also seeing my mother naked. She was so skinny, all the bones sticking out from her skin. Most of the women around us were no better off. We entered Auschwitz-Birkenau nothing but skin and bone.

It was here that some women also suffered humiliating oral and vaginal examinations, as guards hunted out hidden valuables. Women who were pregnant or sick and had somehow managed to avoid the ramp selection were also spotted here and marched to the gas chambers. The naked women were herded like animals up a long corridor, known to the SS as 'the dirty corridor'.

Everything happened so fast. 'Stay close to me,' my mother whispered. At the end of the corridor, prisoners in striped uniforms were shaving off all the hair of the new arrivals.

My mother was pushed towards a female prisoner holding a blunt razor and I watched as Mama's beautiful thick, dark hair fell to the concrete floor. They left nothing, not a hair on my mother's whole body. All the women in our transport had every hair cut off their body, from the hair on their head, to their underarm and pubic hair. These young Nazi guards were watching it all, laughing and joking like they were at a party.

After my mother's hair was shaved, I didn't recognise her. I was spared because my hair was nothing but short curls after it had been shaved off in the infectious diseases ward in the hospital in Łódź. Starvation meant that I hadn't gone through puberty, so there was no pubic or underarm hair to shave.

It was dreadful. My mother's beautiful hair, gone. She didn't look like herself any more. Try to imagine your mother with no hair and how strange she would look.

We were all in such a state of shock.

AUSCHWITZ-BIRKENAU

They were each now one of the mass of nameless, indistinguishable people at Auschwitz-Birkenau. The entire experience of the *Sauna,* as the building they were in was called, was designed to disinfect and dehumanise all who stepped through its doors. Their clothes were already being piled into one of the large *Sauna* ovens and baked to disinfect them, all external traces of their former identities stolen and sent to 'Kanada' storage huts for processing.

The human hair from prisoners, including those murdered in the gas chambers, was collected to package up and sell to textile factories where it was used as yarn for mattresses and socks for U-boat crews, as well as fuses for German bombs. Many tonnes of human hair made their way out of Auschwitz-Birkenau in bags stamped 'KLAu *Konzentrationslager Auschwitz'.*

Every fragment of a Jewish prisoner's identity would be stolen, shorn and stripped from them, and recycled into the Third Reich.

Outside these walls of horror lay a complicated maze of officialdom. How could it be that a typist, far away on the other side of the camp in Auschwitz l, would be calmly typing up accounts on the fifth day of every month reporting on deliveries of human hair, while the prisoners shivered naked?

The dehumanisation process was not yet complete for Renia.

They pushed us through some doors into what looked like a shower room. Several hundred naked women were pressed into the large empty room with concrete floors and walls. I heard the prisoner's voice echo in my ear.

'You are here now in Auschwitz-Birkenau. This is the place where people are being taken straight to the gas chambers.'

One by one, the women looked up to the long metal pipes and shower heads that ran over the ceiling. Everybody was saying prayers in Polish and Yiddish, hugging and kissing each other as we thought this was our last hour.

But then, instead of gas, cold water trickled over us. Water, not gas. Water! Can you imagine how we felt? We were the lucky ones.

There was no time to register their relief. '*Raus!*' screamed a guard. Dripping and slithering on the concrete floor, they were herded, still naked, up another long corridor, running parallel to the one through which they'd entered the shower room.

In the next room, old clothing was piled up in heaps. Prisoners flung clothes at us. You couldn't choose.

'Schnell! . . . Schnell!' *bellowed a guard.*

I was still wet and wanted to cover my body. I was given an old and dirty man's pyjama jacket and a skirt so big that it immediately fell down. Thinking quickly, my mother tore a strip from the bottom of the pyjama jacket and used it to tie the skirt tight round my waist. No underwear. No shoes. Nothing else.

These were to be my clothes until the end of the war.

Everybody else got similarly ill-fitting clothes. Dresses and skirts that were either too large or too small. Big people got small clothes; small people got big clothes. We all looked like we had come out of a lunatic asylum. We couldn't recognise each other. I kept staring at my mother; she looked so strange.

They gave us an oblong piece of white linen with a black number on to pin on our clothing, one on the front, one on the back. I don't remember the number, I only remember that there were a lot of 2s and 3s, and that it was one number different to my mother's. I don't know why we weren't tattooed.

AUSCHWITZ-BIRKENAU

Some prisoners arriving at Auschwitz-Birkenau were still being tattooed on arrival by 1944. The last recorded tattoo at the camp was on 5 January 1945, just twenty-two days before the camp was liberated. But for Renia, her mother and the other Łódź ghetto prisoners, the Nazis had other plans.

The women were pushed from the T-shaped *Sauna* building and ordered to sit on a patch of dirt outside the building. As the women from the Łódź ghetto looked at each other, their eyes raking over each other's bald heads and absurdly mismatched clothing, it must have been hard to comprehend their slide into hell.

Renia, her mother and the rest of the women who had survived the selection spent their first night in the same spot outside the block, frozen to the core, their senses assailed by the thick, noxious smoke, which seemed to hang over everything like a blanket. They weren't offered any food or water. As the light bleached from the sky, a stunned, disbelieving silence fell over the group as their new reality sank in.

At least in the ghetto, there had been some vestige of a normal life. Yes, it was a life of pain and starvation, overcrowding and labour, but they had at least been living among their families with a fragment of privacy. Few had believed Biebow's assurances that they were going somewhere better, with food, medicine and work, but this place was simply beyond imagination.

How had we found ourselves here in such a place? It was freezing, so cold that I thought I wouldn't live through the night. I had no underwear or shoes. I looked at my mother and realised she was as frightened as me. She looked so strange, so strange and so frightened.

What unimaginable terror. What was a mother to do? Sala had already had one daughter stolen from her. Her husband was missing. She was powerless to protect her surviving daughter. How much pain could one woman bear?

Renia leant against her mother's frail body and stared at the smoke-smudged horizon beyond the barbed wire, aching for the chance to give her father one last hug goodbye.

My thoughts went round and round. Where was he? Where had he been taken? Would I ever see him again?

It took another eighty years before I found out what the Nazis had done to my father.

Chapter Eight

Lost Hope

As Renia and her mother shivered their way through their first terrifying night in Auschwitz-Birkenau, a biting wind scouring their flesh, their fates were being decided by the SS. They were what the Nazis termed a 'deposit prisoner' held 'in transit' (*Durchgangsjuden*).

The smoke they saw billowing into the sky over the camp the previous day was the charnel dust of their friends and neighbours from the ghetto; the very people whose fragile bodies they had been pressed against in the freight wagons on the journey from Łódź. Of the 67,000 Jews transported from the liquidated Łódź ghetto to Auschwitz-Birkenau, approximately two thirds were murdered in the gas chambers within hours or days of their arrival.

Those selected as unfit for work were marched by the SS into one of four gas chambers at Birkenau and ordered to undress in special undressing rooms before being herded naked into the gas chambers. Victims were told that they were undergoing disinfection and showering. The gas-tight doors were then shut.

SS men in gas masks would then climb ladders and empty a canister of Zyklon B, a pesticide that had been used to control vermin in the ghettos, through special vents in the roof or walls. Once they reacted with heat and moisture, these crystallised pellets became deadly, releasing hydrogen cyanide. Victims could take up to twenty minutes to die, their bodies twisting in agony as they suffocated.

Only when the ventilation system had sucked out all the gas was the prisoner *Sonderkommando* (Special Labour Detail or Special Squad) sent in. They were forced to perform the gruesome task, under threat of death, of disposing of the corpses, extracting gold teeth, cutting off hair and washing away traces of blood and excrement from the floors. Other prisoners from the *Sonderkommando* unit were forced to operate the crematoria furnaces, incineration pits and pyres where the corpses were burnt, or work in the changing rooms collecting personal belongings.

For the bodies that did not burn completely, *Sonderkommando* prisoners were forced to use wooden mallets and pestles to crush larger bones and skulls into powder which was then dumped, along with the ashes, into the ponds at Birkenau, or loaded on to trucks and carried to the banks of the rivers Soła and Vistula, beyond the silver birch woods, where it was shovelled straight into the water or strewn in the fields as fertiliser.

These *Sonderkommando* units were kept in strict isolation from other prisoners and the SS routinely murdered most of each unit, in the very gas chambers and crematoria they had been forced to work in. By the time of Renia's arrival in August 1944, the number of prisoners in the Special Squad, working in day and night shifts, had reached 903.

Renia and her mother had survived after the mass murder of so many of their fellow Jews from the Łódź Ghetto, but they were by no means safe. They could still be selected for the gas chambers at any moment, or transferred to one of a sprawling network of camps located deep in the Third Reich to work as slave labour.

LOST HOPE

By August 1944, Third Reich policy was still the total annihilation of European Jewry. Hitler was determined to fulfil his promise of making Europe *judenrein* – free of all Jews – but that conflicted with the urgent need to use Jews as slave labour to make up for the workforce deficit. Germany and other occupied countries were undergoing heavy bombardment by the Allied forces and they needed the Jews alive longer, but only so they could work them to death on bomb sites or in factories for war industry.

At 4am on the morning after their arrival, Renia, her mother and the rest of their group were ordered to stand up, their limbs frozen rigid.

We were lined up and taken to a hut. All the huts in Auschwitz-Birkenau were the same. I stuck to my mother's side as we moved off under armed guard in the darkness.

I was starving and delirious with thirst. We hadn't eaten or drunk since the morning we'd left the ghetto and I'd lost count of the hours and days. All I knew was that my father had been taken by the Nazis. We didn't know where he was and I was terrified. I wasn't sure how long I could stand up for.

When we got to our hut, a young woman met us, well dressed, well fed, with a whip in her hand, and she screamed at us: 'I am very small, but I can beat you up very hard, don't forget!' Oh, believe me, she kept her word.

We walked into the hut and we were forced to sit on the concrete floor against the walls, five in a column, between each other's legs, packed like sardines. In this position, we had to sit day and night on the stone floor. Can you imagine? Strangers forced to rest their bald heads against the chest of the woman behind them! I managed to sit between my mother's legs.

Few women had underwear and some people with dysentery

A MOTHER'S PROMISE

and diarrhoea couldn't hold it in. Some young women still had their periods. It was awful, so degrading. There must have been over 500 women packed tight in that long hut on both sides. There wasn't a bunk bed that I saw. Just a long empty barrack with wooden walls and a stone floor. A row of small windows at the top of the barrack let in a little light.

A barrack at Auschwitz-Birkenau

LOST HOPE

It was August, so it was very hot, smelly and stuffy in that hut. Think of it, all those women pressed together so tightly in that suffocating heat. It was unbearable.

Within minutes, my legs went numb and my limbs were aching, and yet you couldn't stretch out.

Along the length of the hut ran a long, low concrete channel running from one end to the other. It was designed to be a heater to keep horses warm, but of course, no fires or heat for us. The boss of the hut, called the Kapo, walked up and down the channel with her whip in her hand beating anyone she spotted talking. She was a very cruel woman and would crack her whip and scream, 'Nicht sprechen!' No talking.

This was to be our home for roughly the next three weeks, day and night sitting on the stone floor. I had no idea what they planned to do with us.

Renia's hut was in an outlying part in the north of Birkenau, known to prisoners as 'Mexico'. The barracks had been adapted from a German Army field horse stable (*Pferdestallbaracken*) designed to comfortably house fifty-one horses, not several hundred women pressed together in a hot and sweaty tangle of limbs.

Once a day they (prisoner functionaries) came into the hut with a 'meal' for us. They came in with two trolleys. On one trolley were saucepans, on the other trolley was a cauldron of soup. Each column got a small saucepan of soup to share amongst five people. No spoons or cups, mind you. Can you imagine five starving people sharing a small saucepan of soup without a spoon? The person at the front of the column would get it first, then pass it back along the column. There were always arguments going on. 'You already had two sips, I only had one.'

The moment you swallowed more than three times, rows would break out. 'You've had more than your share, come on, hurry up, give us that pot.' Up and down the barrack, the same arguments would be breaking out.

All this over dirty water with a bit of turnip swimming around in it. From time to time, we got a little piece of bread with the soup, which we ate as soon as we could. If you wanted to keep the bread until later on, most of the time it would be stolen. And that was our food for the day.

Twice a day, there was Appell (roll call). The camp was very large and the roll calls were all at the same time, usually around 4am and again in the late afternoon.

We all had to go outside our huts and line up in rows of five. Always fives. It was easier for them to count. First, we were counted by the boss of the huts, the Kapo. When she'd finished, the SS guards came along and checked it all over. If they thought there was one person missing in the whole camp, we had to stand in these roll calls for hours on end while they counted and counted.

Women, who were weak with hunger and thirst, collapsed, or even dropped down dead and were taken away. It was a terrible thing to see. We stood in all weathers, heat, cold, mist, rain. The sun burnt women's bald heads. Numbers had to be correct, including dead ones. Two hours was normal, but sometimes we stood for up to six hours or even longer.

You can't imagine the scenes. The task of counting, until every last prisoner was accounted for, was a torture in itself. Prisoners were forbidden from moving and had to stand to attention. Some, who were too weak to stand, would be propped up either side by their fellow prisoners.

After each incoming transport, we could smell a seedy, sickly stench of burning flesh. We saw black smoke all over the place.

Prisoners who suffered from dysentery had to stand in humiliation as liquid excrement spattered down their legs, while the SS looked on, laughing and jeering.

All the time I stuck to my mother like glue. The guards didn't care about our suffering. They were all well fed, taking their time to count as if they had all the time in the world.

By August 1944, there were 3,300 SS male and female overseers working across the whole camp complex. One SS guard who took particular pleasure in the task of both selection and *Appell* was Irma Grese. Grese became the second-highest ranking SS *Aufseherin* (SS Female Overseer) at Auschwitz-Birkenau aged twenty, stirring panic and fear in every prisoner.

After roll call, we were allowed to use the latrines in a separate block. Inside were long planks of wood with holes cut in, built over a ditch. There was no privacy or dignity. Five hundred women going all together. The smell was impossible to describe.

You were only allowed about a minute and, of course, no toilet paper. They treated us like animals.

The occasional girl, if they were still strong enough, had their periods, but they had nothing to keep themselves clean or stop the blood. They had to cope the best they could.

Straight from the toilet, we went to the washroom. It was a long trough in a separate barracks. It was cold water. No soap. No towels to dry ourselves with. We tried to keep ourselves clean. It was important. It was all we had. We were under guard the whole time, in the latrines and while washing.

Then it was back to the hut where we sat in silence until early evening Appell, *jammed between each other's legs in lines of five. And that was it. A day felt like a year.*

Of all her torturous experiences at Auschwitz-Birkenau, the cruelty of their Kapo stood out to Renia. The SS lived in a well-protected compound outside the actual concentration camp area. Much of the discipline of the camp was overseen by so-called prisoner 'functionaries' appointed by camp authorities.

The decision revealed the psychological warfare of the concentration camp system, to put prisoners in charge of prisoners. These prisoners supervised their fellow captives, carrying out their work as a Kapo or as a *Blockälteste* (block elder).

In 'Mexico', many of these *Blockältestes* were Slovakian Jewish women, deported to Auschwitz in 1942, doing whatever it took to survive the camp. Some were known to be good and fair and did what they could to try to ease the terror prevailing in the camp. Some, however, like Renia's, were legendary for their cruelty. By 1944, some had become hardened, mimicking the aggression of their SS captors in order to curry favour and ensure their own survival.

Renia doesn't know what drove her own Kapo's cruelty, but the memory of the small wiry woman with the whip is seared into her brain.

Some of them were good, and they tried to use their position to help prisoners, but ours was so cruel. She didn't have to do it, to be so cruel and beat women with her whip, but she did. If she caught you speaking, God help you. I often caught the strokes of her whip. She had her own little cubicle at the front of the hut by the doors, with a heater for when she got cold. She entertained SS men there as well.

The hot August days of 1944 crawled by, long drawn-out days of exhaustion, disbelief and starvation, punctuated by violence and death. It would have been so easy for Renia to drown in this ocean of suffering, were it not for Sala.

LOST HOPE

It was my mother who kept me going; it was she who kept me alive. Without her, I don't think I could have managed to survive a single day. In a way, I kept her going too. We lived for each other. We weren't allowed to talk, but just her presence gave me the will to survive Auschwitz-Birkenau.

There were two sisters still together in my block, but not any mothers and daughters that I was aware of. Most women were alone, separated from their loved ones. I knew how lucky I was to be together with my mother. It was all I had to hold on to.

I must have been one of the few older children in the barracks, but I don't remember many people from my hut. We were just lines of sad, bald women. We were numbers, that's all. You saw other women who had given up. You could see it in their bodies and faces. They were known as Muselmänner *in the camp. They weren't fit for anything.*

All the other women in my hut just sat, lost in their own misery, not doing anything, not saying anything, wondering when it was their turn to die.

In the ghetto, when people were taken off, we suspected they were being taken to their deaths, but we never really knew. All along we kept hoping. It will get better. Surely it can't get worse. In Auschwitz, we discovered the truth.

Nights were the worst. You might drop off for a little bit but the discomfort soon woke you up. The cold stone floor, with no flesh on my bones. Oh, it was so terrible. In the morning, you might wake to find women around you had died during the night.

I didn't have the strength to hold a thought in my head. If I had any thoughts it was about my little sister Stenia and my father, whom I missed so much.

Every time we went out for Appell, *we tried scanning the camp to see if we could catch a glimpse of my father, but, of course, we didn't see him. I can picture his back, the last time I saw him, and then nothing. I knew my mother's thoughts were with my father, but I know we never believed we would come out alive.*

Day after day, the routine played out in this nightmarish place of smoke and fury.

Locked in the foul air of the stifling hut, each woman lost in her private hell, they were oblivious to wider events outside the high-voltage barbed-wire perimeter fence.

Auschwitz ll-Birkenau was the largest of the more than forty camps and sub-camps that made up the Auschwitz complex. It was originally the site of seven little villages, the largest of which was called Brzezinka, renamed by the Germans Birkenau, which means 'the area of the birch trees'.

Villagers were expelled from their properties and their homes torn down to create a no man's land of 20 square kilometres.

Hidden by a birch forest, close to the railway line, away from scrutiny, this damp, desolate, misty place was the perfect site to carry out mass extermination. Construction began in October 1941: it opened as a branch of Auschwitz in March 1942 and served at the same time as a centre for the extermination of the Jews.

It served its purpose. The majority – probably about 90 per cent – of the victims of Auschwitz concentration camp died in Birkenau, approximately a million people. The majority, more than nine out of every ten, were Jews.

Renia had long ago lost hope of an end to the war, or the appearance of a liberating army. Her experiences of two ghettos and now incarceration in Auschwitz-Birkenau had obliterated that hope. It felt to her as if they had been entirely forgotten. And yet, Allied command was very much aware of Auschwitz-Birkenau.

While Renia sat in a human chain, concertinaed between so many other starving women, sweltering in the suffocating heat, Allied planes flew overhead.

On 9, 12 and 25 August 1944, American Allied air reconnaissance flew over the camp and took photographs. Late Sunday afternoon on 20 August 1944, an American squadron of 127 bombers and 100 fighter jets bombed the I.G. Farben chemical plant 5 miles from Auschwitz. The chemical plant used the slave labour of prisoners from Auschwitz III-Monowitz.

Five days later, American air reconnaissance, tasked with photographing the damage caused by the recent bombing, took pictures in which, with a tenfold enlargement, the women's camp can clearly be seen: the fencing, the watchtowers, the main gate, the railroad ramp within the camp and a freight train with thirty-three cars and approximately 1,500 prisoners on their way to the gas chambers and crematorium ll.

Through the summer of 1944, the British and American governments had debated whether or not to bomb the camp itself. The US War Department felt that the most effective way of helping the victims of persecution was the swiftest possible victory over the Third Reich, and that all resources should be directed towards this aim. The British Air Ministry took a similar stand.

What could they do? If they bombed the camp, then the prisoners would be killed. If they bombed the train tracks, then they would be repaired the day after. They would risk the lives of all those young pilots and for what? When it would only be repaired in a day or two!

A MOTHER'S PROMISE

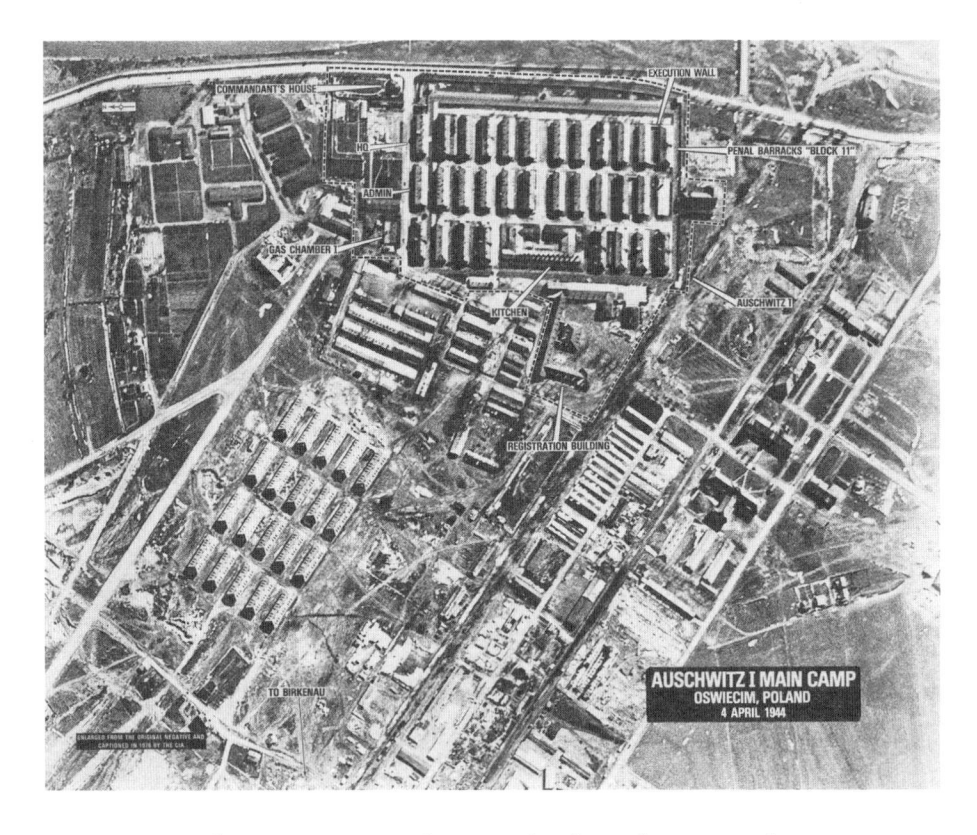

Aerial reconnaissance photograph of Auschwitz, April 1944

Renia had resigned herself to death in the camp, when one morning, quite suddenly, the direction of her life changed.

They woke us up early before Appell *and marched us from the hut through the camp to the same railway ramp we had first arrived at. It was my mother and I, and a few hundred other women.*

No one told us anything; they just ordered us to sit by the tracks and wait.

The sun rose over the high-voltage barbed-wire fences. Guards with machine guns watched down from the wooden watchtowers. Black oily smoke drifted over the camp.

LOST HOPE

Later on, someone came along and threw two old shoes to each of us in the group. Not necessarily a pair. It could have been a boot and a shoe. A shoe and a sandal. Not in your size either. Quickly, we exchanged shoes with the women around us to try and get a matching pair that fitted. I got two old mismatched shoes, but at least it was better than no shoes.

There was some relief that it looked as if maybe we were leaving Auschwitz. At the very least, they weren't going to kill us, we thought, if they're giving us shoes. But quite suddenly, I was taken by an SS guard and marched off alone through the camp. I was so terrified my heart was racing. What did they want with me? I couldn't believe I was being parted from my mother.

He took me to a room somewhere and my hair, which was short tufty curls by now, was roughly shaved off, then he returned me to my mother and the group by the tracks. I must have looked like everyone else in the group. They gave us no bread or water. Then they pushed us on to the freight wagon again.

Renia didn't know it, as she gingerly felt her bald scalp, but she, her mother and the last of the Łódź ghetto prisoners to survive Auschwitz-Birkenau were among the last remnants of the Jews of Poland. Of the 200,000 Jews registered as living in the Łódź ghetto, only around 6,000 to 7,000 would survive the war.

Inside the overcrowded wagon, her mother wrapped her arms tight around her and they lapsed into a heavy silence. With a hiss of steam, the wagons jerked from the siding and the journey began again. Renia clung to her mother, lost in thoughts of her father, and whether she would ever see him again.

We'd escaped the gas, but were we about to face something worse?

Chapter Nine

Germany

Over the previous five years, Renia and her mother had slept in a series of vermin-infested slums, in a blood-soaked cemetery, on a patch of bare earth near a gas chamber and crammed into freight wagons, stables and huts. Their new address was now a vast red-brick warehouse rising on struts out of the River Elbe in the port of Hamburg, Germany. Before the war, it had been a storage facility for tea, coffee and tobacco. By 1944, those goods had been removed to make way for human commodities. The warehouse had become a satellite camp of the Neuengamme concentration camp.

Renia and Sala, along with around 500 Jewish women from the Łódź ghetto, had been transported into the dark heart of Hitler's Reich, via Auschwitz-Birkenau. They arrived sometime at the end of August 1944. Allied bombers had reached it before them.

Hamburg was all smashed up. Everywhere you looked were bomb sites and they needed us to work on demolition and construction. Not gas, but slave labour.

The journey from Auschwitz to Hamburg took a long time, crushed into a freight wagon with no food and a terrible stink. I dozed a bit, I think, pressed into the side of Mama. There was no water and no bread. When we arrived, they marched us to a warehouse in the docks at a place called Dessauer Ufer, right on the water.

GERMANY

We knew we were in Germany because we kept seeing signs in German. Inside the warehouse, we slept on two-tiered wooden bunks filled with straw. After Auschwitz, it was such a relief to at least be able to lie down to sleep.

It was huge, sleeping thousands of prisoners. Outside the high windows, you could just about see the outline of the docks and more water. So this was Germany. I'd never left Poland before, and it made me feel even further from memories of home and family. It felt so strange.

Hamburg, 1945

The previous year, in July 1943, British Bomber Command had orchestrated a devastating night-time attack on Hamburg that had wiped out vast swathes of the city and docks, known as

Operation Gomorrah. The morning after the raid, residents of northern Germany had crawled from their shelters to find a glittering array of metal-foil strips draped like Christmas decorations over hedges, houses and farmland, or drifting through the smoking ruins.

It was a new scientific device, that, when released, would fog German radar screens. The United States Army Air Forces (USAAF) returned to Hamburg by day and engulfed the city in a firestorm of flame and smoke. Bombs tore through the city, pulverising factories and homes. From above, the city looked like a furious glowing carpet of light and explosions. A million refugees fled.

One year on, vast swathes of Hamburg were a grey wasteland of shattered masonry and powdered glass. And, of course, the dangerous job of demolition fell to concentration camp prisoners. No matter if they were crushed by falling buildings, trapped under debris, or blown up by unexploded bombs.

Working under the so-called Geilenberg programme, a programme of immediate measures for rescuing Germany's destroyed petroleum industry, Renia and her mother, alongside the other prisoners, were forced to carry out clearance work for large Hamburg oil refineries such as Rhenania-Ossag, Ebano-Oehler, J. Schindler and Jung-Öl. Renia now found herself no longer making German Army uniforms, but deployed into back-breaking slave labour, helping to clear rubble from their bombed refineries and in other factories in the Hamburg docks.

As soon as we arrived we were put to work and marched to a bomb site under armed guard. The site was filled with huge bombed buildings, some parts destroyed, others with brick walls still standing. It was so dangerous. It could have come down on top of us at any moment. Our job was to remove the bricks by hand.

GERMANY

Whole bricks went into one lorry, broken bricks into another lorry.

Try to imagine, I was a girl working in demolition on a bomb site. I wore the same thin, dirty man's pyjama jacket and skirt I had been given in Auschwitz. I didn't even have underwear, or anything to protect the skin on my legs and arms.

It was physically back-breaking, having to remove bricks and masonry. Were we given anything to protect our head or hands? Of course not.

My head was still bald from where it had been shaved in Auschwitz, all the women's were, and we didn't even have a headscarf to protect us from the wind and rain. Within days, my hands were raw and my bare scalp was numb. If we tried to rest for a moment, or stretch our aching backs, the guard would scream at us to work faster, ordering, 'Schneller, schneller!'

There were no latrines, so if you needed the toilet you had to crouch down behind a pile of debris, always under the eye of the guard.

There was nothing ahead of Renia and her mother but rubble and more rubble. The towering mountains of pulverised brick seemed like an appropriate metaphor for her life.

I had nothing left apart from Mama. My own life, my precious family, my happy childhood back in Zduńska Wola, all gone.

I kept thinking of Tatuś. The final moment where I saw his back disappearing at the ramp in Birkenau played over and over in my mind. I tortured myself with images of him going into the gas chambers, my lovely, gentle father suffocating to death.

Mama must have been thinking the same thoughts. We didn't talk about him. We couldn't. It was too painful. How could my father simply vanish like that without a kiss or a goodbye? How can you even begin to grieve for someone when you don't know what has happened to them? That was the worst part, the not knowing. At night, they gave us a ladle of soup to eat, then we fell on to our bunks in total exhaustion. Some nights when the sirens went we were taken down into the basement to shelter.

On 13 September 1944, Renia and her mother were on the move again. The SS had established another satellite camp of the Neuengamme concentration camp, 12 miles from Hamburg city centre, called Sasel. This camp was to be their new home.

Under brutal living conditions, starving and exhausted, the women had to level the grounds in the nearby district of Poppenbüttel, as well as lay tracks and transport the construction materials, mostly prefabricated parts cast in the clinker factory of the Neuengamme concentration camp, to the construction site and process them. Jewish slave labour was used to build 370 prefabricated houses for German war workers and their families who had been bombed out of their homes.

Any woman the SS deemed no longer fit for work could be sent back to Auschwitz in the so-called return transports, the *Rücküberstellung*.

This new camp wasn't like anywhere else we had been. We slept in little huts. Each hut had five double bunk beds, covered with a bit of straw and a thin blanket. Here we woke at 5am, or earlier, and went straight to the washrooms for a wash in ice-cold water. No towels or soap. I couldn't dry myself so when there was a big frost my damp clothes would freeze to my body.

It was still dark when we were all ordered outside the huts for Appell, or roll call, like in Auschwitz.

After that we got our rations for the day. Now what was the rations? It could be a little chunk of black bread and sometimes a tablespoon of either sugar or marmalade, or a little slice of liver salami, one of the three. And that was the food for the day. Also, a cup of dark black water they called coffee.

The women desperately needed the calories this meagre meal provided because the day's work ahead was brutal. Aside from clearing rubble with no gloves to protect their hands, the women from the camp had to make slabs of concrete from rubble, carry out excavation work, transport building materials and level roads.

The SS were making money from their hard labour. German companies generally paid the SS a maximum of 4 Reichsmark per working day for a female concentration camp prisoner. This 'wage' was lower than that of an unskilled labourer and went from the SS to the state treasury. Mother and daughter sweated among the dust and smoking remains, broken with exhaustion.

I remember at one point we had to help lay a road and that involved carrying sacks of cement on my back. Ever since then I've suffered with back pain from carrying those sacks. We had no shovels, so everything was done with our hands. Before long I couldn't even feel them; they were frozen solid.

Nearly every day, there were Allied air raids as the US and British came to bomb Germany day and night. The sirens sounded often, sometimes up to three times a day, and again at night. That was a godsend, believe me. You'd think the sight of Allied bombers would be frightening, but all I felt was relief to hear those bombs dropping. Yes, I was so happy to see those bombs fall.

As soon as the sirens sounded, we were all ordered into huge concrete shelters and it gave us some time to rest. They didn't care if we were bombed; they only took us into the shelter so we couldn't escape.

We sat near our SS guards in the shelters, listening to the bombs. The more we heard bombs dropping, the more we thought it would all come to an end. Maybe there was a chance we could survive. We were all too exhausted and scared to show any reaction in front of the SS. We sat huddled in lines in the darkness.

As soon as the all-clear sounded, they sent us straight back to work. Immediately after bombing raids, we worked between burning buildings and were in danger of collapsing buildings and unexploded bombs. Again, we were removing bricks and collecting them for reuse.

Many prisoners were also killed in these Allied bombing raids. Six weeks after they left the old coffee, tea and tobacco warehouse on the River Elbe, it received a direct hit and at least 150 prisoners died.

Far more disconcerting to Renia than the sight and sound of an Allied bombing raid was the approach of winter. Leaden clouds barrelled over the docks and temperatures plunged, the cold wrapping their bones in an icy compress.

I came to learn that there was something worse than hunger. Cold! I've never known cold like it. We thought it was cold back in the ghettos, but the winter of 1944 in Hamburg . . . How can I explain the feeling? My hands were solid blocks of ice. I forgot what my toes felt like. The SS did provide us with some old thin coats, but only so we didn't freeze to death and could carry on working.

I still had no underwear, and nothing to protect my head or my hands. As winter came, the snow fell thickly and we were ordered to clear it from the road. I can never describe the cold. Soon I had frostbite on my toes. The wind seemed to cut into my flesh like a knife. I felt half dead. By the time we got back to the camp in the evening, it was all we could do to queue up in the snow for a ladle of soup before collapsing into our bunks.

The draughty, thin-walled wooden huts had no heating and

GERMANY

everything was covered in snow. The barbed-wire fence, the huts and latrines. We woke up freezing, and out on the bomb sites, yet more wind and snow. You could never get warm.

I can't imagine what we must have looked like out there on the bomb sites, in our frozen pyjama jackets and bald heads, our bony feet in mismatched shoes. Our clothes were so filthy they were stiff like cardboard. Our skin was covered in sores. My toes were frostbitten. Our eyes were sunken, dark holes in our skulls. We looked so horrible. So strange and horrible. Barely human.

Every morning we were escorted under armed guard to work on a different bomb site, travelling either by barge through the foggy docks or on freight wagons. There was no hope of escape. Even if we did have the energy, looking the way we did, who would have taken us in and offered us shelter?

Occasionally, we were marched past a baker's shop. The aroma of fresh baked bread that drifted out of the door nearly knocked me out. We would have eaten anything by that point, even wood.

I remember once, a German woman walked past us as we were working on a site. She stopped in her tracks at the sight of us.

'Who are these people?' she asked our guard in German.

'Yiddisher, politisch, Häftling,' was the guard's response.

Jewish. Political. Prisoner.

A political prisoner? I was a fifteen-year-old girl, that's all. Very often, German civilians walked past us as we worked. They knew bad things were happening, but they didn't want to risk their own neck and there wasn't much they could do.

There was the odd one who would stop and ask who we were. We didn't look like humans; no wonder they asked.

Many women in the satellite camps of Neuengamme concentration camp already knew each other from their home towns and some, like Renia and her mother, were related. Others, who had lost many relatives in ghettos or death camps, came together to form 'camp families', relationships which had been formed in the darkest of times to provide that all-important ingredient for survival – hope.

The women shared their food rations, cared for the sick and gave emotional support to one another. The bonds were so close that survivors still speak of their 'camp sisters'. Renia's memories are more elemental.

I was so weak by then that I can barely remember the women in our hut. They were mostly from the Łódź ghetto; that I know. By the time we got back from work, it was dark and we all just collapsed from exhaustion, too tired to talk. I never allowed myself to think of the future. Every bit of energy was focused on Mama, staying close to her and hoping to stay alive.

As 1944 dragged into a freezing new year, some of the most bitter and bloody battles of the war were being waged on land, sea and air.

Something powerful was on the horizon. Not a bomb, but just as lethal.

Chapter Ten

∼

Mama

Every day, Mama got thinner and weaker. She'd always been the strong one. Working hard, pulling us together, exchanging cardigans for cabbages, rescuing me from the hospital, crossing a selection line to stay by my side. Staying strong for us all. Yet that last winter in Hamburg, I could see something changing. First, her younger daughter was taken by the Nazis and then her parents, next her sister, then her husband, taken on arrival at Auschwitz-Birkenau.

I knew she was hanging on for me. Everything she did was for me.

I loved my mother so much. She was the most important person in my life; by then, the only person left in my life.

She was the first person I saw in that hut when I opened my eyes, her prayers the last thing I heard at night. I was a part of her, as she was me. She held my life in her hands, as I did hers.

Without each other, we wouldn't have lasted a day. We were both so fragile, our bodies so weak. Our love was the only strength we had, and we clung to it. We both prayed that 1945 would see an end to our torture.

In Hamburg, Germany, that end was still out of sight. Unlike in Poland. On 19 January 1945, Soviet tanks had rumbled into the Łódź ghetto. The half-dead ghetto prisoners who had been left behind to clear up after the liquidation, staggered, blinking and dazed, from their cellar and attic hiding places to greet their liberators. Two days later, Zduńska Wola was liberated by Soviet forces.

From 17 to 21 January 1945, the Germans marched approximately 56,000 prisoners out of Auschwitz-Birkenau and its sub-camps in evacuation columns, mostly heading west. An estimated 15,000 prisoners died in what would later come to be known as the 'Death Marches'. While they were leading the Auschwitz prisoners on the evacuation marches, the SS set about their final steps to remove the evidence of their crimes, making bonfires of documents on the camp streets and blowing up the crematoria. On 27 January 1945, Soviet soldiers confronted the full horror of Nazi atrocities at Auschwitz-Birkenau.

Every place through which Renia's tragic journey had taken her was now free. Imprisoned deep in the heart of the Reich, however, her liberation was to be drawn out to the bitterest of ends. Renia had been one of the first to fall under the Nazi boot in Poland on 1 September 1939. Five years and four months on, it began to look as if she would be the last to escape from under it.

By January, Renia and her mother were staring again into the abyss. The cold would kill her, or the hunger, she was sure of it.

Snow lay heaped in the streets and on the bomb sites. Picking up frozen bricks would send searing needles of pain through her fingers. Almost as bad were the days when the blacked-out skies spat icy rain and everything was coated in a thick, slippery mud that sucked at her battered old shoes.

In the depths of such misery, hope sprang from a surprising source.

One day, something strange happened. They marched us out of the camp one morning to work, in our usual columns of five. The guard insisted I walk on the outside of the column. He ordered me to carry his briefcase, and at the same time he slipped something into my hand. I looked down, surprised, to see he had put a small green apple in my hand. He said nothing, just looked straight ahead as we marched, and so I said nothing.

As soon as I got to the working site for that day, I managed to whisper to Mama and we huddled behind a wall and very quickly ate it before the guards spotted us. Oh, that apple. It tasted like heaven in my mouth. Mama and I devoured it in seconds, core, pips and all.

After that, the same guard would, from time to time, slip me an apple as we walked to work. I've never forgotten that man and his acts of kindness and often wonder who he was. Maybe he had a child or a grandchild at home? He might have done other bad things in the war, but at least he did one good thing. For the first time, a German had treated me like a human being.

Until 1942, concentration camps and their satellite camps were guarded exclusively by members of the SS. During the course of the war, however, the SS were no longer able to meet the personnel requirements needed for the rapidly expanding concentration camp system as SS men were increasingly called to the front.

In Hamburg, customs officers, police officers, *Reichsbahn* (German National Railway) employees and members of the Wehrmacht who were not 'fit' or were too old for front-line service were assigned to guard female prisoners outside the camp.

That might explain the brief flash of humanity that Renia was shown. Was it a retired customs officer or a railway guard, who allowed his heart and conscience to be pierced by the sight of a child slave? Or maybe, with the end of the war so close, his thoughts were turning to how he could frame his war when questioned by Allied intelligence.

That faceless man could never know that the memory of those smuggled apples would linger for the next eight decades.

During that same winter, some of the women had started wrapping their blankets from the huts around their bodies, hiding them under their coats and smuggling them out of the camp so that they could try to keep warm on the demolition sites. This was strictly forbidden by the SS guards and if they caught the women taking their blankets outside the camp, they would beat them up.

One morning in the hut I saw Mama wrapping her blanket around her body. I was terrified. I knew she would get a terrible beating if the SS guard inside the camp spotted her. Sometimes they did checks on the way out of the camp.

I was so worried in case she should be caught. So I found the guard, the same one who used to give me apples. Luckily, he was on duty that day. I told him, 'My mama is taking her blanket.'

He turned to me and said, 'Don't worry,' and waved me away. Do you know what, that morning, as he marched us out of the camp, he looked the other way! Mama got away with it. I was so relieved.

The incident, which could have gone so badly wrong, revealed a subtle shift in the dynamics of Renia's relationship with her mother. The war had honed her caring instincts to a razor-sharp point and she had become just as adept at protecting as her mother. She was no longer a bewildered child but an expert in survival. Yet for all her resilience, Renia could never have predicted or prepared herself for what was coming next.

One morning, Mama and I were split up and she was sent to a different work site for the day. I didn't like it when this happened; nor did she. I was delivered back to the station near our camp and I waited on the platform for her to return.

Some women who had worked with my mother that day walked towards me and I could tell from their faces that something terrible had happened. Then my mother was unloaded off the train on a stretcher. I ran over to her. She looked awful. Her cheek and her mouth had been ripped open, and her face was covered in blood.

A million thoughts went through my mind. I imagined maybe she'd been injured by falling bricks, or perhaps she herself had fallen on the bomb site, but then one of the women prisoners told me what had happened. Mama was in too much pain to talk herself.

She'd been working near a slaughterhouse and for 'fun' the SS had opened a gate and let the bull out. It had attacked my mother, cutting her face. Can you imagine? My poor, gentle Mama attacked by a bull.

I started to shake and cry.

Mama was taken to the camp infirmary and from that moment on, she wasn't able to work. That was the moment everything changed. I was so upset to see Mama like this, to think of her being trampled and torn. How could they allow such a thing to happen? How? There was no wickedness or evil to which the SS could not sink. Believe me, they weren't human beings; they were monsters.

Everyone in my hut held a collection for Mama from their rations. A drop of sugar, to a crumb more bread, to build up her strength. But she was never good after that. She lost so much strength.

When the attack happened, Sala had been working for the companies Moll, Kowal & Bruns by the imposing red-brick Beef Hall (Rinderhalle) and slaughterhouse in the Heiligengeistfeld area, grinding rubble so that it could be made into concrete slabs. From that moment on, Renia saw the shadow of death in the contours of her mother's face.

At work, I couldn't concentrate because all I could think about was Mama. At the end of the day, they allowed me to visit her briefly and I fed her sips of soup to try and get her strength up.

But she looked so thin and so terribly ill. No one had stitched or dressed her wounds, I don't think. She didn't talk any more, she couldn't, she was in too much pain. Her lip was swollen, her cheek hanging open.

When I went back to our hut alone, I would look over at her empty bunk. I couldn't sleep.

Every time Renia closed her eyes, she imagined a bull charging towards her, the thunder of its hooves, her mother lying on the floor like a rag doll, twisted and torn. She woke for *Appell* each morning, tears frozen to her eyelashes. By April 1945, everything was shattered and broken around her.

Finally, the Allied advance got too close to the camp for the Germans to ignore. On 7 April 1945, the SS evacuated the camp.

We were loaded on to a freight wagon and taken on another long overnight journey. I was still wearing the same pyjama jacket, skirt and shoes that I got in Auschwitz. Mama was loaded into another part of the train on a stretcher. I wanted to go with her but, as usual, it all happened so fast and I was sent to another part of the wagon. To this day, I don't know why Mama was brought, injured, on this journey. I only know that they didn't leave anyone behind.

Again, the same awful conditions. Again, no food, water, no facilities to go to the toilet. The wagon stopped, the doors slid open and we were ordered out.

The usual SS commands of 'Raus, raus, schneller!' and barking dogs, always barking dogs.

I looked about for my mother but I couldn't see her. There was no train station, just tracks in the middle of what looked like a forest.

MAMA

There were no selections. We were lined up in columns of five and then marched for miles through thickly wooded country.

The paths through this forest were littered with dead bodies, stick-thin limbs sprawled among the spring flowers.

They were prisoners from earlier transports who had dropped dead from exhaustion.
There was no chance of escape, even if I had the energy. On the edge of each column of prisoners was an SS man with a gun. The sights just made me more scared. I felt so alone. I didn't know where Mama was. I didn't know whether she'd died on the way. I was very, very frightened.

Renia was not alone. All over occupied Europe, prisoners were being taken on Death Marches as the Nazis began evacuating their network of concentration camps. Some of these Death Marches lasted for weeks, during which thousands died from starvation, cold, disease and exhaustion. Those who fell behind or stopped to rest, even for a moment, were shot. For those left behind in the camps, too sick to walk, the SS, and other local German forces, often shot them and set fire to the camps to erase all trace of their crimes.

She had been walking for several hours when out of the trees she saw a gate. Renia was about to enter one of the Third Reich's darkest secrets, hidden in a dense German forest. The camp gates swung open.

Chapter Eleven

∼

Bergen-Belsen

I think I can fairly describe Belsen as probably the foulest and vilest spot that ever soiled the surface of this earth.
Harold Le Druillenec, schoolmaster from Jersey,
the only British male survivor of Bergen-Belsen

Renia walked soundlessly through the simple barrier, a war-ravaged wisp. She hadn't the energy to register much about it but, within minutes, the stench enveloped her, snapping her back to her senses.

She gagged, covering her mouth and nose with her hand. This wasn't the smell of Auschwitz-Birkenau, of sickly burning flesh and bone, but one of decay, urine and faeces. An abominable stench of something deeply rotten smothered the air over the camp.

Renia looked around her new surroundings, waiting for the usual commands, the lash of the whip, the lunging dogs and sadistic guards, but she couldn't see a single uniform in sight. Just row after row of long wooden huts that stretched into the distance. It looked like an army barracks.

After a walk along the long dusty camp road to the women's section, the new arrivals staggered into the nearest hut, desperate to get into the shade or lie down and sleep, but Renia only had one thing on her mind.

BERGEN-BELSEN

I must find my mother.

This single-minded quest burnt through her skull. If she could only get back to her mother, she could survive this hell. Side by side, they had survived so much. For five years and seven months, they had navigated each brutality together. Often in stunned and terrified silence, but it hadn't mattered. Her mother's presence had been a weapon stronger than any grenade or gun. It had offered her a *reason* to live. Her mother, even shaved, shorn, gored and flame-thin, was still the strongest woman she knew and without her, she was lost.

All that mattered was finding my mother. I was so scared without her. Had she died on the freight wagon? Had they left her there?

I pushed open the door to the nearest hut. 'Have you seen a woman brought in on a stretcher?' I asked, but no one answered.

The scene that met me, you cannot describe. The hut was dark, a thick layer of grime covering the windows. It was a long hut, with perhaps enough room for up to 500 people, but bunk beds for only about half that number. It was already badly overcrowded, even before our transport got there.

Women were crammed on each bunk. Some were alive. Some were dead, their limbs hanging over the sides of the bunk. And there were those somewhere in between, on the verge of death.

The living were too weak to get off the bunks. The dead were lying on top of the living, the living on top of the dead.

The floor was covered in faeces, diarrhoea and vomit. People sat and rotted in the mess and filth, their heads lolling limply against the wooden walls.

In the bunk next to me, a woman was resting her head against a corpse, using it as a pillow.

I found a corner and straightaway fell asleep from exhaustion.

Something tugged me from my sleep. My skin was prickling all over. I looked down at my legs and arms. I was covered in lice from top to bottom. Big, black, long lice. I was so terribly frightened. All I wanted was my mother. I knew this was the end of the road.
  'Where on earth am I?' I thought.

Bergen-Belsen was established in 1940, south of the small town of Bergen and the village of Belsen and north of the picturesque town of Celle.

Until 1943, Bergen-Belsen was exclusively a prisoner-of-war (POW) camp. In April 1943, the SS Main Office, which administered the concentration camp system, took over a part of Bergen-Belsen and converted it into a concentration camp.

Over the course of its existence, the Bergen-Belsen camp complex held prisoners of war, Jews, political prisoners, Roma (Gypsies), asocials, criminals, Jehovah's Witnesses and gay men.

In December 1944, while Renia had been slaving on bomb sites, SS Hauptsturmführer Josef Kramer was sent from Auschwitz to be the new Camp Commandant at Belsen, imposing an even stricter and more vicious regime.

As Soviet forces advanced into Germany in late 1944 and early 1945, Bergen-Belsen became an internment camp for thousands of Jewish prisoners evacuated from camps closer to the front. The arrival of thousands of new prisoners, many of them survivors of forced evacuations on foot, overwhelmed the camp. Renia's transport from Hamburg had arrived at the Wehrmacht barracks' railway platform located between Bergen and Belsen and the dreadful march to the camp had been 6 kilometres long.

BERGEN-BELSEN

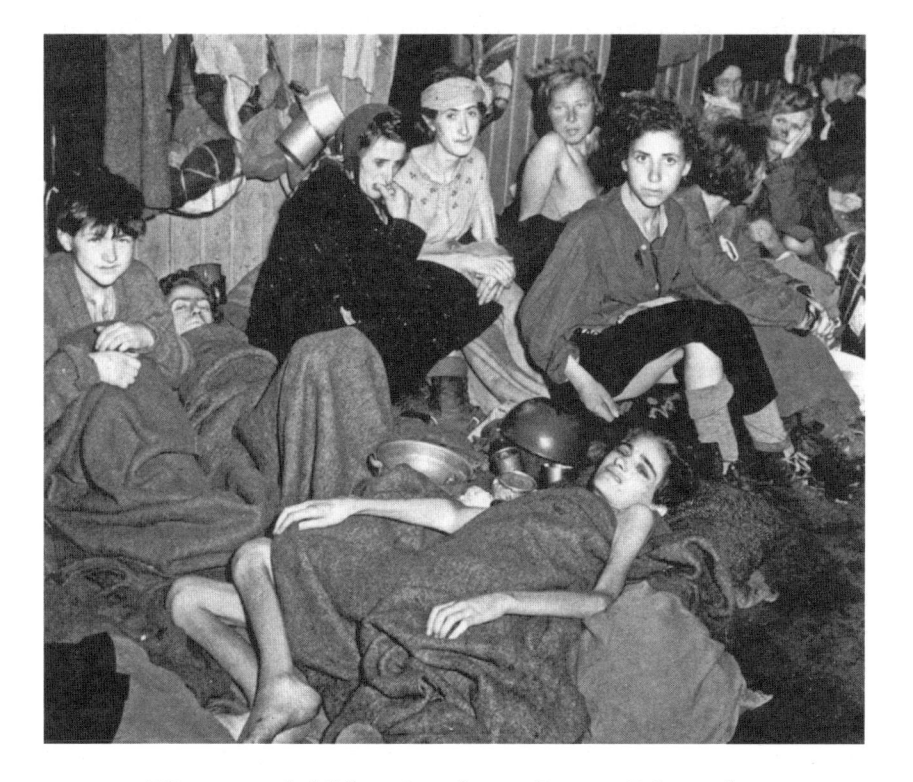

Women and children in a hut at Bergen-Belsen after their liberation

By April 1945, camp authority had largely broken down. Belsen was no longer a slave labour camp like those Renia had just come from, or even a place of streamlined, mechanised mass murder like Auschwitz-Birkenau.

The concentration camp had become a place where people had been brought to rot and die.

The water supply had been cut off days before Renia arrived. When Allied bombs destroyed Belsen's water pump, the guards made no effort to bring water for the inmates from a nearby creek, which meant no sanitation either. By the time of her arrival, no bread had been distributed for two weeks.

There was no more law or order in the kingdom of death in which Renia found herself and, with blinding lucidity, she realised it wouldn't be a bullet, gas or a beating that would kill her, but disease. The camp was infested. Dysentery, typhus and tuberculosis were rife. The hot, infectious breath of the dying hung like a blanket over everything. And where airborne germs couldn't reach, rats, flies, fleas and lice continued the process of infection. The camp was only a few days and a few degrees away from a cholera epidemic.

Renia brushed the lice off her body and lurched back outside.

It's just impossible to describe the scenes. Here, I saw skeletons walking, their arms and legs like matchsticks. Their eyes bulged out from their skull-like faces.

Some were dressed in rags, others were naked. The smell that arose from that camp, it's not possible to describe. I was so terrified.

Like leaves falling from a tree, people were falling down and dying. Naked or just covered in a few rags, people staggered about like an army of the living dead, walking aimlessly, bones sticking out through the ragged remains of their skin.

Roll call had stopped. There was no point counting. For every thousand people alive in the morning, there would only be about 700 people alive by the afternoon. That's how fast people were dying. It was chaos.

People shuffled out of the drifting yellow dust, or simply sat and waited for the end. The stench of death shimmered over the dry, scorched earth. Apart from the sporadic gunfire, there was barely a sound, just the wind tugging at the barbed wire.

Renia slipped from hut to hut like a ghost. The effort made black spots dance in front of her eyes.

BERGEN-BELSEN

The camp was so big. In each hut, I asked: 'Have you seen a woman come in on a stretcher recently?' But no one had the strength to answer.

Outside, I hadn't been walking long when I spotted two tall hills in the distance.

When I got closer, I realised these hills were actually bodies, piled up to heaven. There was no one to bury them and the smell was terrible. We were lucky it wasn't a little bit warmer, otherwise, as I found out later, cholera would have broken out there.

'Am I in hell or on earth?' I wondered, not wanting to look, but at the same time, unable to look away.

Layer upon layer of dead bodies, tangled in a jumbled mass of discoloured limbs. Some were nothing more than polished skeletons.

Renia didn't weep or cry out. She just stood and stared, unblinking. Her innocent childhood had been shattered years ago, but she was still a girl standing in the shadow of a pyramid of corpses.

All those years ago, in what felt like another lifetime, when her mother had told her to look the other way at men swinging from the gallows, she could never have conceived of this.

No human brain could comprehend or process the sight of so many bodies stacked together in a grotesque mountain of death.

In the distance, she heard a boom and turned away from the bodies, her determination to find her mother redoubled, her need both fierce and primal.

For two days, I walked from hut to hut, backwards and forwards. I had no idea where I was going. I didn't care whether I was shot. I could only focus on finding my mother.

Finally, at the end of the second day's search, I saw a body lying on a stretcher on the rough wooden floor in the corner of a hut. I knew that face. It was my mother! You can't imagine how I felt to have found her. 'Mama . . .' I wept in relief, falling to my knees beside her.

She was alive, but only just. She looked terrible. I could see she was dying. She knew it herself.

What hair Mama had left was tangled in matted ropes, and her body was covered in lice. She looked like everybody else there, not like human beings at all.

'Mama, it's me,' I told her. I held her hand in mine, hoping it would give her the strength to hold on. But as I looked closer at my mother, I was so scared. All hope left me. Like everyone else in this hut, she was on the edge of death. I only wished I had water and food to give her, or blankets to cover her with, but I had nothing.

Nothing.

My mother's gaze slowly turned to me. It took her a long time to find the strength to speak, her lips opening and closing.

Finally, she spoke in Yiddish, her voice barely above a whisper. 'Vayn nisht ven ikh shtarb.' Do not cry when I die.

Do not cry when I die.

With that, her mother seemed to crumple further into the ground. Renia held her mother like a child, cradling her fragile, delicate body, skin to skin.

Renia wanted to protest, tell her that they could survive this, but the truth was, she didn't believe it. She could sense her mother's life force ebbing away.

In the oppressive heat and darkness of the hut, Renia lay down next to her mother, held both her hands in hers, and exhaled.

My mind was so weakened; nothing registered any more. I was so ill by then.

Hours drifted past sluggishly. Renia fell in and out of consciousness, unable to stand or talk, able only to make sure her mother's cold hand was pressed against hers.

Survival was a remote possibility by now, and so to die together was her only aim. Life had shrunk to two elemental pinpricks.

Her heartbeat. Her mother's heartbeat.

I was asleep next to my mother. That's when I had a dream. Her two younger brothers, who adored her, and she them, took her away on a stretcher up to heaven. That's when I knew for sure she was dying.

When I woke up, I became aware of someone feeding me sips of sour, vinegary soup, which immediately gave me diarrhoea. I needed air. I stood unsteadily and walked out of the hut, almost blinded by the bright light outside.

As I was walking through the camp, a woman said to me: 'There's a British tank near the gates.'

I just couldn't take it in. My mind was so weakened. Nothing made sense any longer. I was so ill by then, it didn't make a difference if there was a tank there or not.

The British Army liberated Bergen-Belsen on Sunday, 15 April 1945, with no shots fired. 249 Battery, 63 Anti-Tank Regiment (Oxfordshire Yeomanry), Royal Artillery was the first British military unit to go into Bergen-Belsen, shortly followed by more soldiers and tanks.

What they witnessed changed the course of history. Renia did not greet her liberators with rapture, but silence, incredulity and dead-eyed incomprehension.

White dots danced at the edge of her vision, and the ground came rushing up to meet her.

I collapsed, and that's the last thing I remember of my liberation.

Chapter Twelve

Liberation

If the whole of the sky was turned into paper and all the trees were pens, and all the seas were full of ink, we would still have insufficient material with which to describe the horrors and sufferings at the hands of these bestial Nazis.
Welsh Jewish padre Reverend Leslie Hardman, speaking at the close of the first Shabbat service for survivors at Bergen-Belsen

While Renia was unconscious, her fragile young body putting up its last fight, a Jewish man from Stepney in East London took his first steps through the gates of hell. Armed only with a bar of army-issued milk chocolate and the will to help, 28-year-old military policeman Charles Salt gazed about the camp.

His brain was unable to reconcile the piles of corpses with real people. He scanned the horizon, horror mounting.

'What on earth . . .' he began, trailing off. There were thousands upon thousands upon thousands of bodies. He had never, even in five and a half years of ugly warfare, come close to witnessing anything like this.

Some were walking slowly in faded grey-and-white-striped uniforms, some were stumbling, others crawling on their hands and knees through scattered bodies and dry earth. They looked at him as if he had just landed from outer space.

Women in Bergen-Belsen have access to running water for the first time since their liberation by British troops, April 1945

The sun was shining but all around was death, starvation and disease. This was the first time that he, as a British man, had seen the full extent of the Jewish genocide, the Holocaust as it would come to be known, on German soil.

Born among the narrow, terraced streets of the Jewish quarter in Stepney, East London, on 10 March 1917, Charles was no stranger to antisemitism.

He had been nineteen years old when he had joined the anti-fascists and turned back far-right fascist Oswald Mosley and his thuggish Blackshirts, chanting *No Pasarán,* You Shall Not Pass, at the Battle of Cable Street in London's East End in October 1936. In England, it had been a watershed moment in the fight against prejudice and stood as an example of social solidarity in the face of hatred.

And now, here he was, nearly nine years on, witnessing the culmination of that fascist ideology.

He hadn't planned to be here, but when a memo came round appealing for a unit of seventeen volunteers from the Military Police to go to a newly liberated concentration camp and help, he hadn't hesitated.

It had felt like the right thing to do. Besides, this was personal. His father, Mark Salt, had been killed in his home in Stepney on the eleventh day of the Blitz, 17 September 1940. The terraced house, so old that locals joked it was only the wallpaper holding it up, had taken a direct hit. They'd had nowhere to take cover, no deep-level government-built shelter or Anderson shelter to protect them from the Nazi bombs. In the early days of the Blitz, few in Stepney did, with many civilians having to resort to hunkering down in railway arches, crypts, the Tube stations, basements and even cupboards under the stairs.

After a debrief and an anti-typhus vaccination Charles had imagined himself ready. But nothing on earth could have prepared him.

He gagged, unable to catch his breath. His fellow operatives in the Military Police did the same. As they plunged deeper into the camp, conversations trailed off into stunned silence. Picking his way past the bodies and grappling with the visions of the damned in hell, an awful thought occurred to Charles.

This could have been me.

Had the Germans successfully invaded Britain in that fateful summer of 1940, had he found himself living under German occupation, *he* would be the one being pulled out of those wretched huts, not witnessing the unimaginable in a British uniform.

Charles Salt in Military Police uniform at Bergen-Belsen in 1945

The sobering thought snapped him out of his torpor. There was work to do, manning the gates, setting up information points, preventing looting and assisting the survivors who could still be helped.

The most urgent task confronting Charles and the liberating troops and medics was a major medical and humanitarian rescue operation of unparalleled proportions. The relief effort was a combined one, involving British and US servicemen, relief workers, medical students, doctors, nurses, Red Cross workers, volunteers, stretcher-bearers and ambulance drivers.

Initially, they had little more than aspirin, bandages, water,

LIBERATION

Dettol, glucose tablets and Bengal famine mixture (powdered milk dissolved with water and mixed with flour and sugar). Amid such chaos, mistakes were made when survivors were given food that their bodies simply couldn't digest. Many died from eating rich foods that they hadn't eaten in years, like meat and chocolate.

Mervyn Kersh, ninety-nine, from north London, who received the French Legion of Honour in 2015, had been among the first to land on Gold Beach on the Normandy coast on D+4.

'Every time I saw a column of captured Germans, I would shout out to them, *"Ich bin jüdisch,"* (I am Jewish) in defiance.'

By April 1945, Mervyn realised he was just 3 miles away from a newly liberated camp called Bergen-Belsen. He says he knew what had gone on there, but nothing could have prepared him for the scale or the sights. 'I wasn't allowed in the camp because of typhus so I waited outside the gates to talk to the survivors who were strong enough to walk.

'They were walking skeletons. It was a wonder they could stand. As a soldier we got rations every week, a bar of chocolate and sixty cigarettes in a brown tin. I didn't smoke so I swapped my cigarettes for chocolate.

'At the gates on that first day, I gave the survivors all my chocolate. Their faces! They hadn't seen chocolate in years. I didn't speak Yiddish (apart from a few curse words) or any languages apart from English and a little French, so I communicated with hands and kindness.

'The next day, I collected more chocolate from other soldiers and took quite a lot with me and gave it out. It was only years later I was told that chocolate was the worst thing you could give to someone who had been starving, but I didn't know that then.

'I spoke to hundreds of survivors in those two weeks and everyone wanted to go to Eretz (Land of) Israel. Only one man said he was going to go to South America, marry a Catholic girl so his children would not be Jewish and run the risk of antisemitism. There was nothing for the survivors to return to in Europe. Their homes had been taken over, their possessions stolen, their lives in Europe over.'

Charles Salt at one of the grave sites in Bergen-Belsen after the camp's liberation in 1945

Every minute, a sight or a conversation would draw Charles up short, like the reasonably well-fed Jewish woman who told him she had been forced to be the mistress of an SS officer. Or the woman whose legs were so emaciated she looked like a walking skeleton.

As the hours ticked by, the sights grew more awful.

Cannibalism. Bodies that had been cut open with glass and the livers removed by people driven mad with hunger. A bulldozer digging mass graves into which corpses were thrown, slithering and tumbling, heads cracking. Rescue workers vomiting and passing out. It was little wonder the camp quickly became known among the British troops as 'The Horror Camp'.

That evening, Charles and his fellow military policemen sat in silence trying to eat a meal in the mess hall, attempting to forget everything they had witnessed that day, when a strange moaning sound drifted in through the open window.

Charles hurried to the window. Survivors were huddled by the bins, scraping out what they could find with their fingernails. A heel of bread, potato peelings, fruit rinds and ersatz coffee grounds, all were feverishly turned over and devoured. As they ate, the survivors moaned. '*Essen, essen.*'

The man next to him looked confused. 'I don't understand, Charles. Why do they want to stay in Germany?'

'They don't,' Charles replied. 'It's Yiddish for "eat". They're starving.'

That night, when he got back to his billet, dog-tired and sick at heart, he realised to his disgust that he was smothered in lice. From then on, the Army began spraying everyone who came in and out of the camp with DDT, a strong chemical powder, to kill off the typhus-carrying bugs.

He took out a pen and attempted to compose his thoughts into a letter to his mother, Sarah. He had found the words easily enough to tell her about the bullet in the knee he'd taken on the beaches of Normandy on D-Day, or of the heavy shelling he'd endured while guarding bridges and roads. No problems either at reliving in his head his excitement at crossing the Rhine and witnessing the Allied paratroopers dropping into Germany. But this?

'I can't believe what I'm witnessing,' he wrote simply.

All the time that this was going on, the body count was rising. Tragically, in the days after liberation, former prisoners were continuing to die in their thousands. They had made it to liberation, but their bodies, weakened from disease and starvation, were too frail to recover.

Teams of doctors, many of them medical students, were flown in from Britain and worked around the clock, risking their lives to cut down the death rate.

Medical student Ian Reginald Davidson was flown in from Britain by Dakota and housed in a former SS officers' mess, a few miles from the camp.

'I was allocated to hut 42, on the male side of the camp,' he recalled. 'We walked in and held our noses and looked at each other in disbelief. Where did we even start? It was frightful. Wooden bunks occupied by the most emaciated people I've ever seen in my life.

'There was a toilet at one end, which went up to the top of one's boots in excrement, but people were too weak to use it. They were lying in their own faeces, and it was dripping down the bunks.

'We were told we had to cut down the daily death rate from 1,200 to 600 a week. We brought many back from the brink. Every morning the Hungarian guards took out the dead who hadn't survived the night and left them outside the hut for the wagons to collect.

'The mass graves were terrible, the bodies dumped in very unceremoniously, bodies thrown on top of other naked bodies, heads cracked on the ground, slung into the pits at all angles. Such an awful end for so many human beings.'

At least 52,000 prisoners from all over Europe were killed in the Bergen-Belsen concentration camp. Despite the extensive rescue and relief efforts of the British Army and volunteers, 14,000 children, women and men died in the first weeks after liberation as a result of disease and malnutrition. Some had even had a glimpse of a future.

Charles was stunned by the sight of a young woman who lay

LIBERATION

dead on a rutted track, clutching a lipstick in her hand.

It turned out she had just visited the clothing store for survivors nicknamed 'Harrods', where survivors could throw away the vile and filthy clothing they'd been liberated in and pick out dresses, underwear, shoes and even lipstick to try to restore their sense of self.

One young survivor had picked out her new clothes and was walking back to apply her lipstick when death claimed her. She lay sprawled in the dust, emaciated and shorn, her precious lipstick gripped between her fingers.

As disbelief gave way to anger, questions around retribution, justice and collective guilt drifted round the camp.

The British Army erected prominent signs at the gates to the camp, one in German and one in English. Charles had his photograph taken next to the latter.

Charles Salt at Bergen-Belsen after the camp's liberation in 1945

Next, they rounded up the mayor and dignitaries from the towns nearest to Belsen and forced them to watch the burials. They stared as captured SS men were forced, under armed guard, to carry the bodies to the pits.

The man next to Charles was a local dignitary.

'Didn't you know what was going on?' Charles asked him, unable to hide his contempt. 'You can smell this place for miles around.'

'If anyone ever went in there, they never came out,' the man replied. As if that explained it.

Easier to look the other way more like, Charles thought. Well, there was no avoiding the truth now.

They continued watching in silence as men, women and children were placed in the pits, a tangle of matchstick limbs. Ordinary, decent people. Accountants. Teachers. Artists. Diarists. Shopworkers. Tailors. Housewives. Students. Brothers. Grandmothers. Fathers. Sisters. Mothers and daughters.

Ignoring the danger to his own health, Jewish chaplain Leslie Hardman held services over those mass graves and recited Mourner's *Kaddish* over the pits before they were filled in.

Charles had already met Reverend Hardman at the Purim service earlier that year in Eindhoven in Holland and had the greatest respect for the man and his kindness and compassion. How it shone out now in the grimmest of surroundings.

'How are the survivors ever to lead a normal life again, padre?' he asked Reverend Hardman after the service.

'The Jews are born civilised, and nothing will destroy them completely. Give them a chance. Give them a warm, human word,' he replied, in his soft Welsh accent.

'But how do we help?'

'You have hands and you have lips, do you not? Show them the milk of human kindness. Be patient with them. Tell them they are good, that they are brave, that they are still beautiful and lovely, despite their shorn heads and emaciated bodies.'

Charles took in the padre's soothing words and watched him work tirelessly in those weeks after liberation, ignoring Army protocol and doing things in his own humane way, holding services over the pits, writing long letters to survivors' families, persuading soldiers to part with their precious rations of cigarettes, bars of soap and chocolate to give to survivors.

He was there to administer physical and spiritual solace to the sick and dying, but his response was also practical. He even took to task an eminent Bengal famine mixture expert who had been sent to Belsen by the government to help feed the survivors.

'Padre, they're not eating my stuff,' the doctor complained.

'Forgive me if I'm talking out of turn, but you need to adapt it,' Reverend Hardman replied. 'It's too sweet.'

The padre's outspoken views made him unpopular with certain British military personnel. As well as acting as an unofficial mouthpiece for the survivors, many of whom feared returning to their old homes, desperate instead to go to Palestine, he also criticised the slowness of certain relief workers to help survivors or go into the huts.

Reverend Hardman took his orders from a higher calling.

Even when he was ordered by his military superiors to leave Belsen and return to his normal military duties of providing support to Jewish troops, Reverend Hardman refused. 'I'm not prepared to leave. If the authorities want me, they will have to come and get me.'

Charles laughed and shook his hand when he heard. 'Good luck to you. You'll have to become a kind of Jewish Scarlet Pimpernel.' And that's exactly what the padre became, remaining in the disease-infested camp, helping everyone in every single way he could. No one in authority could find the heroic padre for weeks.

Taking inspiration from Reverend Hardman, Charles learnt that bending the rules was sometimes the right thing to do.

'Please can you help me?' begged a young female survivor in Yiddish. 'I have no one left except an aunt and uncle in Palestine, but I have no way of getting in contact with them.'

There was no postal service in the camp, and she had neither pens nor paper. Charles gave her both.

'Write a letter and I'll put it in the Army post,' he promised, breaching strict Army rules. 'Whether it will get past the Army censor I don't know, but I'll send it anyway.'

She wrote the letter in Polish and Charles sent it off with his office address at the camp as a reply address. The woman came back every day at 5pm on the dot when the post arrived to see if there was a reply.

Days passed with nothing. Charles began to fear for her uncertain future. But on the fourteenth day came a reply. As she walked up the path towards him he waved the letter over his head.

'You've got a reply,' he cried. Despite her weakened state, she ran up the path towards him, her face wreathed in smiles and hugged him tightly. 'Thank you, thank you.'

Charles never saw her again but how he hoped she had found her way to a future.

Gradually, the putrid huts began to be cleared, with people either transferred to hospital or to the burial pits. What now for those who had endured and seen too much?

After they were cleared, the huts were burnt to the ground. There was a ceremonious torching of the last hut, bedecked with a large picture of Hitler and a swastika flag. Speeches were made by those in command and a flamethrower was used to light up the wood.

LIBERATION

Crowds watch as British soldiers set fire to the last remaining hut at Bergen-Belsen

Charles watched as black smoke mushroomed into the blue sky. Could the memories of what he'd seen here be so easily erased from the landscape of his thoughts?

As the 'Horror Camp' was slowly evacuated, Renia's eyes opened.

Chapter Thirteen

∾

Do Not Cry When I Die

I found a girl; she was a living skeleton, impossible to gauge her age for she had practically no hair left on her head and her face was only a yellow parchment sheet with two holes in it for eyes. She was stretching out her stick of arm and gasping something. It was 'English, English, medicine . . . medicine.'

Broadcaster Richard Dimbleby, recording his first broadcast from the camp

White. Everything was white. Soap. Uniforms. Skin. The woman was washing her gently, soaping her with warm water. It ran in rivulets down Renia's protruding ribcage, the bones of her spine, along the arms so skinny – she could have circled them with her fingers. Then the woman washed her hair, using her fingers to work loose the matted clumps of filth. Renia's hair, growing back in the eight months since it had been shaved in Auschwitz-Birkenau, was flecked with grey at the back.

She slumped as helpless as a newborn baby in the woman's arms, unsure of her surroundings, or what was happening to her. It was Wednesday, 25 April 1945. She had been unconscious for ten days.

When I came to, I was in a delousing centre, on a table being washed by a nurse. It's hard to fully remember that time as I was so weak, so very weak and ill. I was naked, that I know, and a nurse was washing me. I wish I could explain what it felt like to have warm water on my body after so many years, but I was so very muddled and mixed up in my head. I didn't know what was going on. Then the nurse started to put a white powder on me.

All around me were more skeleton-like people, like me, also being dusted with white powder. It was so very strange. The only thing that made sense in my head was finding Mama, but I was too weak to get off the table or speak.

Then I tuned in to the voices around me. The nurses were speaking German! We were being treated by German nurses. I was so confused. Did that mean we were still prisoners of the Nazis? Not that I could have got off that table, or run, or done anything to get away. Then I saw Mama on the table next to me. I felt so relieved. How were we still together? I'd collapsed outside the hut. Somebody must have carried me back in and put me next to her maybe? It didn't matter. We were still together.

Renia was in a former Wehrmacht barracks that had been converted into a makeshift delousing centre, where newly liberated prisoners were washed and dusted with DDT insecticide to kill the lice that spread typhus. It was nicknamed the Human Laundry.

From there, Renia and her mother were wrapped in clean blankets and taken to buildings within the barracks that had been converted into a makeshift emergency hospital set up by the British Army. And so began the long journey to recuperation.

Just one week after liberation, the British Red Cross joined forces with Army medics in providing civilian medical care.

German doctors and nurses were also pressed into service by the British authorities. Later, they would be joined by British medical students, Queen Alexandra's Royal Army Nursing Corps, Swiss doctors and nurses and a group of Vatican sisters. By the middle of May 1945, Belsen had become the largest makeshift hospital in Europe, housing over 13,000 patients.

Mother and daughter were now free, but not out of danger.

We were moved into a small ward. There were about four to six beds. Mama and I were next to each other in single beds with white bedding. Can I describe to you the feeling of this bed? Clean white sheets against my skin. Being able to stretch out. The feeling of this, after five and a half years of concrete floors, straw beds and rotting wooden bunks. It is indescribable. Though, at that stage, I was still too ill to appreciate the feeling. There were two other women in beds on the other side of the room. They were just as ill as we were.

Out of the window, there were no high watchtowers or barbed wire, but a beautiful sun-dappled forest of fir and silver birch, their branches stretching into blue skies. After so many years of cruelty, darkness and horror, her brain could hardly make sense of it. Renia only had one powerful need.

When I felt strong enough, I turned my head to the right until my eyes found my mother. The woman who had kept me alive, whose presence of mind, strength and love had been the one thing that had given me hope.

I tried to reach my arm out to her, but I was too weak. I could tell she was dying. I could tell there was no recovery. Her eyes were closed. She looked so ill and I could tell that it was too late for her. I'd already had the dream back in the camp, of my two uncles carrying her away on a stretcher to heaven. I knew. I just knew.

Renia sank back into the numb fog of incomprehension. The only thing that pierced it was a strange sensation on her tongue.

The nurses were giving me food. Drops of water and a spoonful of stewed apple on a quarter of a slice of white bread. Don't ask me what I weighed when I was liberated, but it can't have been much. I was nothing but skin and bone.

The doctors and nurses were already learning about the dangers of overfeeding, so they were careful to just give me tiny amounts of food. A quarter of a slice of white bread, that was all to begin with. It was manna from heaven. Pure heaven. I can still taste it today.

Then, two days later, it happened. I could see something had happened to Mama. She had slumped, she was sort of falling out of the bed. I tried to use my voice to call the nurse to push her back on.

The nurse came over and she looked at Mama. She shook her head. 'I'm sorry,' she said.

They took her body away, and I was left on my own.

～

Sala Berkowicz, Hebrew name Sura Bajla, died twelve days after her liberation from the Bergen-Belsen concentration camp in Germany on 27 April 1945. She was forty-two years old. Sala was one of an estimated 14,000 women, men and children who died in the days after liberation of disease, abuse and malnutrition.

From September 1939 to April 1945, Sala had survived two ghettos, Auschwitz-Birkenau, a slave labour camp, Bergen-Belsen, and navigated an ocean of unimaginable darkness. Motherhood had given her the will to survive, to keep her only living child safe. She had stayed alive until her daughter was safe, but could her daughter keep her promise?

'Do not cry when I die.' Those, it turned out, were her last words. I didn't cry, not then.

I felt destroyed and numb. My heart was crying, but my eyes were dry. I had no tears. I couldn't do anything for my mother, and to this day, that's what hurts me the most. I wanted to get out of bed, arrange a proper funeral for her, but I couldn't move my legs and I had no clothes. If I could only have walked, I could have arranged a single grave for her.

In the days after, I didn't care if I died as well. I drifted in and out of consciousness, waking to find tiny pieces of food by my bedside. Every time I opened my eyes, I looked over to see Mama's bed was empty and the pain and grief hit me all over again.

The nurses encouraged me to eat and drink, to try and get out of bed and move to the open window and look out at the trees and the sunshine. But what good was food, clean sheets and freedom, when I was no longer with Mama? My beautiful, kind, loving mother.

How was I supposed to live without her? What was the point?

I'd watched as they took her body away and I had no idea where they were taking her or what had happened to her.

I later discovered my mother was buried with hundreds more in a mass grave. What kind of final resting place was that for people who had already suffered so much? But what could the British Army do? There were thousands upon thousands of bodies. Mothers, sisters, wives, husbands, brothers, grandparents. Every one was a precious human being. Every one had a story. Every one deserved a proper burial.

Sala was buried in a mass grave in the grounds of the displaced persons camp, approximately 2 kilometres from the Glyn Hughes Hospital – named after Brigadier H. L. Glyn Hughes, the first Allied medical officer to enter Bergen-Belsen – her body buried with 160 others on the same day.

Where BBC journalist Richard Dimbleby led, others followed, and soon the Holocaust was on cinema screens and kitchen tables around the world. Bergen-Belsen seared those images of death into the collective consciousness of a generation.

In the former concentration camp, various padres and priests did what they could to lend some dignity and solemnity to the burials. After the Jewish Reverend Leslie Hardman had recited the traditional Mourner's *Kaddish* over the burial pits, two Anglican padres, Reverend Thomas James Stretch of Holy Trinity Church, Aberystwyth, and Reverend Cuthbert of St Paul's in Seacombe, Merseyside, gave the last sacraments over the mass graves. Roman Catholic priests also said prayers.

My mama went to heaven. This I know, and no one can tell me any different. That gave me some solace to hold on to, the thought that one day I would see Mama again.

I stayed in that hospital room for a few weeks, the nurses encouraging me to eat. Each time, they gave me a little more bread and stewed apple.

'You should look out of the window,' one of the nurses said to me when I'd gained a little strength, but I didn't care. My body was getting stronger, but my mind was very muddled. It was like something had stopped in my brain. The world had stopped the moment Mama died.

The windows had wide sills which you could sit on to look out. Eventually, one of the nurses picked me up and gently placed me on the windowsill next to the open window. It was so beautiful outside and the sun was shining, but I felt so afraid. I was all on my own. I was just fifteen years old, and I had no one. I assumed my entire family had been murdered. I was an orphan with no one and nothing to live for.

Most days, the nurses took me to the window to look out, but I couldn't see a reason for living. I was no longer a Häftling, *a prisoner, but I didn't feel free.*

British Army Rabbi Leslie Hardman in front of an open mass grave

Renia was buried too deeply under the rubble of her memories to see a future. And yet, beyond that room, history was being made.

Three days after Renia's mother's death, on 30 April 1945,

Hitler committed suicide in his underground bunker. Allied forces accepted the unconditional surrender of German forces. Victory in Europe was celebrated on 8 May 1945 and in the Channel Islands the following day. For survivors like Renia, liberty didn't come with pealing church bells, bunting and street parties. Nor was she a part of any emotional public celebration with singing, dancing and bonfires.

Liberty instead began with a search: *Who am I now?* and *How do I wash clean the stench of my memories?*

Renia's war was far from over.

Inside that room, I didn't know anything. I didn't know anything about Hitler, or VE Day; it passed me by. I don't remember whether the nurses washed me again, whether I cleaned my teeth or brushed my hair. I do remember taking shaky steps to the window.

When I got a bit stronger, I remember chatting to another Jewish survivor, a lady in the same hospital room. She told me that I should come and live with her and marry her son. She was trying to be kind, but she didn't even know if he was still alive. I wasn't interested though. I just wanted Mama.

When I was strong enough to walk, they discharged me from the hospital, and I was sent to the Displaced Persons camp at Belsen.

They gave me a bed in a barracks with about ten other women. Once a week we got Red Cross parcels and, believe me, that was like heaven. Inside was a little bar of chocolate and a tin of condensed milk. There were also little tins of luncheon meat and sardines. I was scared of eating it all at once, so I tried to ration it to last. When you've hardly had food for over five years, to suddenly receive it is a wonderful gift.

I was given some clothes. I didn't get it from the clothing store they called Harrods because they'd run out, I think, by the time I got out of hospital, so I got a wool skirt that had belonged to an SS woman! There was nothing else for me to wear. After eight months in that same man's pyjama shirt and the oversized skirt tied up with a strip of material, I was only too pleased to be given clean clothes.

After initial appeals for clothing from the local population proved insufficient, the British military ordered the following appeal to be published in the local newspaper, *Cellesche Zeitung*: 'The Military Government has demanded from the town of Celle that 10,000 unfortunate people from Belsen, ¾ of them women, receive full sets of clothing ranging from dresses or suits, underwear and coats to stockings and boots. The results of the collections that have been carried out so far hardly cover a tenth part of what is needed. If we do not hand in enough things, we will have to fear sharp measures on the part of the Military Government.' The article concluded: 'Give immediately and generously. This is a matter of removing a blot from the German name.'

There were women of all nationalities in that place, but German and Yiddish were the international languages. Most people spoke and understood German; we'd all heard enough of it after all. We all got along with one another in a way. All these women had their own stories to tell, but we didn't share too much. It was all too painful for everyone. Everyone was wondering who was left of their family. What would they do next? I think I was the youngest person in there, but nobody seemed interested in me. Everyone was just lost in their own grief.

So, I slept, I ate food from the camp and my rations, to try and get stronger. My teeth were in a terrible state because I hadn't been able to clean them for over five years. My back was in so much pain from carrying sacks of cement. I still hadn't gone through puberty, so I had the body of a child.

I went for little walks. It was so strange to think we were in a place that had once been a training school for Nazis. In the late May sunshine, it was so beautiful. Years later, when I went to Bournemouth, it reminded me of Belsen.

They laid on so much for the survivors, the liberating troops and all the rescue teams. The actor Laurence Olivier came and performed a play. Yehudi Menuhin, the famous violinist, put on a concert. They even had a cinema there. I didn't see any of the plays or concerts, but I did manage to watch a film that had Deanna Durbin in it.

There were dances there too and lots of romances going on between female survivors and British soldiers. I was too young for that.

It felt so strange to be watching films, eating chocolate, all the things I'd dreamed of for so long.

Renia was once more a member of the human race. Except she didn't care. She just wandered about, watching other people learning to live, wondering what would become of her life.

Renia had no idea, as she walked past military policeman Charles Salt, whose job it was, on occasion, to let people into the cinema, that there *was* someone out there who not only could help her to heal, but who had seen what she had seen in those hellish Belsen days. There was someone out there who understood. Someone to love. But in those chaotic and surreal summer days of 1945, Renia didn't feel free or hopeful. Not even close. She was a tiny, bird-boned orphan, living in the shadow of incalculable loss.

Renia was numb to the extraordinary events unfolding around her, of the dances that took place under strings of brightly coloured lights with music supplied by the Royal Air Force.

A MOTHER'S PROMISE

Or the recovery of sexuality as young women survivors began romances with soldiers, or the little library set up by the British, or the Red Cross sewing circles and the theatre clubs. Some survivors were determined to enjoy their freedom to the fullest and get back to the business of living. But not Renia. Not yet.

Nearly six years before, I'd been a normal ten-year-old child with a future and a close and loving family. There'd been a close community in my city, Jewish traditions and holidays to observe, long summer holidays with Bubbe and Zayde. And who knew what else beyond that? Maybe my father's dreams of a Parisian education would have come true!

Instead had come dehumanisation, death and despair. What was freedom without her family?

I knew of Mama's death, I had seen it with my own eyes after all, but where was my little sister Stenia? What had happened to Bubbe and Zayde? And Tatuś at Auschwitz? What had happened to him after we got separated on arrival? He couldn't have survived, could he? I'd seen and smelt the smoke from the chimneys over the camp. It wasn't possible he had survived and yet . . . and yet . . . Not knowing was more torture.

My thoughts always came back to Mama. She'd fought so hard to keep me alive; she crossed an SS selection line so that she could remain by my side.

In all those years, when she could so easily have given up, especially after Stenia was taken, she hadn't. Somehow, she had held back death until I was safe.

Mama had lived with such grace and dignity, right up to the end.

When I felt strong enough, I walked to her grave. It was a mass grave; the earth was still fresh. I stood over this patch of brown earth, marked out by rows, and I was still too numb to cry, my feelings buried deep. It was too much to take in. How could it be true that my mama was buried in this pit with so many others? I couldn't do anything for her. Without Mama, I didn't know what to do, where to go. I had no plan.

And so, Renia wandered aimlessly about the Displaced Persons (DP) camp, watching, waiting, for what she wasn't quite sure.

The burning question was what to do with survivors. For many, their homes had been destroyed or stolen, their families murdered.

The Allies created the legal status of 'displaced persons' for the former concentration camp prisoners and slave labourers who had been deported to Germany from all over Europe. They were entitled to special support from the Allies.

In September 1945, a Jewish camp committee was transformed into the Central Committee of Liberated Jews in the British Zone, with its headquarters in the DP camp.

The Central Committee set up a police force, courts, schools, and cultural and social institutions. Many survivors started families in the camp and found new hope for the future. In the first two years after the liberation alone, more than 1,000 Jewish couples got married in Bergen-Belsen, and well over 1,000 Jewish children were born in the DP camp before it was finally dissolved in the summer of 1950.

Displaced persons camps were scattered all over Europe. In 1943, the United Nations Relief and Rehabilitation Administration (UNRRA) had been founded to provide relief and provision of food, fuel, clothing, shelter and other essential services for victims of war. DP camps had been formed in former military barracks, factories, airports, hotels, castles, hospitals and private homes. Displaced people were crammed into every corner of Europe. There was even a DP camp formed in the grounds of Hamburg Zoo.

But a new life within the DP camp was not to be Renia's experience. Sometime during that first summer after the war's end, a stranger pushed open the door to the barrack, her eyes scanning the rows and rows of young women. It was difficult for her to tell what age most of them were; they all wore the same haunted expression and baggy second-hand dresses.

'Is Renia Berkowicz here?' she asked haltingly.

Chapter Fourteen

～

Learning to Live

In the dark abyss of the Holocaust, the sacred prayer Shema Yisrael – *'Hear, O Israel: The Lord our G-d, the Lord is One' – became a beacon of light, a lifeline to the soul* (neshoma) *of every Jew. This ancient invocation, recited for millennia, represents more than mere words; it is a testament of unwavering faith, whispered by parents to their children before going to sleep at night.*

After the Holocaust, Rabbi Eliezer Silver of Cincinnati (originally from Lithuania) went to Europe on a mission to rescue Jewish orphans hidden in convents and monasteries by the Nazis.

In an orphanage, filled with children whose identities had been obscured, Rabbi Silver faced an insurmountable task: How to identify the Jewish orphans among them? He began to chant the Shema. As the words filled the air, a miracle unfolded. Tiny voices echoed back the prayer. Tears streamed down the faces of those children as they remembered the sacred words their parents had whispered to them. The prayer, taught at the cradle and destined to be the last uttered at the grave, revealed the hidden Jewish neshomas *within.*

Rabbi Silver looked at the priest and said, 'These children are mine.'

Ilana Greenblatt, Jewish Culture and
Faith Manager for Jewish Care

The sister-in-law of my Aunt Miriam, my father's older sister, whom I'd last seen in the ghetto, had found me. She explained that she'd come to the Belsen DP camp to search for survivors of her own family and spotted my name on the DP list.

'Your Aunt Miriam is at a camp nearby called Braunschweig,' she explained. 'Will you come with me back there? She'll be so happy to see you.'

I didn't need asking twice. I was only too happy to learn that someone from my family had survived. I had nothing to pack so I stood up and left in the only clothes I owned. Just like that. I travelled with this woman back to my aunt's DP camp, in the grounds of her former camp.

Braunschweig was a small satellite camp about an hour from Bergen-Belsen. Approximately 800 women were housed in the stables which had held the horses of the SS-Junkerschule (SS Officers' School). The women had been sent there from the women's camp at Bergen-Belsen. In the final months of the war, they, like Renia and her mother, had been used in demolition, helping to clear rubble in Braunschweig.

I was so pleased and relieved to see my Aunt Miriam. Like many from the Łódź ghetto, she'd been sent to Auschwitz, where she got separated from her husband and fifteen-year-old son.

She asked me about my father, her younger brother, and all I could do was shake my head and say, 'Auschwitz.' She wasn't a warm or affectionate woman. I don't remember her hugging or kissing me. But she was practical and determined, and immediately began exchanging some coffee for a pair of new boots for her son Heniek. She didn't know if he was still alive, but she was determined to get back to Łódź to see if she could find him. She gave me his boots to wear for the journey back to Poland. There was no question that I wouldn't go with her. What else could I do, after all?

Renia and her aunt drew the summer air into their frail lungs and began the difficult journey home. As fragile as two feathers in the wind, the survivors made their way eastwards, back to Łódź. The men, women and children released from Nazi terror now faced futures shaped by the impact of war.

It took us weeks to get back to Poland. The journey was very difficult because we had no money and the trains didn't run properly. We walked part of the way, hitched lifts and travelled on the roofs of trains. We lived on potatoes or whatever scraps we could scrounge from local farmers. We didn't talk much, but sat lost in our thoughts.

One day, we were sitting in a goods train on the Polish border. I was holding a parcel containing my old shoes – on my feet were the boots Miriam had got for her son if he was still alive. They were two sizes too small, but the idea was that if we were robbed, the new shoes would not be taken. Of course, we were robbed – by Russian soldiers who swept through the train and left us with nothing. They took the parcel with my shoes.

To others it might have felt like a blow, but Renia was resigned to having things and losing them. Besides, if the rumours she was hearing were true, she was lucky her shoes were all they took from her.

There was nowhere to wash, or keep clean, so I ended up getting a terrible skin rash along with all my other troubles. I was told to rub salt into the open itchy wounds which stung like anything. I wasn't in a good way by the time we reached Poland, in a pair of boots two sizes too small.

For survivors like sixteen-year-old Renia, returning to their old homes and the places of their persecution was intensely traumatic. She arrived back in her homeland a broken, exhausted shell, skin on fire, teeth rotting, back bowed.

Łódź too was a very altered place. Many people returned in the hope of finding relatives. Sadly, very few had the good fortune of being reunited; the more common story was finding kith and kin murdered, homes and businesses taken.

Miriam was one of the lucky ones. She found her husband and her son alive. I was happy for her, but worried about what I would do next, when her husband told me some news. 'Your Aunt Gitel is here in Łódź!'

Aunt Gitel, Mama's younger sister, was alive! We'd always been very close, she and I. I don't remember how I got to her address, but I do remember going there barefoot, her opening the door and me falling into her arms.

After we hugged, she stood back, gripping my arms and looking at the empty space behind me. I'll never forget the look on her face.

'And where is Mama?'

I didn't want to answer her. I couldn't say the words, so I shook my head instead and with that I saw all her hopes die. She started to cry and, finally, so did I.

Wrapped in the safety of her favourite auntie's arms, Renia's tears flowed, scalding and raw. The pair clung to one another, hardly able to believe they had found each other. In Poland, apart from Aunt Miriam and her husband and son, and two more of her father's sisters called Mania and Lonia, Renia and Gitel were the only survivors from an extended family that had once run to over two hundred members.

Her mother had been one of four; her father one of eight.

LEARNING TO LIVE

The majority of the aunts and uncles, cousins and two sets of grandparents that Renia had grown up around had all been murdered by the Nazis.

Poland had the largest number of victims of the Holocaust. The Nazis and their collaborators murdered at least 3 million Jewish citizens of Poland, destroying communities that had thrived for centuries. Now it was left to Renia and her Aunt Gitel to somehow forge a new life from the wreckage of their old ones.

Renia looked up shyly as a strange man entered the room.

Gitel introduced me to her new friend, a man called Lejzer Tondowski, originally from Zduńska Wola. He'd also been in the ghettos and two camps, Auschwitz-Birkenau and Mauthausen. His wife and six children had been shot in front of him. Gitel's young son and husband had been shot after they were found hiding in the attic back in Zduńska Wola. Lejzer had a tattoo from Auschwitz. He never tried to cover it over. Some survivors covered their tattoos with plasters.

The pair had a relationship built out of a shared understanding of each other's suffering and grief.

Gitel was a handsome woman. War hadn't changed that. She was tall, with very clear skin and thick, dark hair. In fact, as long as I knew her, her hair was always a dark colour. She became my rock.

Gitel shared everything she had with me, immediately giving me a pair of her shoes and insisting I come and live with her. So, I moved in and she became like my mother.

When Gitel was deported out of the ghetto in February 1944, Renia and her mother assumed she had been sent to her death in one of the extermination camps, but in fact she had been sent to a slave labour camp in Częstochowa, a city in southern Poland, where she was put to work in a munitions and armaments factory. After her liberation in January 1945, she had returned to Łódź, where she met Lejzer. They had known each other back in Zduńska Wola, where he had owned his own textile workshop. They had found solace in each other's arms. Such situations were commonplace after the war, with survivors marrying other survivors.

Renia doesn't remember much about her return to Łódź, other than a gradual sense of a return to life.

Gitel shared everything she had with me: her clothes, her food, her affection. We were all in a terrible state physically. Poor Lejzer had ulcerative colitis from years of starvation. I had constant toothaches and backaches, and the frostbite I'd endured from working through that last winter on the bomb sites in Hamburg left me in terrible pain. Every time there was a change of temperature, I got a burning sensation in my toes. It drove me crazy.

Gitel was such a strong woman, like Mama, and took over the care of us all. She made the most delicious chicken soup to try and build me up.

Renia's senses reawakened, but with them came a fresh onslaught of memories. Bubbe's yeast cake, still warm from the oven. Blackberries in the forest with her little sister. Her mother waking her with a soft kiss on the forehead, cherry juice and sponge cakes.

Gitel tried to get me to talk about what had happened after we were split up, to tell her my experiences of Auschwitz-Birkenau, Hamburg and Bergen-Belsen, but I just couldn't talk about it. I wasn't ready to. Gitel didn't push me to talk; she had her own grief to deal with and the memories of the little boy she'd last seen hiding in the attic.

In Łódź, I was given the opportunity of a new life. I can't remember who exactly I spoke with, most probably a Jewish aid organisation, but they offered me the chance to emigrate to

LEARNING TO LIVE

Canada, to live in a children's home and start a whole new life.

In Auschwitz, 'Kanada' was where they had stored all the stolen prisoners' possessions and it was called that because they believed Canada was a land of plenty, so I thought it would probably be a good place to live.

Canada and the US, along with Palestine and Australia, were the most popular places for Jewish survivors to emigrate to and attempt to start over. Renia was tempted to go, but couldn't leave Gitel and Lejzer and so decided to stay with her little patched-together family.

I often wondered, years later, what my life would have been like if I'd moved to Canada. If I'd taken up the offer, I'd have missed the wonderful man who was coming my way.

Around that time, Gitel and Lejzer got married and we decided to go back to Zduńska Wola. Lejzer had owned a big building, which the Germans had taken over and run as a fur factory, and he wanted to see if he could reclaim the property.

Renia had many firsts in Zduńska Wola. Reading a newspaper, listening to a wireless, combing her dark hair, which was now growing back thick and strong, her first period. Returning to her childhood home of Zduńska Wola in 1946 also uncorked all Renia's fears.

It was awful. We walked along the once-friendly streets of my childhood, and I saw conversations trail off. People stopped and openly stared, or whispered behind their hands. Some muttered comments, like 'Why's she come back?'

Hardly anyone had returned to Zduńska Wola, maybe fewer than 100 out of a community of over 9,000 Jewish people.

We were made to feel so unwelcome, as if people were disappointed we'd survived the camps. They didn't want to see us Jewish people coming back. Believe me, the antisemitism was terrible, just terrible. It made us feel very vulnerable.

Renia, Gitel and Lejzer moved back into his old home at 7 Stężycka. They were among the fortunate ones. Many Jewish survivors had great difficulty reclaiming their homes and businesses and were left destitute.

Immediately after the war, Poland was, in places, still virulently antisemitic. As Renia's memories testify, survivors were not always welcomed home, rather the opposite. On 4 July 1946, a pogrom erupted in the south-eastern city of Kielce, Poland, 110 miles from Zduńska Wola.

A mob of Polish soldiers, police officers and civilians murdered forty-two Jews and injured over forty in the worst outburst of anti-Jewish violence in post-war Poland. Jewish men and women were stoned, robbed, beaten with rifles and stabbed with bayonets.

Their mothers, many of whom were survivors, wept bitter tears over their children's coffins. Coming just one year after the end of the war, the massacre triggered terror in an already traumatised Polish Jewish community and shocked people around the world. But not Renia.

We weren't wanted. We tried to settle back in and pick up our old lives. Lejzer was a hard worker and immediately set about making clothes, which Gitel and I tried to sell in the market, but it was obvious we weren't wanted. We didn't feel safe.

On top of this were the memories. I didn't dare return to the site of the old ghetto, or our old home, or the square where Stenia had been taken. It was too painful, but the ghosts of my family were everywhere. Every tall, slim man I saw reminded me of my father. It was all I could think about. My mind replayed the moment he was taken at Auschwitz-Birkenau over and over, and I knew I wouldn't rest until I got answers.

Whenever I met a man who had returned from the camps, I asked him whether he had come across a man called Szaja Berkowicz. It was always the same answer. 'No.'

Renia tasted the disappointment, hot and sour on her tongue. In the ensuing decades, she would ask this question over and over, tormented by images of her father swallowed up into the crowds at Auschwitz-Birkenau.

I never stopped asking. Wherever we went I asked, 'Have you seen my father?' I just wanted to know, in case by some miracle, someone had seen him. Eventually, years later, I finally gave up. I never believed I would have news of him.

Unbeknownst to me, Aunt Gitel had written to some old family friends who had managed to move to Palestine before the war. They wrote back and sent some photographs.

There, looking back at me, were Mama and Tatuś. They were walking down the street together before the war, so smart and handsome. There was another photo. This one was of Stenia, my little sister, taken in a toy car when she was about six or seven years old. I couldn't believe my eyes.

Her big eyes stared back at me, so serious and clever. Just as I remembered her. My murdered sister. My tears flowed. Having her photo in my hands! It was just like a miracle.

I would never let the photos out of my sight again. Those photos were the most precious treasure you can ever imagine. I only wish they had been able to send one photograph back of me, so that I could remember what I looked like before the war.

In that first year after the war, Renia was a physically fragile, emotionally vulnerable girl. Without her aunt's strength to guide her, she's unsure how she would have coped with her new-found freedom.

Over the years, Gitel taught me many precious lessons, but looking at the photos of my lost family, the most important one was that I had to somehow go on living. I owed it to them. It wasn't enough to survive.
  I had to learn to live.

Teenage Renia faces the future

Chapter Fifteen

Paris

April 1947

The night was as black as pitch. Renia and the man slipped silently through the yard. There wasn't a breath of wind. Just the soft slap of their booted feet and shallow breathing. As they reached the wooden gate, the guard dogs suddenly started up, snarling, snapping and lunging on their chains. Renia froze. The racket was sure to alert the guards.

'Run,' hissed the man, pushing open the gate and hurtling headlong into the inky darkness. Renia didn't need telling twice and followed him, her heart thumping. Renia Berkowicz had had to do many things in her young life, but a moonlight flit out of a French detention centre was a first.

You want to know why I was arrested? I'll tell you. I still can't believe it myself.

Eventually, we decided to leave Zduńska Wola, sometime in 1946. The antisemitism was just too bad and none of us felt safe there. There were just too many bad memories. It wasn't our home any longer, so we decided we needed to try and find a new home where we could feel safe.

Lejzer decided that we should try and get to France. He'd heard things were good for survivors there. We packed up our things and began our long journey west. All I had were a few pieces of clothing, my old skirt, a second-hand pullover and a lilac coat I'd got in Zduńska Wola. Like so many other survivors all over Europe, we were desperate to find a safe place to rebuild our lives.

So, we left Poland. Over the course of many months we travelled through Czechoslovakia, across Austria and into Germany. Now what did we see? Europe was shabby and bomb-damaged. Highways and whole cities were destroyed. People were living a hand-to-mouth existence. But we also saw great beauty, like the mountains and meadows of the Austrian Alps.

It was quite a journey, believe me. We hitched lifts on the back of farmers' wagons, or just walked for mile upon mile, stopping at DP camps run by the Americans, where you could get a bed for the night and food.

With every new town or village they stopped to rest in, Renia's past came, too.

Everywhere we went, I asked the same question to any Jewish male survivors I met: 'Did you ever meet a man called Szaja Berkowicz in Auschwitz?' No one could ever tell me anything, but it didn't stop me asking.

Eventually, in late 1946, they arrived in the Landshut Displaced Persons camp in Bavaria, southern Germany, run by the United Nations Relief and Rehabilitation Administration (UNRRA). By the time it closed in 1947, UNRRA was still running nearly 800 resettlement camps for people just like Renia, Gitel and Lejzer.

Once there, Uncle, as I had started to call Lejzer, found some old friends he'd known from his days in the concentration camps and

PARIS

they helped us to find a small flat, where we lived for quite a while, at least until early 1947.

It was a simple life. We collected rations every week from the Jewish committee. Like us, most people were determined to put their past behind them. Some wanted to emigrate to Palestine. Others, like us, wanted to get to Paris.

It was here that I tried peanut butter for the first time. I liked it very much and this helped me to put weight back on.

I needed the strength because we were determined to try and get into France. But this wasn't easy. We didn't have papers and it was very difficult and slow to get official papers to get residency in France, so we tried to smuggle ourselves in.

Uncle managed to get some forged visas on the black market, but they can't have been all that good. The first couple of times we tried to cross the border into France, we were stopped and turned back.

The French police weren't unkind when they turned us away, and they didn't seem antisemitic either, but without proper papers they wouldn't let us in. By the second failed attempt, we decided we might be more successful if we split up. The idea was that we would meet up if successful in Paris. If this sounds a bad plan, it's because it was, but what else could we do? We had no other options open to us. I was scared, but by then, the worst had already happened to me. I had been a prisoner of the Nazis for nearly six years. What could French border police do that was worse than the Nazis?

So, I said goodbye to Gitel and Uncle and arranged that we'd meet at the home of a cousin we'd discovered had survived. He was called Szachna and lived in Paris. Gitel hugged me as we left each other. 'Stay strong, look after yourself.'

This time, I met a man on the train, another survivor like me, who was trying to join his wife in Paris. I don't remember his name, but we were both arrested together at the border and placed in either a detention centre or an open prison, I forget which.

Should I have been scared? Perhaps, but like I say, the worst had already happened.

I trusted the Jewish man I was with, so when he told me he was leaving, I didn't want to be left behind. I was frightened to be left on my own there so I went with the Jewish man.

One night, under cover of darkness, we walked out. It can't have had high security, but I was still frightened, I can tell you, especially when the two guard dogs at the gate started barking like mad. We both ran and made our way to the nearest station. As soon as morning came, we went to the ticket office and the man bought me a ticket to Paris.

To this day, I wish I could remember the name of my Good Samaritan, or more details about who he was. It was this small act of kindness that gradually helped to restore my faith and trust in humanity.

I'd gone through so much torture and brutality that the simple gift of a train ticket was so very moving. Practically, it was a huge help to me too.

Arriving in Paris was very emotional and overwhelming. After the destruction in Poland and Germany, the buildings in Paris seemed so very grand. Hardly anything had been bombed. I was finally in the city my father had dreamed of for Stenia and me.

My kind friend delivered me to the home of my mother's cousin Szachna. I thanked him and we parted ways.

Szachna lived on rue la Condamine. His war had been very different to mine. His wife and son had managed to escape to the free zone in the south of France. He'd managed to stay in hiding in Paris right through the Occupation. He owed his life to his neighbours, who had looked after him by sneaking him food. He only came out of hiding after the fall of Paris. He'd been very lucky not to have been found by the Germans.

I stayed with him while I waited for Gitel and Uncle to make it *across the border. Eventually, I registered with a local Jewish relief committee and they sent me to a home for young displaced people near the Palace of Versailles.*

The house was very grand, surrounded by nice parks and buildings. Here we were well fed and cared for by a rabbi's wife.

After many months, Gitel and Uncle managed to get papers to come to Paris legally and they came to fetch me. What a happy reunion that was. 'My little Renia,' Gitel cried, hugging me. 'You can't imagine what we went through when we heard you'd been arrested.'

Uncle rented a room and a small tailoring workshop and, here, my life began.

Renia and her uncle in Paris

Paris in 1947 – City of Lights. To Renia, city of new beginnings. After all the years of torture and persecution and the restless months of travel, finally, here was a place she could put down roots.

Paris woke something in Renia which the Nazis had nearly destroyed. *Hope.* In Paris, everything seemed brighter. When she wasn't working in her uncle's tailoring business in the 18th arrondissement, or learning to speak a little French at night school, Renia wandered the streets, soaking it all in.

The moon that washed the Seine with silvery light seemed luminous in Paris. The bakeries with their perfect lines of jewel-coloured *macarons*. The golden lights of the Eiffel Tower dancing over the rooftops of Paris. Cafes with waiters in crisp white aprons serving French wine. After years of darkness, it was dazzling. The young woman from Poland, who had loved her mother's stylish dresses, had found her spiritual homeland.

I loved Paris. I enjoyed watching the people, especially the beautiful women, walking through the streets in their haute couture. Oh, the dresses! I could have sat all day and watched those women walk past in their Christian Dior 'New Look', which had just been released in Paris in 1947. Were those women stylish. And how!

Renia watched them carefully, saw the feminine way they moved their hips, the jaunty way they wore their divine little hats.

The city seemed so glamorous to me. After years of concrete, barbed wire and mud, I loved it. They seemed to have so much of everything too. I'd stop and stare at the fruit vendors with barrows of figs and oranges piled up to heaven! We could only have dreamed of such a sight in the Łódź ghetto. We ate them like there was no tomorrow.

PARIS

Renia sitting by the Seine, Paris

While Renia was sampling the delights of Paris, back in Poland, justice was finally being served. In 1947, Hans Biebow, Nazi Head of Administration for the Łódź ghetto, stood before a Polish tribunal in Łódź, accused of war crimes. After the war, he had managed to escape to Bremen, but was recognised by a survivor of the ghetto and extradited back to Poland. Responsible for theft, systematic starvation and the murder of thousands of Jews, including Renia's sister, grandparents, uncles and nephew, Biebow was sentenced to death and executed.

We didn't hear of this in Paris, but today I feel that justice was finally done.

In Paris, it seemed that along every boulevard, there was something new to marvel at. One day, she and her uncle were walking through a smart Parisian shopping mall.

I saw something that stopped me in my tracks.
    'What's that, Uncle?' I asked, pointing. He looked puzzled for a moment, then smiled.
    'They are moving stairs, Renia.'

They both stared as the escalator slid effortlessly up, transporting Parisians to the floor above, so that they didn't even break a sweat.

The pair stood in reverent silence, watching as Parisians hopped on and rode upwards. To Renia, that escalator stood for so much more than progress. It was a sign that the world was once more civilised. And she was free to step with ease into this new world. *Free.* For the first time in years, an emotion surfaced inside her, as effervescent as a champagne bubble. Not happiness. Not yet. But something more durable. Hope.

We got on it, I remember, and it felt strange and miraculous.

Renia could have ridden that escalator all day long. Just because she could.

Uncle was a good worker and he started over from scratch and worked hard to build up his business. I worked alongside him, sewing pockets and buttonholes. It was hard to begin with as I didn't have papers and I could have been arrested at any moment,

PARIS

but little by little, we began to do better. Eventually, I got papers which allowed me to stay in Paris.

By 1948, I even had a little money to buy my own clothes for the first time in my life. The first dress I bought myself was only a cheap dress, but wearing something brand new, only worn by me, made me feel so special. Oh, it was wonderful.

Gitel was so proud of me. 'You could put on a sack and you'd look good in it,' she exclaimed. I loved the feeling of wearing new clothes.

After eight months in the same dirty old pyjama jacket from Auschwitz, Renia's cheap new dress might have been Christian Dior's 'New Look' for all the effect on her morale.

Renia in Paris

My teeth still hurt, and my back and neck ached, but my body was gradually healing. I had filled out and my hair grew back. I was once worried it would never grow back after it was shaved in the hospital and then again in Auschwitz, but it did. It grew back thick and shiny, like Mama's had been. But if you looked closely, you could see grey hairs in the back.

I wasn't the only young female survivor in Paris. From time to time, I saw young ladies in the street, with long plasters on their arm, so we knew they were covering up an Auschwitz number.

Renia was nineteen by now and in many ways, still a shy, fearful young woman, but after so many years of making herself as small and inconspicuous as possible in order to survive, she was beginning to take up space in the post-war world. Starting with her hair, which stood high and defiant. In post-war Paris, women still styled their hair with the Victory wave, or scooped it up under a towering, brightly coloured turban, as an emblem of victory and personal survival.

Those Paris days burn bright in Renia's memory. Those who have never lost their freedom can never realise how precious it truly is. To walk on a pavement, simply because you can. To turn left or right at will. To throw your arms wide, or sing. To exist without fear of persecution is a privilege.

Gitel and Uncle had started to make new friends, mainly through a small Jewish group they'd found of survivors from Zduńska Wola.

They'd get together and share memories and home-cooked food. I went along too and again asked if anyone there had seen my father, which, of course, no one ever had. I was pleased they'd found a community once more. Gitel had lost her faith after all she'd been through, so in Paris we weren't that observant.

But I could see they were settling down to life and learning to live again and, gradually, so was I.

And maybe it would have remained that way; Renia growing old in Paris, becoming fluent in French, perhaps even getting that smart office job her father had dreamt of for her. But, in early 1949, Renia received an invitation that was to change the course of her life.

Szachna and his wife invited me round for a family dinner. Gitel and Uncle couldn't make it, or were working, I can't remember. Anyway, it was just me and I got the Metro alone to their apartment.

'Renia,' Szachna said, leading me to a man's side. 'Let me introduce you to your mother's first cousin. This is Charles Salt.'

Chapter Sixteen

∼

Charles

Charles Salt had many fine qualities. He was scrupulously honest, with a strong sense of justice, a wicked sense of humour and intellectual curiosity. The 32-year-old former military policeman with the impeccable war record had come to Paris with his mother to visit family.

Charles adored his mother Sarah and older sister Pat. He worked hard as a tailor in a smart Bond Street firm, always giving his mother some of his wage packet at the end of the working week. He had bright blue eyes and a mouth that seemed to curl upwards at the edges. He was a man easy to fall in love with. A man to lean into. At thirty-two, he might have been considered old to be unmarried, but he had been fighting in a six-year war.

Renia was shy. She wore her experiences of the Holocaust like a protective shield. She worried there was a gulf between them, not just because of the twelve-year age gap. Renia didn't speak English. Charles spoke no Polish. But they found common ground in Yiddish.

How could I ever explain to this tall Englishman what I'd been through? His family had emigrated from Poland to England before the First World War and changed their name from Zalc to Salt.

CHARLES

Charles was my second cousin, but we'd never met before that first meeting in Paris. How could I ever tell him what had happened to me, or explain the sights I'd seen?

We'd been chatting a while when the conversation inevitably turned to the war. It was four years on from my liberation, but some days, it still felt like only yesterday.

Charles turned to me and said: 'I was at Bergen-Belsen.'

I replied: 'Me too!'

We talked for a long time that first night. Just knowing that he'd seen what I'd seen made me feel that I was with a man who could understand. I wouldn't need to try and have a difficult conversation about the war. Charles had seen it for himself. In many ways, he knew more about the liberation of Belsen than I did. I'd been unconscious for ten days after my liberation, after all.

'It was a race against time,' he explained. 'If the liberation had taken place five days later and the temperature been one degree hotter, there would have been a cholera outbreak. Then there would have been no survivors at all.

'There were thousands of bodies, and at first we didn't know what to do with them,' he went on. 'I was able to talk to the survivors in Yiddish and in some cases help them get letters out to their families, or arrange separate burials.'

'I couldn't arrange a burial for my mother,' I told him, 'and that's what hurts me most. I was in a hospital bed. I couldn't move.'

Renia stared down at the floor as she spoke, consumed with a shattering and complex mix of grief and guilt. When she looked back up, she realised Charles had tears in his eyes.

Charles had such a way with words. I could see everything so clearly by the way he described things.

A shared understanding forged an instant bond between the pair, but it was more than just a mutual experience that drew Renia to Charles.

He was funny too. A natural storyteller.

'What did you do after the war?' I asked him.

'I was at Belsen from April to September 1945,' he replied. 'Once the huts had been burnt down and the survivors all transferred to hospital, I stayed on and helped out with the Military Police. One of my jobs was working at the cinema in the DP camp.'

'I used to go there,' I replied, remembering the feeling of being so alone. It felt so odd and so amazing to know that he'd been there at the same time, perhaps even within arm's reach.

'One day, we were working when a jeep pulled up,' he went on. 'A knockout pair of legs slid out. My friend said, "There's only one person with a pair of legs like that and it's Marlene Dietrich."

'"Don't be silly," I mocked. "What would she be doing in a place like this?"

'"I might not be a good soldier," he laughed. "But I do know a good pair of legs when I see them." Sure enough, it was her.

'Then there was the time I was standing in the DP camp theatre when I politely asked one of the actors waiting in the wings to please pipe down so as not to disturb the performance. That was before I realised it was Laurence Olivier!'

His stories were so interesting.

'After Belsen, I wangled nine days' leave back in London for the Jewish New Year,' he explained. 'When I rejoined my unit, they'd moved to Hanover. Apparently, the men had requisitioned a German-owned property and gave the inhabitants five hours to get out.

'"You can't expect us to pack up our life in five hours," they protested, and do you know what they said? "You're right. Let's

CHARLES

give you the same amount of time you gave people before they were sent to ghettos and camps. You've got two hours!"' He shook his head. 'We were very angry with the Germans.'

I nodded. 'That I can understand. We didn't even get two minutes.'

'You know the best thing about Hanover?' he went on. 'I got to hoist the Union Jack over a prestigious building, and I laughed to myself as I did so. Imagine that, Renia: a Jewish man raising the flag in Germany. But that's war I suppose.'

I listened to his stories, spellbound. The evening passed in no time. 'I'd better go,' I explained when it got to 10pm. 'My aunt and uncle will worry about me.'

'I'll walk you to the Metro station,' he replied.

I was so shy and, though we had so much in common, I wasn't looking for romance. But I think Charles was. When we reached the steps to the Metro he turned to me and said, 'Would you like to live in London?'

'How would I know?' I replied. 'I don't know London. I don't know if I'd like it or not.'

'You should come and have a look around. See if you like it,' he replied.

Blushing, Renia shrugged and walked down the steps to the Metro. But Charles was not a man easily deterred.

He wrote to me from London, asking again if I'd like to come for a visit. I wrote back saying that I couldn't travel by myself. He replied, 'I'll come and fetch you then.'

And return he did. Not once, but several more times over the spring and summer of 1949, clearly determined to win Renia round. It can't have been a hard decision for Charles to leave behind the streets of his home in Hackney and return to the French capital. Paris in 1949 was where everyone wanted to be. The streets were teeming with Americans, ex-GIs taking advantage of the educational grants provided by the GI Bill of Rights to study in the city they had helped liberate. The vibrant energy of Parisian nightclubs, cafes, restaurants, theatres and haute couture acted like a magnet to journalists, writers, artists and diplomats. Charles had travelled to Paris for one reason only, though. A certain young woman who he felt bore a striking resemblance to Ingrid Bergman . . .

The woman who captured Charles's heart
– Renia in Paris

CHARLES

He came back and bought a pair of nylon black-market stockings for me and took me dancing. Charles loved to dance. Before the war, he used to win dance competitions at the Hackney Empire. He was so good at the tango and the quickstep.

Every time he returned, I got to know him a little better. He was a man I could rely on. With Charles, I'd never have to explain. He was a safe pair of hands.

When they weren't dancing, the pair talked over long walks through the city and, each time, Renia unpeeled a piece of her painful past.

I told him I didn't know what had become of my father, that the last time I saw him was when we got separated on arrival at Auschwitz-Birkenau. He told me that his father had been killed during the Blitz when a bomb landed on his home. I saw how painful that was for him.

'We were living in Stepney at the time,' he explained. 'There were no good shelters in the East End provided for a direct hit. The truth is our country wasn't prepared for war.'

'Nor Poland,' I replied.

We'd both suffered. Charles wasn't a flashy man. He was a gentleman. Gitel and Uncle liked him; everyone seemed to; he had that way about him. What's more, he was religious and observant, like his whole family. After having lost my way with my faith after the war, that was an attraction. It seemed to me that Mama would have liked him too. What can I say? I just trusted him. I could see he felt protective of me and maybe, in a way, I liked the fact that I knew he would look after and care for me.

Renia can't remember the exact moment Charles proposed, or when he first kissed her.

I just know that, sometime in August 1949, Charles came back to Paris with some papers which would allow me to enter England, and an empty suitcase for my clothes. He got stopped in Calais by customs who wanted to know, 'What's in the suitcase?' He replied, 'Nothing.' The customs officer thought he was taking the mickey and demanded he open the case. Charles opened the suitcase and smiled.

But I had barely anything to put in it. Uncle had made me a beautiful grey suit to get married in. He and Gitel were sad to see me go. They came with us to Gare du Nord train station and we all cried as we hugged each other goodbye. We'd all been through so much together after liberation, but they were happy for me that I'd found such a good man to start my life with.

'Take good care, Renia,' Gitel said, hugging me tight. 'Come and see us as soon as you can.' And that was that. I knew they wouldn't come to the wedding. They didn't have papers to come to England. I kissed them both. Charles picked up my suitcase and we got on a train heading for Calais.

Charles and Renia's engagement photo, taken in Paris in the summer of 1949

CHARLES

And so Renia, who had only just turned twenty, found herself crossing the Channel. To others, it might have felt reckless to leave behind your patched-up family to go to a country where you know no one and don't speak the language, but life was offering her a chance of happiness, and didn't she deserve that?

The crossing was bumpy. Everyone was being sick. I stood up on the deck the whole time. I was so shy and nervous. I held Charles's hand as the cliffs of Dover came into sight through the dark. I didn't know what to expect. I just knew I had to make a go of this. It was a very long journey from Dover to Hackney in East London by train and bus, and I was exhausted by the time we arrived.

The plan was that I would stay with Charles's older sister Pat, who was married and lived in Farleigh Road, and, as soon as we were married, I would move into the house Charles shared with his mother nearby in Clapton Way, just down the road from Hackney Downs.

Pat was lovely and immediately made me feel at home when I arrived. But in the weeks that followed, it became obvious that my mother-in-law-to-be wasn't so keen on our relationship. It wasn't so much what she said, or did, but I felt it. Maybe she didn't want her son marrying a poor Polish girl, and a survivor at that.

I had nix, nothing. I can see why, looking back, she wasn't keen. It wasn't a good match in her eyes. I was made to feel that I shouldn't talk about my experiences of the war and what we'd suffered in the camps and ghettos. No one in England wanted to know.

I remember once raising the war in Poland and immediately people said, 'We had a war here too, you know. We had it bad.'

Homesick for Paris and bewildered by Hackney, Renia had never felt so estranged from her Polish roots. What she needed was support, not comparisons.

There was a wall of silence. No one wanted to talk, and so I didn't. At least with Gitel, I knew I could raise the subject, but straight away in Hackney I knew that I mustn't talk about the war. The subject was taboo.

Charles's mother wasn't trying to be unkind. She'd lost her husband in the bombings and lived through the Blitz, the rockets and rationing.

I came to realise that if I wanted to fit in in England, I had to pull myself together and not talk about my feelings.

Renia's past was packed up and put in a metaphorical box under the bed marked '*Wartime. Do Not Open*'. The trouble was that, in Britain, memories of the war were everywhere.

It was four years since Victory in Europe, but Hackney, in common with the rest of the bomb-battered East End, was smothered in bomb sites, known to the curious kids who played in them simply as *the debris*.

The strange roofless buildings and rubble-strewn patches of wasteland were sprouting drifts of purple buddleia and willow herb, which helped to hide the scars of war. There was a bleak kind of beauty to be found in these desolate places, but not to Renia. No flowers or weeds could cover the memories she carried in her heart and mind, of barbed wire and hangings, people stuffed into freight wagons, smoke pumping from chimneys and pyramids of corpses. Nor would any amount of 'pulling herself together' ever obliterate the image of her little sister running towards a covered truck, tears streaking down her face, or her father vanishing into the crowds at Auschwitz-Birkenau.

Sadly, for Renia, the transition into her new life in London didn't prove easy.

CHARLES

In 1949, Paris and Hackney were as different as night and day. What a comedown! Hackney was dreary and shabby back then, full of bomb sites and queues. And Schnorrers *everywhere.* Schnorrer *is a Yiddish word meaning 'scrounger'. Hackney was very poor at that time, so everyone looked patched up and shabby. Food and clothing were all still on the ration. But after fashionable, elegant Paris, it was quite a shock, I can tell you.*

I remember queuing up for a couple of hours for a pair of tights. So, you know, in comparison to Paris, London was poor and miserable.

Hackney didn't have escalators or oranges piled up to heaven, but it did have fog.

'Peasoupers' they called the heavy fog. Getting caught in the fog was terrible. You choked on the air and it made you quite ill.

The darkness of the streets wasn't helped by the re-emergence of the ugly face of fascism. Fascist leader Oswald Mosley, who had been interned during the war, was back, stirring up yet more tension and hatred. Under his newly formed fascist party, the Union Movement, he and his bullyboy Blackshirt supporters made antisemitic speeches in Hackney and attacked Jewish people and their property, as well as smashing up synagogues. Ridley Road in Dalston was a favourite venue for open-air fascist meetings. The anti-fascist 43 Group set up by decorated Jewish ex-servicemen after the war, ambushed them, leading to violent confrontations. After all they had witnessed in the war, the 43 Group did not wait to be attacked and this time took the fight to the enemy.

Luckily, I didn't hear of this. Charles would have known about it. He was very well informed about politics and current affairs. He must have heard about it, but decided to keep it from me. It would've been easy to do as I didn't speak English, so I didn't understand the radio, or many conversations.

I just hoped that things would get better after I married Charles. I just hoped that once we were married and living together as man and wife, it would all settle down. Pat was lovely and when Charles was at work, she took me under her wing and I spent my days with her, shopping and learning to cook and keep house. She gave me the English newspapers and Woman's Own *to read and, gradually, I started to pick up the language.*

Pat and her husband Arlie started calling me Renee, an anglicised version of Renia. I didn't mind and soon everyone started calling me Renee, even Charles.

There was one good thing about coming to London. Charles and his family were religious, so it felt wonderful to be able to observe once more, attending synagogue and observing Shabbat. It felt good. It made sense to me.

It would take longer to understand the psyche of post-war Britain.

'Least said, soonest mended' might have been the prevailing attitude, with so many people determined to put the war behind them and look forward, but for Renee, as she was now known, some memories couldn't be so neatly tucked away. The images that had been swallowed into the hungry, dark throat of the war were about to climb back out.

Three months after her arrival in Hackney, Renee's past came back to haunt her.

Chapter Seventeen

Surviving

On a blustery November day in 1949, Renia Berkowicz and Charles Salt exchanged vows under a chuppah in a Hackney synagogue. Renia stood nervously in her good grey suit and felt a soft fluttering of hope. She wasn't Renia any longer. She was Renee, about to become Mrs Salt. An ordinary, working-class, British housewife.

I was marrying into a good, honest family. They didn't have much money and the wedding itself was modest, but none of that mattered because I was marrying the man I loved. Charles was everything I could have hoped for and more. He was a family man, a hard worker and very handsome. When I looked at him, I felt such hope. I hoped that our wedding day was the start of the rest of my life. A chance to put the past behind me. After the ceremony, we went to a local hotel for dinner with the family. As for a honeymoon, it was a few days in a boarding house in Westcliff-on-Sea. Nothing fancy. It was all Charles could afford.

As she strolled along the seafront, arm in arm with Charles, all bundled up against the cold, only one thing stained Renee's new-found happiness.

At the wedding, apart from my father's two uncles who'd come from Croydon and central London, I had none of my family. I thought of Mama, Tatuś, Stenia and both sets of grandparents. Would they have loved it? And how!

Tatuś would have been so proud to walk me up the aisle. Stenia would have been my bridesmaid. But when I tried to think of the details of her mannerisms or her exact features, I couldn't remember, and that was so very painful.

Renee's mind groped for a gesture, a characteristic by which to remember her sister, mother, father and grandparents by, from before the war. The awful realisation hit her. She didn't know, and now never would know, which characteristics she had inherited from her mother and which from her father.

So much about a person is intangible and time blurs the edges. All the little habits, the mannerisms, the natural smells were fading from her memory. And that, Renee realised with a bitter sting, was the worst of it. The Nazis hadn't just murdered her family. They had stolen her memories.

After the wedding, I moved in with Charles and his mother into their home, a Victorian semi-detached in Hackney.

It was difficult to be living together as man and wife under my mother-in-law's roof. It was her home, not mine. At times, she made me feel as if I didn't know anything. How to clean, how to cook, how to run a home.

Charles was kind and caring to me. Every morning before he set off up west on the bus for his tailoring job, he kissed me goodbye.

My mother-in-law got me a job round the corner, machining ladies' coats. I'd learnt how to sew after making German uniforms in the ghetto. Like the ghetto, we worked in a production line, with one woman sewing one part and then passing it down the line for the woman next to her to sew the next part. That's where the similarity ended though. The factory was noisy and cheerful. The wireless blared Music While You Work *all day long. Clouds of steam from the Hoffman press filled the air. Friday was payday and our wage was delivered in a brown paper envelope.*

The East End was the heartland of the rag trade, filled with mainly Jewish-owned firms turning out everything from gents' suits to children's clothes, millinery and women's clothes.

The women there had also been through the war, and many of them must have lost loved ones fighting, or in the bombs of the Blitz, and later the V1 and V2 rockets, but they were kind to me. They had no idea what I'd been through and, by then, I knew better than to share. Not that I could as my English was non-existent. We communicated with a little bit of Yiddish and hand gestures.

Many of them would have seen the footage of the camps on cinema screens and in newspapers, but although they knew I came from Poland, no one ever asked if I'd been in one of the camps.

Working there helped me to learn the language and got me out of the house. At home, in the evening, when Charles got back from work, he did the football pools, read the Daily Herald *or listened to the news on the wireless. My mother-in-law had already prepared the dinner for us so there was nothing for me to do.*

The post-war population of Britain was around 50 million. It was a simple, ordinary life, as in so many other working-class homes in post-war Britain.

But as the Singer sewing machines rattled and hummed, Renee's subconscious was unravelling.

Not talking about her murdered family, or even being able to acknowledge that they had existed, wasn't healing Renee, but harming her. With no opportunity to share her story, no acknowledgement of her trauma, or counselling to help her process her grief or the horrors she had witnessed, her pain wasn't fading, but festering. The reverberations of her trauma were about to make themselves felt.

It happened a few days after the wedding. I suppose you'd call it a breakdown, but the doctors just called it 'nerves'. I'd got back from work and was in the kitchen with Charles and his mother when I started to see terrible things.

Under my feet, the ground split in two. It began to break apart. It felt as real as the hand in front of my face. A terrible feeling of fear and panic gripped me. I started to shake. I can't remember if I screamed and cried. Then I saw a pure white elephant.

It was so strange and unreal, and yet, it felt so real. As if it were there in the kitchen with me. I trembled, my body reacting to these strange visions.

Charles and his mother were upset and mystified. They didn't know what to do to calm me down so, in the end, they took me to a hospital, not far from where we lived. I don't remember much about the time, except that I felt I was going mad. I was so terribly upset, scared and confused.

'It's her nerves,' the doctor told Charles after checking me over. He gave me some pills. To this day, I don't know what they were; sedatives maybe? We got home and Charles put me to bed. I was so terribly shaken and scared. I hoped it would be the first and last experience like that.

But it wasn't the last time. Even though the sedatives hit her bloodstream and dulled the roar, they did nothing to stop the barrage of terrifying images, which always followed the same pattern. The ground breaking apart and a jagged chasm opening beneath her feet. Gigantic white elephants. After an hour or more, the attack would pass, and Renee would realise she *was* in a safe place. The danger was inside her.

After that, these attacks grew more regular. It was such a terrible and frightening time. They could last for what felt like hours and could happen anywhere. At home, in the street, or at work. When it happened at work, the women were very sympathetic, patting my arm, making me hot, sweet tea and, when that didn't work, the boss would send me home. Soon they were happening day after day.

It was usually the same images. I'd be in a terrible state, crying and shaking. I knew it couldn't be real and yet it felt so real, so terribly real.

Charles was always so kind. He knew some of what I'd been through. He'd seen it for himself after all, but he was still bewildered as to how to cope with it. He did try though.

First, he got me an appointment with a nerve doctor round the corner from Great Ormond Street Hospital, then he paid for me to see a private doctor. He was kind and gave me more pills. I don't recall anyone ever asking me about my experiences of the war. Maybe Charles explained to them, but no one discussed them with me. They just sent me away with prescriptions for pills and told me it was my nerves.

But pills and a pat on the hand cannot eradicate five and a half years of torture, and in tandem with her declining mental health, Renee's physical health plummeted.

Oh, my health became terrible. All the bones in my neck were so very painful. My teeth and gums were rotting and I had terrible stomach pain.

The newly formed National Health Service was very helpful and I was sent to hospital, where they diagnosed me with stomach ulcers. I had to go in and have a tube inserted through my nose and down the back of my throat and into my stomach. Then I was attached to a drip on a stand and an alkaline mixture dripped into my stomach. I was in hospital for a month on that drip.

I also started seeing a dentist in a dental hospital in Gray's Inn Road, who began the long process of fixing my decaying teeth. For nearly six years, I hadn't been able to clean my teeth and I was starved, so it's no wonder my teeth and gums suffered. Once a week for two or three years, I was under the care of that dentist, who cleaned my gums and filled a lot of my teeth.

It was a strange and frightening time. My brain and body seemed to be falling apart. I was a new bride. I should have been in the honeymoon period. Charles was kind but I felt so isolated and alone.

It was test after test. To be honest, that time is a bit of a blur. Few people seemed to know about how to treat Holocaust survivors back then. Charles's love, patience and kindness were everything. He was such a tower of strength and a support to me, but it put a strain on our new marriage, not helped by living with my mother-in-law.

No one ever talked to me about my breakdown. Not my mother-in-law, nor my sister-in-law Pat. Not because they were unkind, but you have to remember, back then, people didn't discuss their feelings in the way we do today. I learnt to carry on taking the pills and kept soldiering on.

How many other Renees were out there, just 'soldiering on'? The field of psychotherapy bloomed in the post-war years. The end of the Second World War brought about a new understanding of psychiatric health.

SURVIVING

Some survivors were able to access this professional help in dealing with their trauma, but not Renee. She found herself tightened in a veil of silence, not daring to speak out, dreading the uncertainty of when and where her next attack might happen. There was no respite to be found in sleep, either. Her memories had claws and scratched their way out by night.

I had terrible nightmares. I was facing a selection, waiting to see if I was going to live or die. I would see SS men in their shiny boots and hear gunshots. My father's back disappearing. My sister running towards the SS man. Mama's face ripped to shreds by the bull. I relived my experiences night after night.

As the nightmares continued, Renee felt trapped once more in the unrelenting horror of it all. The mornings after, in a grey blur of exhaustion, she would clock on at the factory and muddle along. The phrase she heard the most from doctors was 'pull yourself together'. During the war, expressions of grief had been suspended in order to survive and then, in her so-called freedom, her grief was denied again. And yet she was drenched in it.

In the end, in early 1950, Charles took me back to Paris. He thought that seeing my aunt and uncle would help, and it did. Being with Gitel made me feel secure.

My aunt took me to a doctor too and he gave me blood transfusions to try and build me back up. I was there for three weeks. Being back in Paris was a tonic too; just being in the city I loved was uplifting.

Aunt Gitel must have had to fight her own demons too, and so did Uncle. She never said as much, but being around people who had gone through the ghetto and camps helped me. I didn't feel I had to cover it all up. I felt more at home. There was maybe more understanding towards survivors in Paris than London. After that first visit, I started to go back more regularly, at least a few times a year.

Looking back, should I have felt angry towards those doctors I saw and all the people who didn't want to know? Perhaps, but maybe they were ignorant? They could never have known what I and so many others had been through. They just did what they had to do.

Chapter Eighteen

New Beginnings

Renee endured a deep, dark well of trauma in silence, internalised and repressed as, somehow, she tackled each new day. At times, just finding the will to get out of bed in the morning took colossal reserves of strength, never mind carrying the burden of her grief.

All around her, Britain was changing, casting off the shackles of the past and looking to bright futures. The Greater London Council (GLC) started huge slum-clearance programmes, rehousing communities out of the bomb-shattered East End and into newly built suburban housing estates, with such luxuries as indoor plumbing and hot and cold running water.

The newly formed Welfare State meant times were changing, horizons widening. Most working-class women wanted more than a sub-divided portion of a damp, terraced house built in the last century and a dependence on the tally man and the pawnbroker for survival. The 1948 Education Act raised the school-leaving age from fourteen to sixteen, opening up a university education for the first time in history to working-class children.

In the immediate years after the war, not just in Renee's Hackney, but all over Britain, there was a desperate desire for a return to peace and stability. The men who came home from the war got their old jobs back. The women who had stepped in to help, the so-called 'place holders', had to work out a new identity for themselves. Everything was back in its supposedly rightful place, and women were encouraged to embrace their traditional feminine roles, cooking dinners, scrubbing steps, running sheets through a mangle in the yard.

The 1951 Festival of Britain showed Britain a 'beacon of change', in the form of a clean, bright and modern future.

The post-war baby boom took hold and women who had once worked for the war effort now found themselves washing terry nappies and juggling babies.

But Renee didn't feel like other women. And she knew no one who had experienced a fraction of what she had survived in the war. Dehumanisation. Subjugation. Erosion of her civil liberties and rights. Persecution. Violence. Selections. Disease. Starvation. Ghettos. Camps. Slave labour. The murder of almost her entire family.

How could she even begin to fathom a future, never mind a bright and shiny one? Especially when reminders of the past were everywhere. Her mind constantly reached for associations.

A trip to Bournemouth triggered memories of the DP camp in Bergen-Belsen. The beautiful heathland reminded me of the landscape around the camp. When my toes, once frostbitten, began to burn, I'd be back in the freezing German bomb sites.

In October 1951, Renee's life changed once again.

I discovered I was going to have a baby! Believe me, that changed everything. Being a mother changed me. I had to pull myself together. I had no choice.

Sharon was born in a Jewish maternity hospital in Lordship Road, Hackney, on 12 July 1952. When I held her in my arms, so perfect and innocent, I knew it wasn't about me any more. I had a responsibility to get better for her.

Sharon was such a beautiful baby, like a little doll, with fair hair and dark eyes. When I looked into those eyes, I could tell she was going to be clever.

'She's a born teacher,' said the midwife.

Renee and Sharon

Four years after Sharon, I had a boy, Martin, on 6 August 1956, an early birthday present for me.

'You should have a dozen like him,' everyone said.

After being starved for so many years, it was a miracle that I managed to have children at all. I loved being a new mother. The pure love that they passed on to me made me feel so wanted again. Being a mother was a healing experience. Charles was a natural father, very loving. He adored his children. He was a hands-on father. He enjoyed giving them their bottles, winding them and holding them. We took them out for walks in a big black carriage pram. There was a time I thought I'd never live, never mind push beautiful babies in a pram down the street.

Becoming a mother of course reminded me of my own mother. I missed Mama even more after Sharon and Martin were born. She would have been there every day and taken over. Mama would have helped feed the babies and me. She would have been the greatest help a young mother could have and she would have taken such pride in being a bubbe herself.

Life began to get a little easier from then on. In 1952, we also began the process of applying to Germany for compensation. It was a long process. We had to get proof that I'd been a prisoner in the ghettos and camps. No amount of money could compensate for my loss, but we felt that Germany should compensate at least for some of the work that I did for them in the ghettos. It wasn't a huge amount, but it was enough to help improve the quality of our life.

When Martin was eighteen months old, with money lent to us by my Uncle Lejzer, we bought a little grocery shop in Albion Road, Stoke Newington and built a business. It wasn't much, just a few rooms above a shop, but it was our own. Being in our own place, out from under my mother-in-law's feet, also helped me. We were very grateful to Lejzer for the opportunity. He always helped me whenever he could. His tattoo never faded, you know.

In the early 1960s, we moved out of Stoke Newington and lived in Finchley for a year. Then we moved to Hendon, north-west

London, and bought a delicatessen at 91 Bell Lane, with a flat above. We changed its name from Denbies to Charles. We were so proud of it! It was also a chance for the children to go to schools where they'd be able to make Jewish friends.

We saw this as our chance and we worked so hard, delivering food all around the area, staying open all the hours except for the Sabbath and half-days on Wednesdays and Sundays.

Every day I was so busy: caring for my children, washing, cooking, cleaning, helping Charles in the shop, doing the accounts. Our hard work paid off and a few years later, we were able to buy a house a few streets down from the shop in Kings Close.

Charles and Renee in their shop

A MOTHER'S PROMISE

Charles behind the counter of the deli

Renee dealing with the accounts

NEW BEGINNINGS

With her own house at last, Renee became a *balabusta*, just like her mother. In its own way, cooking became Renee's therapy, calming the turmoil in her soul, as if she could funnel the memory of Mama and Bubbe into flaky pastry and warm bread.

I learnt to cook on instinct. I just knew how I wanted food to taste like from my childhood. Cooking gave me a connection to my Polish roots. The first time I baked my bubbe's yeast cake, it turned out perfect, delicious, just as I remembered it.

That cake was more than just yeast, butter and eggs. It was a time machine to the past, back to those happy summers in Kalisz with her bubbe. But this was Hendon, not Zduńska Wola, and so she also cooked rice pudding, liver and onions, roast chicken and roast potatoes, sardines and tomatoes on toast.

I used to cook and bake from scratch. Freshly baked bridge rolls, cheesecakes, walnut cake and sweet cheese buns. Whenever we had family and friends around, I put on a big spread. It made me happy to see it all laid out on the table. I took pride in being a wonderful hostess. My chopped herring became famous. Nobody could make chopped herring like mine!

Renee and Charles worked hard behind the Formica counter of the deli. Six days a week, they served freshly cut wafer-thin slices of smoked salmon, cream cheese and beigels to their loyal customers, dispensing smiles and cooking tips. In the sticky British summers, they dished out Snowcrest pyramid kosher ice cream sorbets in lemon, orange and pineapple.

People came from miles around to buy Renee's famous chopped herring, served up in little tubs. In the build-up to Passover, they delivered dozens of food orders around the area.

Renee and Charles became embedded in their community, as much a part of Hendon as yeast is to bread. It was a traditional, honest life, made up of hard work and the occasional trip to the coast for some sea air.

Renee and Charles on holiday

Renee came to think of Charles as 'the guv'nor'. A loyal and gentle man, he was old-fashioned, perhaps, to the next generation, but typically self-effacing, like so many of his wartime contemporaries. He had taken a bullet in the knee on the beaches of Normandy on D-Day, lost a father in the Blitz, volunteered to go into a concentration camp, but he would never talk about it. Even when Sharon expressed admiration at his boxful of war medals, he shrugged and told her that every returning soldier got them. Why were his experiences any more important than anyone else's?

Charles, like Renee, discovered that 'keeping busy' was a good camouflage for pain and grief. He had also learnt the hard way, during the Depression of the 1930s, that work was a blessing, as was reading widely, dancing and his keen interest in politics.

After the children, I still got the nightmares, but the visions and attacks began to fade. I learnt to live with it. Or the few times I did bring up the past, or talked about Bergen-Belsen, it wouldn't be long before Charles had tears in his eyes. He just couldn't talk about it without crying. 'I can't talk about it,' he told me, and I respected that. He never wanted the children to see him upset and always took care to protect them.

He was my best friend as well as my husband. We rarely quarrelled. It was a marriage built on love, trust and mutual understanding. I'd been to hell, and he'd experienced a part of it.

Renee and Charles made an unofficial pact: to never speak of the past. And so began a fifty-year silence. Renee remained silent, year after year, walking a tightrope of trauma. Just one wrong step, and she felt she could have toppled into the past.

Keeping busy, busy, busy all the time. We used to take the children out on different outings, occasionally on a holiday. Because of the business, sometimes Charles took the children, and sometimes I took them, to visit Gitel in Paris.

As Sharon and Martin grew up, I became very protective of them. I remember one day, when Sharon was sixteen, she was late home from school and I was hysterical. Half the neighbourhood were out looking for her. Eventually she walked in. Turned out she'd been having extra English tuition at school.

Logically, I knew she was fine, but after all that I had experienced and witnessed, I was unable to control my fears. The worst had happened to me, over and over, so how could I not fear it? If I lost sight of her for even a few minutes, I was hysterical.

I also couldn't bear to see them leave good food uneaten on the plate. The memories of the starvation years were still so clear in my mind, when a piece of bread meant the difference between life and death. How could I stop myself obsessing about food when I'd had none for so many years? It's impossible.

When I saw them not finishing their food, it reminded me of how I used to hide food under the table. That reminded me of my regrets. At times, mealtimes were a battle.

All Charles and I wanted was for the children not to go short of anything and have a happy, safe childhood. We worked so hard to give them everything that could make a child happy. Warmth, food, toys and, most of all, love.

Chapter Nineteen

~

Revisiting the Past

SHARON

The summer of 1962 was thrilling. I was ten years old and my brother Martin was six. For the first time, my parents were able to afford a family holiday for the four of us. Luxury! Bliss! And what a holiday – Butlin's Bognor Regis, where everything was provided, from meals to sport and entertainment. I'd just devoured Billy Bunter at Butlin's *and this was a dream come true.*

We climbed the stairs to the bedroom we'd been assigned on the first floor of a huge concrete block and entered the little bedroom. To my amazed delight, the walls were lined with bunk beds. What could be more adventurous than sleeping in the top bunk bed? (Naturally, I would take the top bed, and Martin could have the lower bed.)

As we stood in the doorway, my mother spoke out, clearly, plaintively: 'This place is like Auschwitz.'

I didn't understand. I understood later . . .

I knew from a very early age that my mother and her family had been taken away and deported. One of the things I do remember that might explain why I knew more than she thought was that when I was born, at that point, my mother couldn't speak very good English and my father couldn't speak Polish at all, but they both spoke Yiddish. That was the language in the house for quite a long time. They spoke Yiddish quite frankly and openly in front of me, on the assumption that I wouldn't understand it. Actually, I understood every word perfectly. When you are small, you are primed to pick up the first language you are exposed to.

When I found out there were other Jewish children whose parents or mothers had not been through that experience, I remember being very puzzled and wondering whether they were really Jewish at all.

Looking back, I know that there are some things about the way that we were brought up that are a direct reflection of Mum's experience. One thing I remember in particular was that if you left a scrap of food, she'd get hysterical. Understandable, because she'd experienced starvation.

My earliest memories of my father were when he was helping me learn to walk and I could feel these hands holding me up by both elbows, standing behind me as I took little faltering steps. Then he'd take the hands away and I'd sink gently to the ground. Father was there to support me. He was always there to protect me and not to moralise or lecture.

One of my favourite stories of his was when he was at Bergen-Belsen. He went into the administrative buildings and picked up some stationery. Crossing out the SS headings, he wrote: 'Under new management.'

My parents worked hard as we were growing up. Their relationship was a traditional one, based on the idea of providing security for the family and for each other. Growing up in the 1950s, we were never showered in kisses and hugs.

Bubbe was a great matriarchal figure. She who must be obeyed. She used to sing us old Yiddish melodies and songs from the First World War. She had come to England in the early years of the twentieth century, fleeing pogroms.

Gitel was a very vibrant, strong-willed woman. Mum took me to stay with her and Lejzer in Paris. I remember when I was very little, looking at her and thinking:

'That's funny, such an old person and her hair is completely black.' It never occurred to me it must have come from a bottle.

When I went to stay with them when I was fourteen and I tried to talk Yiddish with them, Gitel turned to Lejzer and said, 'Zi redt Hitlerdaytsch' – she talks Hitler German. That has to be the most back-handed compliment I've ever received!

Sharon and Martin on holiday

MARTIN

Mum and Dad never talked about the Holocaust, so I grew up not knowing what they'd been through during the war. When I went to school, there were no Holocaust studies either.

But growing up I could tell something wasn't quite right. At mealtimes, I was told never to leave anything on my plate and to eat everything up, even if I was full. Mum would make huge spreads of food, far too much, and she would make everything from scratch. She'd probably win Great British Bake Off today!

Cakes were her favourite: walnut cakes, bridge rolls, pastries with icing on the top.

In the week, she and Dad would be busy in the shop, but on Sunday afternoons, if they had people round, she'd be in the kitchen all day.

They worked so hard in the shop. It was always open, even on Christmas Day. The only time they'd shut was Wednesday afternoons and Saturday for the Sabbath, but then back open again on Sunday.

At seventeen, I started helping out, running deliveries and, on Sundays, working in the shop. They'd sell smoked salmon, which my dad would slice really thin, fresh beigels and great wagons of Gouda cheese. None of this pre-packaged stuff you get today. They also sold tins of fruit and beans, which would be stacked up high on shelves. Dad had a long gripper so he could take tins off the top shelf.

They had a huge till on the counter, which made a great thunk when it shut. It'd look old-fashioned today.

Mum and Dad would deliver food for Pesach, but no one wanted to take it too soon before, so it would all be stored in our lounge and by the staircase, and we weren't allowed the heating on then as the food would have gone off.

They really worked hard. They were a part of the landscape of the community.

Mum was in hospital a lot when I was growing up. She had an ulcer and a hernia. I never really knew what it was she was in for.

Gitel and Lejzer came over from Paris to stay with us a lot. They were very stern people. If you didn't do what they said, you'd be in trouble, but they loved us all, especially Mum.

When Mum was in hospital, we'd stay with Auntie Pat, Dad's sister. I loved that. She had a little tortoise which used to hibernate under the stairs in a warm box full of straw and she'd give me bottles of lemonade. My grandma, or bubbe, used to give me half a crown when we went round.

Mum and Dad worked hard so that we didn't go short. Like most parents, they wanted better for their children – which included piano lessons every Sunday. They wanted us to have the things they could never have.

Finding out about Mum's past was a big discovery.

Life in the shop had its own rhythm, but as Charles and Renee got older, the long hours got harder. Charles's knee, where he took the bullet on D-Day, throbbed after a day on his feet. Renee's neck, never right from lugging sacks of cement in Germany, bothered her all the time, especially when she was hunched over the books. Great pleasure, however, came from their children's achievements.

When Sharon got a first-class degree in English from Oxford University, the whole neighbourhood came into the shop to congratulate us. I always knew she was clever, that one. We were so proud! Sharon used her brilliant mind and became a tutor, teaching English, just as the midwife predicted when she was born. Sharon married a fellow Oxford student called Simon, who qualified as a chartered accountant three years after they married. They had three lovely girls, Rebecca, Daniela and Shoshana.

Martin did us proud too, getting a good job as a fixed assets manager and travelling to work in the West Indies. He married Hilary and had two wonderful boys, Adrian and Benjy.

Being a grandmother, or a bubbe, myself was the best revenge on Hitler. He didn't expect me to marry and have children and grandchildren!

Charles and Renee in later life

In 1983, the same year their first granddaughter, Rebecca, was born, Charles and Renee sold the delicatessen and took a well-earned retirement. When they weren't going on cruises and dressing up for dinner and dancing, a pastime they both loved, there was a lot of spare time. Time to think. In the back of Renee's mind lurked memories of Germany and of a dry, unloved, unmarked grave. It was time to go back to Belsen.

Fifty years after I was liberated from Bergen-Belsen, we returned. We went back on a cold November day in 1995 to have a stone-setting ceremony for my mother.

We were booked to go via the Channel Tunnel, but a fire broke out in the tunnel. After a last-minute panic and a few urgent phone calls, we managed to book on a ferry from Dover to Calais. The group was made up of me, Charles, Martin, Sharon and my son-in-law Simon, who insisted there would be no problem driving from Hendon to Hanover in one day, provided we only got out of the car for thirty minutes in thirteen hours.

So, 7am on the morning of Wednesday, 20 November 1995 saw us on the road to Dover, prepared for the campaign with three flasks of coffee and enough sandwiches to feed an army for a week. When we got to Dover, we couldn't believe it when they said the ferry was full and we would have to wait for the next one. With many hundreds of miles to travel on a dark November day, it was obvious someone would have to start an argument if we were going to catch our ferry. Luckily, Simon is good at that sort of thing. He exchanged a few words with someone and then we were boarding the ferry.

Soon, we were speeding through Belgium, into Holland, and then into the industrial heartland of Germany. Smoking factories against a background of dark skies sinking into total blackness made the journey feel emotional. As we got closer, all I could see out of the window were thick, deep woods.

In our hotel, it felt strange and uncomfortable, spending the night somewhere so clean and modern, yet so close to the site of that evil concentration camp.

The next morning was dull and cloudy with a bitter, driving wind. In the pretty town of Bergen, there was time for a quick stroll before the stone-setting ceremony. Children were walking neatly dressed and tidy on their way to school. Shoppers were out buying thick loaves of dark rye bread. I wondered how they could live in a place with such terrible associations.

Then we made our way to the British Army base, near to the Belsen camp. We were shown to the cemetery, which contained the remains of thousands of people who died in the weeks and months after liberation. I'd been anxious to try and locate as exactly as possible the spot where Mama was buried. The memorial staff told me it was most likely that she'd been buried in one of the first three rows to the right of the entrance.

Her death had haunted me all my life. It was time to properly honour her life.

Renee had left the Bergen-Belsen displaced persons camp in 1945, a traumatised orphan with no plan other than to search for her missing family. She returned fifty years later, a 66-year-old woman with her own family.

The camp was a very different place. The time of our liberation had been hot, the sky blue, with hardly a breath of wind. When we returned, it was cold and foggy. The cemetery was immaculately maintained, a beautiful and peaceful spot. I got comfort from knowing that Mama and the other victims lay in such peaceful surroundings. The headstone we'd chosen was flat, in light-grey marble, with the names of Mama, Tatuś and Stenia inscribed in Hebrew and Berkowicz in English capitals at the top.

Simon had arranged for seven Russian men to come from Hanover to join him, Charles and Martin in prayer. In the Jewish religion, a prayer service requires the participation of a minyan – ten men aged thirteen or over.

We assembled around the simple grey marble stone and, fifty years on, Kaddish *was said for my mother, father and sister, to the accompaniment of the wind in the trees and the distant muffled sound of gunfire. It was a reminder that we were in the midst of a NATO training exercise. But here, with so many reminders of the past, it was easy to forget that, and to imagine that the distant sounds marked the advance of the British Army in 1945.*

I tried to remember Mama not as she was when she died, but as she was before the war, walking through the streets of Zduńska Wola on my father's arm, elegantly dressed in a powder-blue wool suit. Elegant, beautiful and dignified. I remembered how protective she was of me, how warm and loving.

After the simple, quiet ceremony, we thanked our new friends who made up the minyan and they left. It was then that the first few drops of rain began to fall, as if it had been waiting for us to finish. We placed three Yahrzeit candles beside the stone and lit them.

It was a moving service, a closure of a sort and a chance to look back and reflect.

A mother's job is to keep her children safe and loved as they grow up. My mama managed to keep me safe in the face of unimaginable horror. Even on her deathbed, she was thinking of me, finding the strength to say, 'Do not cry when I die.' What must it have taken to say those words? To be thinking of my happiness in her final moments! Those words are always in my heart.

Mama didn't want me to suffer and cry. She wanted me to go on and live a long and happy life. I have always been grateful to her, not only for her love, but for giving me the gift of God's love.

Tucked behind the image of her mother, though, lay another. Her father's back, disappearing into the smoky dawn at Auschwitz-Birkenau. After fifty-one years, the question still haunted her, battering relentlessly in her mind. What had happened after he vanished? Where was his body now? Renee reconciled herself to the fact that some questions can never be answered, but the grieving and the yearning would never end.

Afterwards, we were welcomed by Colonel Wilkins, whose kindness had made the ceremony possible, and then returned to the Bergen-Belsen camp itself. The site of the former camp is 2 kilometres further down the road. Nothing from the road gave any clue as to the terrible secrets hidden behind the thick forest of trees, apart from the creepy-looking path into the woods, which was once the main entrance to the camp.

A new and modern entrance to the camp now greets visitors. A large car park led to a low, modern museum and information centre. It looked just like any English Heritage tourist centre. Only when you enter do you realise that it's no ordinary tourist spot.

We met with a curator and walked around the camp. It was a strange and eerie experience. In the bitter cold and biting wind, we were the only visitors, the only sound the muffled explosion of shells in the distance, which gave me a weird feeling that fighting was still going on.

We walked around in silence, Charles and I both lost in our private memories. It seemed impossible that anyone who hadn't been there at the time could ever believe, let alone imagine, what it had been like. In my mind, I could still vividly picture those huts, the walking skeletons, the piles of corpses . . .

As we left, we saw two German coaches full of teenage schoolchildren drive into the car park and I wondered what they would be told and what they would think of it.

Back home in Hendon, we looked over photographs. The most important thing I brought back was the memory of something very necessary finally achieved. It was a deeply moving experience for all of us. For me, it meant completing some unfinished emotional work, helping me to cope with the past and carry it with me into the future.

Renee could never have imagined what that future would hold. Or what she was truly capable of.

Chapter Twenty

∼

Testimony

Two years after Renee's return from Germany came a surprise invitation.

In 1997, when I was sixty-eight, a friend of mine, whom I'd met when she came into the shop, suggested I come with her to a support group she attended. It was called the Holocaust Survivors' Centre (HSC) and it had been set up by an organisation called Jewish Care.

There were a lot of survivors in Hendon and the surrounding area. I could tell other survivors when they came into the shop. They heard my Polish accent and asked where I came from. We'd get chatting and you soon knew. It was interesting to me to chat to other survivors over the counter, but I'd never heard of an actual centre for survivors.

I was interested and I went along to the Holocaust Survivors' Centre, not far from where we lived in Hendon. The centre had been set up by a specialist called Judith Hassan, whose mother was a refugee from Nazi Germany.

'What do you have to lose?' I told myself. Charles dropped me off at the centre, but preferred not to come in. I was a bit nervous to begin with, but I didn't need to be. Everyone was so very friendly.

Judith, then Director of Services for Holocaust Survivors and Refugees for Jewish Care, explained how since the beginning of the 1980s, a mutual support group, the Survivor of Shoah (SOS), had been meeting regularly in premises she had found for them, funded by World Jewish Relief. She facilitated the group and what she learned from them helped to give her the blueprint for the Holocaust Survivors' Centre. Survivors needed a place where they could belong and call 'home'.

There were many survivors in the centre, over 200 at least. The room was busy and noisy, everyone chatting and drinking coffee. I saw men and women with numbers tattooed on their arms and I spotted the subtle signs of trauma, the look of pain in people's eyes. These were people like me, who carried deep wounds.

I looked around the room and I felt a sense of belonging. There were others like me.

I was asked to introduce myself. I stood up and cleared my throat.

'My name is Renee Salt. I was born in Poland . . .' I began.

By the time I finished my story, I could see people nodding their heads as I explained about my losses and how isolated I'd felt after the war.

After I'd introduced myself, so many people came up to talk to me. There were a lot of Polish and Hungarian survivors. Everyone had a different story to tell and though it wasn't like a formal sharing, I got to hear so many people's experiences. People were talking quite openly.

There were many camp and ghetto survivors like Renee. Memories of tragedy, despair and suffering were not the exception; they were the rule.

TESTIMONY

'Renee, I was at Auschwitz working on the railway tracks when your transport came in from the Łódź ghetto,' one lady told me. 'I couldn't believe how bad the people looked from that ghetto.'

I nodded. 'We'd been starving for four years by that point.'

Another survivor shared my feelings about people in England not wanting to know about the Holocaust.

'It was the same for me,' she explained. 'When I arrived at Dover after the war, my uncle collected me. He turned to me and said, "Don't tell the family about the camps. I don't want them upset."'

I tutted and shook my head, the old feeling of isolation surging back.

The room was packed with survivors. It felt so good to talk freely and openly. It felt good to be understood.

Looking at the many male survivors, something clicked in my mind. 'Did you ever meet my father, Szaja Berkowicz, at Auschwitz-Birkenau?' I asked them. I must have asked that question so many times over the years, and I realised then that it was still as important. Despite many of the men having been in Auschwitz, none of them had come across my father.

'Will you come back next week, Renee?' Judith asked.

I knew I would. And so began the next stage of my life. Sharing my testimony.

Renee had found her second home. The centre was more than just a place to go and get a hot kosher meal and share experiences. Under the caring umbrella of Jewish Care's Holocaust Survivors' Centre, Renee found a way to continue the long, slow journey to emotional healing.

Faith is the touchstone of Renee's life. Kindled in the darkness of her persecution, it is a beacon of hope that has burnt bright and nourished her ever since, but that is not a universal experience. Some Jews completely lost their faith during the Holocaust. There are others too for whom faith had little, if any, meaning or relevance. As Renee was learning at the centre, no two survivors responded to their traumatic experiences in the same way.

Eventually, I became a secretary for the centre and I got even more involved. I took the minutes of the meetings, helped to organise social outings and welcome new members. Often, I would cook mushroom and barley soup and bake apple pie. On a Wednesday, everyone waited eagerly for my soup.

Judith was always very clear that it was their centre; a place where their voices could be heard. During the Holocaust, they had every last shred of power stripped and stolen from them. By having an advisory committee consisting of nine elected survivors to ensure the needs of the centre were heard, the survivors regained some of that power.

We always came back to talking about the same thing – our experiences in the Holocaust. There was therapy on offer with professionals. I didn't take it up. I felt it was too late. Maybe, looking back, I should have had some treatment, but just going to the centre was a form of therapy. It really helped me to feel more stable and settled.

The more I went, the more I realised what a wonderful place it was. Each person who worked there was fantastic. I started to go more and more as it's open all week.

With the children all grown up and getting on with their own lives, I became even more immersed in the Holocaust Survivors' Centre. Occasionally, Charles would come and listen, but it was more my thing.

Then we were asked by Jewish Care if any survivors would go and speak in schools about the Holocaust.

I hesitated. Talking with other survivors was one thing, but talking to other people about it, and schoolchildren at that, was something else. Nervously, I agreed.

But as the day dawned, I was eaten up with nerves, I can tell you. It was hard, very hard, but I reminded myself that God had spared me for a reason. I believe that reason was to tell others what I had experienced. It wasn't enough to just speak with other survivors. I had to go out into the world and tell my story.

On the day, I wore a smart royal-blue wool suit. I made sure my hair was done and I looked nice. Sharon helped me to write a speech which I had rehearsed dozens of times at home, but I was still trembling as I was introduced and I looked at all the faces. I prayed that I wouldn't break down in front of the children. But once I opened my mouth, the story just flowed out of me. My nerves melted. The children were so interested in what I had to say and had so many questions for me.

Afterwards, and in fact for days, I thought I was coming down with the flu. I felt so exhausted, but it still felt good to have got the story out of me.

After that, things really took off. I joined forces with the Holocaust Educational Trust, a British charity whose aim is to educate people about the Holocaust, and they helped me to present more talks. In time, I visited the Foreign Office, the Treasury, the Home Office and the Cabinet office. I even spoke with a group of footballers from Liverpool Football Academy. I met a lot of Cabinet ministers too. A highlight was when Charles and I met with Dame Vera Lynn. Charles, like a lot of the men who were in the forces, loved her so it was a treat to meet her.

I was also invited up to the National Holocaust Centre and Museum in Nottinghamshire. The centre, also affectionately known as Beth Shalom (the House of Peace), was founded by a Christian family called the Smiths.

That place became like another home to me, I visited that many times. James and Stephen Smith, together with their late mother, Marina, are a really wonderful, loving and kind family.

The Smiths set up the charity after a visit to Yad Vashem, Israel's national Holocaust museum. Upon their return they found that there were no plans for a memorial site in the UK, so they took matters into their own hands and set up a place of education, with exhibitions and a permanent memorial to victims of the Holocaust. They were so dedicated to this that eventually, they gave over their own family home to the centre, an old farmhouse near Sherwood Forest. Today, the Smith family are still involved but no longer run the NHCM. James Smith is Life President of the charity.

They invited me up to the centre to give a talk. Afterwards, Mrs Smith, the head of the family, came up to me and hugged me. 'Your story is so emotional,' she told me.

That really meant something to me. There were so many good and kind people in the world. Mrs Smith personified this. I felt very close to her and her family. Sadly, Marina passed away in 2022, aged eighty-seven. I will forever be thankful to them. They aren't Jewish, yet they care so much. That made that support valuable. That mattered.

In 1999, the centre invited us to come and see the unveiling of a white rose bush within the memorial garden, planted in honour of my family, which we sponsored.

Charles and I travelled up north once more. It was so emotional to see the plaque next to the bush, which read: 'In loving memory of my beloved family who perished in Poland/Germany. This rose is dedicated by Renee & Charles Salt.'

The memorial garden gives us survivors a place to commemorate our loved ones. Today, there are over 1,000 beautifully scented white roses which flower every spring.

TESTIMONY

In June 2015, a gentleman called Victor Huglin from Merseyside also paid to have a rose bush planted in my name after coming to listen to me speak. I felt so very honoured.

I returned again and again to speak to the many parties of schoolchildren who visit the centre. I began to realise that it's often a unique experience when a survivor speaks to a young person. You feel you're doing some good by speaking to the younger generation. Once, a schoolgirl came up to me afterwards with tears in her eyes. She took off her bracelet and gave it to me.

'I want you to have it,' she told me. 'I was so touched by your talk.'

'Thank you, darling, I'll cherish this bracelet,' I told her. Believe me, I was just as touched as she was.

Afterwards, Renee often received letters from the pupils she spoke to about her experiences. 'I felt like I was there in the camp with you,' wrote one. And from their teachers: 'My form were thrilled to meet someone who had survived such a catalogue of trauma . . . May you long find strength to continue your brave resolve.'

The centre facilitated those amazing encounters between survivors and the next generation, helping to bridge a gap. But their thoughts were turning to how to educate them when the survivors are gone. What do we do when there are no survivors left?

The centre came up with something called The Forever Project. They turned me into an interactive experience! Over a week, I was filmed answering over 1,200 questions about my experiences of the Holocaust, and now you can go and see me there, and have an in-depth question and answer session with me and other survivors, without us even being there. Ask a question and my life-sized digital projection will answer you from my pre-filmed replies. They even launched it in Parliament. I saw myself beamed all over the walls of the historic Churchill Room. I came face to face with myself!

The National Holocaust Centre and Museum understand how important it is for future generations to learn from survivors like me when we are no longer around to tell our stories.

'Survivors aren't just a history lesson, but a life lesson,' Dr Stephen Smith MBE said. I only hope that the many schoolchildren who visit the centre will learn the importance of decency, respect and understanding.

Charles had also begun to speak, and he provided his testimony and memories of being part of the liberating forces at Bergen-Belsen, agreeing to be interviewed by the National Holocaust Centre and Museum, the USC Shoah Foundation, the Imperial War Museum in London and the Bergen-Belsen Memorial in Germany. I shared my testimony with all these places too. I felt very proud of him.

Renee believed that it was her duty to share her testimony and approached this new phase of her life with great zeal and professionalism. But she quickly realised that a talk always came at a price. Whether she was chatting informally with a small group, or delivering a talk on a stage in front of hundreds, it stirred the murky pot of memories. Talking disturbed the sediment, allowing those memories to float freely around her mind. For days after, she would be physically and mentally wiped out. But the struggle was a small price to pay.

'Thank you for coming to listen to my story,' I told the audience. 'I will tell you my experiences during the Holocaust . . . I was ten when war broke out.'

People's reactions were so interesting. Sometimes, you could hear a pin drop. Other times, people would break down and cry. I wanted people to know what it really felt like. Not just Auschwitz, but the ghettos, the hangings, the selections . . . The whole range of

TESTIMONY

experience. Please God no one should ever experience it themselves, but I wanted people to try and understand my pain. To feel my pain.

I tried to speak clearly and just focus on telling them what it was like.

Two or three times, I met students who didn't believe what I was telling them. They actually challenged me and told me I was wrong! In such situations, we're always advised to try and stay calm and just tell them in our own words why it was true, but you couldn't change their minds. It made me feel terrible.

On the whole, though, people were very understanding. People would come up to me afterwards and thank me or ask me more questions.

Each time I talked, I felt my confidence grow. I'll say it myself, I became a very good speaker. One time, I was asked to speak to a firm of solicitors in the City of London.

'That was absolutely incredible,' said the Chief Executive of the Holocaust Educational Trust afterwards. I felt so satisfied and appreciated.

And do you know what? I realised that, gradually, my nightmares were getting less frequent. To sleep a whole night through was such a relief.

My testimony meant something. I was even introduced to the Queen and Prince Philip on the fiftieth anniversaries of the liberation at St James's Palace. The Queen was tiny. She was a lovely lady and so interested in the stories of survivors.

The Holocaust Survivors' Centre went from strength to strength, too. Over time, it grew from a small grassroots group to something much larger, helping to support more victims of the Holocaust, including hidden children, refugees and children who had fled Nazi persecution on the Kindertransport, and spouses of survivors.

As the survivors gradually became more open, going out and

delivering talks about their experiences, so too did the centre, opening its doors to volunteers and speakers. Many times, they welcomed the inspiring and charismatic Reverend Leslie Hardman, who had worked so hard to support survivors in Bergen-Belsen after the liberation. After the war, Reverend Hardman worked as Minister of the Hendon Congregation and continued listening and helping anyone who needed it. In 1997 he was awarded the honour of Extraordinary Hero of the Shoah. He even conducted the wedding of Renee's daughter Sharon to Simon!

Since 1995, the Holocaust Survivors' Centre has also offered its members access to Shalvata (Hebrew for peace of mind) service, a specialist team of social workers and therapists available five days a week to assist survivors and refugees with practical and emotional issues connected with past trauma from the Holocaust as well as current difficulties. A social centre right next door to a therapeutic centre was a unique model, allowing survivors easy access to therapy.

Also at the centre now are therapists and social workers you can talk to whenever you feel you need to.
I could never have dreamt of such a thing when I first arrived in Hackney in 1949.
They call you up at home if they haven't seen you in a while. I feel so loved and cared for by them. They are all like my family.

Renee had come a long way from the silent, traumatised young woman who had washed up in Dover, emotionally and physically scarred. She had become a powerful and eloquent speaker. Thanks to the Holocaust Survivors' Centre, the National Holocaust Centre and Museum and the Holocaust Educational Trust, Renee had blossomed into a Holocaust educator herself, providing a crucial eyewitness account.

TESTIMONY

Charles still didn't like to talk too much himself, but he was proud of me, I know he was. I was proud of myself. I met so many wonderful, supportive people along the way. I realised I was surrounded by love.

Along with all the other indomitable survivors at the Holocaust Survivors' Centre, Renee became an unstoppable force of nature. In the ghettos and camps, she had learnt to keep a low profile, to remain inconspicuous and silent in order to survive. In the immediate aftermath of the war, on her arrival in London, the need to stay silent was reinforced by society's stultifying attitude. No longer. As the new century dawned, Renee had found her voice, and the world was finally listening to survivors and waking up to the value of their testimony.

Renee had wrestled a lot of demons since she first joined the Holocaust Survivors' Centre. She had embraced a new spirit of openness. Shared her testimony hundreds of times over with everyone from schoolchildren to politicians, met Queen Elizabeth and planted fragrant white roses in her family's name. She'd even allowed herself to be turned into an interactive experience. There was one final place she didn't want to confront, but knew she must. She had to return to Auschwitz-Birkenau.

Chapter Twenty-One

Laying the Ghosts to Rest

I had to return to Poland, if only to lay the ghosts to rest. The opportunity came in 2004 when the BBC got in touch with me via the Holocaust Survivors' Centre. They were making a documentary called Grandchild of the Holocaust *and were looking for a survivor and their grandchild to film. Who should they pick but me and my grandson Adrian!*

Adrian was thirteen at the time and knew very little about the Holocaust.

'Why did you never talk about the Holocaust, Grandma?' he asked me as the cameras started to roll.

'It was too painful,' I told him. 'And some things I thought you were too young to know, but I think you're ready to hear.'

'I've always known my grandma survived the Holocaust,' Adrian said in a video diary he was asked to keep. 'I've tried to ask her about it, but she won't answer my questions. I know she was in Poland somewhere.'

The filming was a very intense process. The BBC arranged for myself, my son Martin and Adrian to return to Poland. But first they took Adrian to the Imperial War Museum to visit their Holocaust exhibition to try and get an understanding of what I'd suffered.

'I never thought it would be anything like this,' he said, visibly shocked and upset after hearing survivor testimony and viewing footage and photos of the camps and ghettos.

'To kill them in the way that they did. They used to humiliate them, destroy their businesses, make them pay for it. It is hard to believe that one nation or race of people can do that to another kind. I can't believe Grandma actually saw that happening. You could die just from seeing that happening.'

Adrian came back with so many questions. 'Did you experience Auschwitz?' he asked, and I had to admit yes.

He turned to Charles. 'Did you meet Grandma in Poland?' He was surprised when he learnt that we'd met after the war, and that Charles had been part of the liberating army.

'It's amazing to think that Grandma was a survivor and Grandpa had been one of the liberators of the Bergen-Belsen concentration camp,' he said.

Then it was time to go to Poland. I was so nervous returning to Zduńska Wola. If I hadn't been with a BBC film crew, I don't think I could have gone. I'd have been too frightened.

My heart was in my mouth as we wandered the streets of my old home town. I couldn't recognise a thing. Eventually, we found my street. We got chatting to an old lady.

'Of course, I remember how they murdered the Jews and that they were murdered in the cemetery,' she told me. 'From where I lived, you could hear all the screaming. I heard it all,' she said. Later, she told me that they couldn't do anything as the Germans had threatened to kill all their families if they did anything to help the Jews.

It stunned me to find someone who remembered those days,

who'd been on the other side of that cemetery wall. It felt unbelievable, so strange.

Then we walked to the spot where Stenia was taken in the selection. I stood once more in the space where I saw my lovely little sister torn away from me.

'The mothers were screaming and crying, "Almighty God, help us,"' I told Adrian. 'That upset me more than anything. That happened here.'

I stood in silence with my grandson and son, remembering that terrible day as people walked about us, doing their shopping, going about their business. It didn't feel real.

From there, we walked to the overgrown Jewish cemetery. 'Only three children from the whole town survived the massacre,' I told my grandson. 'I was one of them.' Here, I couldn't stop my tears.

'It was really difficult to see Grandma so upset,' Adrian told the cameras. 'I've never seen her cry before. The marketplace and cemetery brought back so many bad memories for her.'

Our next stop was Łódź and the courtyard of our old home where my bubbe was taken.

'I had no idea that Grandma had lived through so many selections,' Adrian told the camera. 'She told me she saw people die every day from starvation and disease. I was beginning to realise how lucky she was to have survived.'

From there, we made the long journey south and I came to the place I was dreading most of all. Auschwitz-Birkenau.

It took Renee sixty years to return to hell. She had left the camp a terrified fifteen-year-old, bundled into a freight wagon. She returned six decades later, a 75-year-old Holocaust educator with her grandson on one side and her son on the other. The trio walked hand in hand along the rail tracks that led into the centre of Birkenau.

Adrian asked me if I remembered getting off the wagon. 'As if it were yesterday,' I told him. 'I remember everything.'

I told my son and grandson the story of our fear and bewilderment and of the selection when I faced Dr Mengele.

'This is the place where I last saw my father,' I told them, pointing to the side of the tracks where we were forced apart. Sixty years melted away as I stared about the vast camp, at the barbed wire and the high watchtowers. To be back in Auschwitz was absolutely terrifying. All the memories came flooding back and I was so terribly nervous.

I was broken-hearted to see that place again. There were no words I could say that could express my feelings. Instead, we all stood in silence. Then we lit a candle and placed it on the tracks.

Auschwitz-Birkenau as captured by Martin, Renee's son, during their visit in 2004

To return to the largest crime scene in human history, the site of Renee's incarceration and the last place she saw her father alive, took unimaginable courage. Words are rendered useless. The swampy ground at Birkenau tells its own story.

'Now I've seen Auschwitz, I realise why my grandma found it so difficult to talk about,' Adrian said in his video diary. 'I started this trip with so many questions and gradually, she's telling me her story and I'm beginning to understand what really happened to her.'

'Do you think it's made you a bit more overprotective?' Adrian asked me when we reached Hamburg.

'Yes, it made me very protective towards my children and my grandchildren. I hope one day to see you all settled and have good jobs. I like to see only good things for my grandchildren. I'm pleased I've been able to bring you here. You'll remember this for the rest of your life. I love you so much.'

In Bergen-Belsen, we were joined by Charles, who told Adrian what he'd seen on entering the death camp.

'They sent us here to die,' I explained. 'The dead were lying on top of the living, the living on top of the dead. There was sheer chaos here. It's impossible to describe. We gave up all hope of surviving.'

I told Adrian my mother's last words. Do not cry when I die. I couldn't last much longer. I thought I was going to die too.

He held my hand. 'Did you think you would survive?' he asked.

'No. I was all on my own after my mother died. I was fifteen years old and I had no one.'

Telling my grandson this story was so incredibly hard, but he had a right to know the truth. He hugged me with tears in his eyes and we all left the camp arm in arm.

Back home in England, we went to a Holocaust survivors memorial service.

'The Holocaust is not history,' said a speaker. 'It is a part of us. The purpose of coming together is not just to remember the past; it's to pass over a message to future generations. That they will keep alive everything that we stood for and we stand for. As we begin another year, my message is, let the children and the grandchildren take over where we are leaving off.'

'Before I went on the trip, Grandma never told me much about the Holocaust because she wanted to hide it from me,' Adrian said in his video diary at the end of the documentary. 'After the trip I realised, she didn't want to hide it from me. What she was actually saying was that all those questions that I wanted to ask her couldn't have been answered in a conversation. I actually had to go there to get them answered.'

After that, we went back to normal, until the TV documentary aired in January 2005. You can't believe the letters we got. Sack loads. Adrian even appeared on Blue Peter *and* Richard and Judy. *I'm so proud of him and all my grandchildren.*

Layer by layer, Renee's past was unfolding as she shared her story with the people who really mattered to her. Not just the backbone, but the softer, in-between details, of the childhood games she played outside her home, the smell of her bubbe's baking and the sound of lively Yiddish conversations drifting through the busy streets of Zduńska Wola. It was important to

Renee for people to know about the cultural richness of Jewish life in Poland, not just its death. For Renee, the need to share had finally overcome the desire to forget.

Chapter Twenty-Two

∼

Now

Six years after the documentary aired, I lost my beloved Charles on 22 December 2011. He was ninety-four. We arranged for him to be laid to rest in Israel in a plot at the Eretz HaChaim cemetery on the outskirts of Beit Shemesh. I have a plot there too. We arranged for a minyan from the local yeshivah, a place where Jews gather to study the Torah. It was a lot to organise, burying him in Israel, but it was what Charles deserved. As we buried him, the sun came out over the Judean Hills and shone brightly.

I'll never find the words to thank Charles. He saw something in me, a broken young woman, and his love brought me back to life. It must have been so frightening and heartbreaking for him to see me having my breakdown, but he never let me down.

We were married for sixty-two years. I still miss him. My favourite memory of him is when we used to go dancing on the cruise ships we both loved going on after we retired. Charles loved to dance the tango and quickstep. Even when he was sitting down in a chair, his feet were always tapping up and down. Whenever I hear dance music, I think of him.

You don't get men like Charles coming around too often. He volunteered to go into Bergen-Belsen when he didn't have to. He worked hard all his life. He was the most wonderful, loving, kind and patient man.

He helped me to see that life was worth living. I knew I couldn't crumble after his death. What can you do? I had no other options; I had to carry on without him. It's what he would have wanted me to do.

The year after Charles died, Renee sold the house and moved into sheltered housing in Hendon where she discovered a wonderful new neighbour to help with her grief. Actually, lots of wonderful new neighbours. The Holocaust Survivors' Centre was right downstairs!

I was told there was an empty flat above the centre and was lucky enough to move in.

I started to go to the group more often. Every time I went downstairs in the lift and walked past the door to the centre, I'd drop in and have a coffee with the group and the organisers. There were tea parties, dances, art classes, Yiddish singing groups, theatre trips, more talks – always more talks – and a lot of laughter.

People might find that strange, that Holocaust survivors should laugh, but we do all the time, believe me. We celebrate our lives.

The group are always served a hot lunch. The soup is always thick, steaming hot and plenty of it. The bread basket is always full and always left out. No more obsessing over food, when or if they will receive it. The room is light and open. The doors never locked. There are never queues for anything. Survivors' birthdays are celebrated with chocolate cake and more singing.

I met so many lovely people, including Hungarian, Austrian and Polish survivors who, like me, survived Auschwitz-Birkenau and Bergen-Belsen.

I also met Arek Hersh, who grew up not far from Zduńska Wola in a place called Sieradz. Isn't that amazing? My community was all but wiped out in the war, and here I was in Hendon, all these years on, sitting next to someone who had lived very near me in Poland. Like me, Arek survived the Łódź ghetto and the camps.

I made so many precious friends with a shared understanding of each other's pasts. We started a discussion group based on current affairs in the news. 'Jews with Views', as we jokingly call it. It's very popular.

There are also lots of opportunities to discuss our faith in discussion groups. My love for God Almighty has only grown over the years. There are plenty of survivors who have turned away from God, questioning how any God can exist and allow the Holocaust to have happened. I understand that, but for me personally, it has only deepened my faith.

I believe in God. The Almighty helped me to survive so that I could inform others of what happened during the Holocaust. I feel it is bashert, *which is Yiddish for 'preordained'.*

It's God's plan for me.

I barely had time to sit still for a moment. Every week it seemed I was delivering a new talk all around the country. Believe me, I clocked up some miles. I delivered hundreds of talks.

In 2016, I was awarded the British Empire Medal (BEM) for services to Holocaust survivors, education and awareness. Martin and his wife Hilary came with me to the Tower of London to collect the medal.

For eight years in a row, starting in 2011, I went on something called the March of the Living, founded and organised by a lovely man called Scott Saunders. It's an intense five-day journey in Poland, which brings together people from all over the world. Students, young people and adults join survivors like me and educators to learn about the devastation and horrors of the Holocaust.

It was, and still is, an incredible experience. You visit the centres of Jewish life in Warsaw and Kraków and the sites of the ghettos. And you bear witness to extermination and concentration camps such as Majdanek and Auschwitz-Birkenau.

On the final day, you retrace the steps of the March of Death, the actual route which so many people were forced to take on their way to the gas chambers at Birkenau. But this time, there's a difference. It's called the March of the Living, with thousands of young people and adults marching shoulder to shoulder.

It really is something to see. All these young people walking with flags and proudly singing songs in Hebrew while you walk. It's noisy, colourful and emotional. Afterwards, there's a moving memorial service at the far end of Birkenau in between the crematoria.

It was never easy going back to Auschwitz-Birkenau. It brought back so many memories. Each time we walked along the side of the tracks that brought the transports into Birkenau, I remembered the pain of seeing my father disappear. No kiss. No goodbye. Nothing. Nothing.

Today, I'm proud to have reached ninety-five. My life is quieter these days. I don't do so many talks, but when I do, I still feel the powerful effect of them, as I hope people do when they listen to my story.

I'm so lucky. I know so many nice people. In February 2024, I met Prince William at the Western Marble Arch Synagogue in London. What a lovely young man, so gracious and natural, just like his mother used to be.

I was nervous to begin with, but he held my hand. 'Don't be nervous,' he said, smiling. I began to talk to him, telling him a little of what I had experienced, and he listened in silence.

'Sadly, my mother died twelve days after we were liberated from the Bergen-Belsen concentration camp by the British Army in 1945,' I told him.

Prince William was fifteen when he lost his mother. The same age I was when my mama died.

NOW

'How did you manage?' he asked quietly, and I shrugged.

'It wasn't easy. Somehow, I survived,' I replied. 'The sad thing is that antisemitism is worse than ever. I never imagined that within my lifetime there would once more be an explosion of hate-fuelled antisemitism.'

Prince William shook his head. 'Antisemitism has no place in this country. Prejudice has no place in society.'

He's right. It doesn't. He urged me to carry on sharing my testimony so that the next generation could understand what it was really like.

I do it when I can, but it gets harder and harder to do. Like most people my age, I have many falls. But I get back up. What else can I do?

Renee with Prince William at the Western Marble Arch Synagogue in London, February 2024

I make fewer plans these days. There's an old Yiddish proverb: 'Der mentsch trakht un Gott lakht.' Man plans, God laughs.

Today, I focus on only being around family and friends. The Holocaust Survivors' Centre is a part of my life. They keep me going. As do my own family. For the last few years, Adrian has been living with me. Sharon and Martin visit me every week. I'm so lucky. They're all very protective of me and I'm so very proud of them all.

People would think that as you get older, the pain fades, but I find it that it never goes away. It actually gets harder.

A natural part of ageing is to remember people and places from the past. The faces that Renee struggled to remember in the grip of her breakdown in her twenties are now, in her nineties, coming back into focus.

I think of my little sister all the time. I miss her more with every passing day. I'd love to know what she would have been like if she'd been allowed to get old like me. Stenia would have been ninety-four if she were still alive today.

I think of my parents every day too, and my grandparents, and all my aunts and uncles, all of whom were so loving and warm. I think of Mama and Gitel cooking together in the kitchen in a cloud of steam. I remember my kind, clever, handsome father and what a gentleman he was.

Many survivors will tell you their survival is down to luck and chance, when a flick of a finger to the left or right decided whether you should live or die.

I put my survival down to Mama and God Almighty. It is thanks to them that I am still alive to tell my story. My relationship with God came from my mother. I watched her pray in the ghetto and eighty-five years on it is the same prayer that I say every night when I go to bed at 10.30pm. It gives me strength and comfort.

NOW

I will never forget Mama, or stop speaking her name, for she will always be a part of me. Sala Berkowicz. Thank you, Mama, for showing me the most powerful and pure love there is.

Renee's mother, Sala, photographed before the war

Today, Renee is ninety-five. Honoured and praised by Holocaust charities and organisations, by our late Queen and Prince William for her services to Holocaust education. Time has gone so fast. It feels to her like only yesterday she arrived at Dover, a stick-thin girl with only a few words of English, a half-filled suitcase and a heavy heart. Other times, it feels like several lifetimes.

Eighty years have passed since the liberation of the camps in 1945. And in that time Renee has seen indifference and denial of the Holocaust. New wars. New genocides. But always the same suffering. And that is what keeps Renee going. Who else can bear witness to the filthy ghetto streets, the sealed cattle carts, smoking crematoria chimney stacks or the tangle of human bodies? Who can give a voice to those obliterated communities and ruptured families? The pool of survivors dwindles until soon, living memory will pass into archive testimony.

Renee is reminded of man's cruelty every day.

Every time I turn on my television and see the little children uprooted and killed by war, I'm reminded of my own past. We're not so clever, us humans, despite all our technology, because if we were, we would have learnt, surely?

My message to the younger generation is this. Please be tolerant of one another. Perhaps the world will be a better place to live in. I'd like people to start learning to live with one another in peace. We must learn to love and not hate.

Over and over, Renee has stared into the abyss. A beautiful and vulnerable young woman who survived against the odds and lived to become a wife, a mother, a grandmother. A survivor.

I hope my story has moved you. Maybe you're wondering, do I forgive? I don't forgive. How can I? It's not my right to forgive. Instead, I choose to live with love.

Epilogue

Answers

'Did you ever meet a man called Szaja Berkowicz in Auschwitz?'

A simple question with a lifetime of trauma attached to it. After nearly eight decades of repeatedly asking that question, Renee gave up hope of ever finding out the fate of her father. And yet, the question was never banished to the recesses of her mind. It was always there, along with the vivid image of her father swallowed up into the crowds at Auschwitz-Birkenau.

Finding answers to questions surrounding the Holocaust are deeply painful and complex. And, yet, as the following proves, it's never too late to try. History is constantly unfolding . . .

∼

The same day Renee's mother drew her last breath in Bergen-Belsen, 370 miles south, a lone American Army jeep drove through thickly wooded countryside. Deep in the heart of Bavaria, the sun-dappled forest was quiet. Too quiet for George Leitmann's liking.

George was serving with the 286th Combat Engineer Battalion as part of the United States Seventh Army. He and his driver were on a reconnaissance mission, patrolling ahead of their unit to see whether they would encounter enemy resistance.

Nazi ideology was deep-rooted in the area. In the town of Landsberg am Lech, just 3 miles from the area George was patrolling, Hitler had been imprisoned in the town's jail in 1924, where he wrote his antisemitic manifesto, *Mein Kampf*. The locals were fiercely loyal to the Führer, earning Landsberg the nickname, '*Hitlerstadt*' or 'Hitler Town'.

George was there to do a job. Finish the war.

'I was nineteen years old. I had volunteered to fight in the war against Nazi Germany. Unlike my comrades, it was personal.'

Ninety-nine-year-old George is both a Holocaust survivor *and* a US Army veteran. Nazi persecution had forced him, aged fourteen, alongside his mother Stella and both grandmothers, to flee their home in Vienna, Austria in 1940 and emigrate to the United States, leaving behind his father Josef Leitmann who was unable to get a visa to join them.

As soon as he graduated from high school, George volunteered to join the United States Army, and in 1944, he sailed back across the Atlantic and returned to European soil, this time as an eighteen-year-old soldier.

By April 1945, George and his unit had already fought their way across Nazi-occupied France before eventually crossing the Rhine into Germany.

'The Nazis were cruel beyond belief. Even to their own people. We were about to cross the river at Würzburg but we were stopped by the Germans on the west side. Two of our people had gone across on reconnaissance and hadn't returned, so my driver and I were assigned the next day to look for them.

'We got to a little village. Hanging from the lamp posts in the village were twelve children. The SS had handed these Hitler Youth bazookas and told them to defend the town when the Americans came, but the children had run away. The next day the SS returned and hanged them all. In my mind, I still see those kids, eleven- and twelve-year-old boys, swaying in the wind.'

EPILOGUE

George and his driver advanced through the Bavarian countryside.

'As we drove, we noticed a foul stench. We had already seen our fair share of dead bodies to know that it was the kind of smell that only comes from death.

'We alerted our unit and hid out in a wooded area until they joined us. The next day, 28 April 1945, my unit arrived, and we advanced through the gates of the camp.

'The SS had evacuated the camp and those prisoners who had not been strong enough to walk, or were too sick, were left behind. In an attempt to hide their crimes, the SS set fire to the camp by throwing gasoline on it. These bodies were only skin and bone, so they didn't burn very well and were still smouldering when we arrived.

'Everywhere were piles of unrecognisable people.'

George and his unit had stumbled upon one of the last Nazi concentration camps, Kaufering, a sub-camp of the Dachau concentration camp and consisting of eleven satellite camps situated around Landsberg am Lech. What differentiated Kaufering from other camps was its unique purpose. Hitler's builders, the Organisation Todt (OT), were managing the construction of enormous semi-underground bombproof bunkers in which to produce the first jet fighter. By 1944, Hitler still hoped to win back German air supremacy by production of these jet fighters and ordered the project be given the highest priority.

Due to the shortage of labour forces, the OT turned to what was left of European Jewry. From June 1944 onwards, Jewish slaves were deported to the eleven Kaufering camps and forced to work in hellish conditions, often underground, supervised by SS and OT guards, who used terror to keep up the demands of production.

In about ten months, 23,500 prisoners, including women and children, went through the Kaufering sub-camps.

By day, their main task was the construction of semi-underground bunkers for the production of the Messerschmitt Me 262, building railway embankments and unloading cement sacks. Fatal accidents happened every day.

By night, Jewish prisoners slept in primitive earth huts, built halfway underground so that only the roof was seen. These quickly became a breeding ground for disease and vermin. Because of these brutal conditions and a typhus epidemic, by December 1944, Kaufering IV had become a quarantined death camp, called 'the cold crematory' by many survivors.

Kaufering IV

'We saw these strange huts and our Commanding Officer, Colonel Johnson, ordered us not to go in for fear of disease transmission. We distributed cigarettes to the survivors and the Army medics set about treating them and giving them small amounts of food, being careful not to overfeed them.

EPILOGUE

'Colonel Johnson was so outraged when he saw the burning bodies that he ordered us to go to all the surrounding villages between Landsberg and Kaufering and pick up local people and bring them to the camp and make them march through it.

'I overheard two women talking to each other. They didn't know that I could speak German. The words stuck in my mind. One said to the other: "Der Führer was right. Americans are barbarians to make us look at this."'

Kaufering IV Camp Commandant Johann Baptist Eichelsdoerfer was captured by American liberating forces and forced to stand amid the corpses of prisoners killed in his camp. He was later tried at the Dachau trials and sentenced to death by hanging in the nearby Landsberg Prison, the same place Hitler wrote *Mein Kampf*.

On 29 April 1945, Dachau concentration camp was also liberated by US forces.

'There were just nine survivors in Kaufering IV. It was mainly bodies. It was something that you never forget.'

Nine days later, the war in Europe was over.

One of the men who passed through the camp gates of Kaufering IV was Szaja Berkowicz. Accountant. Husband to Sala. Beloved father to murdered Stenia. Beloved father to Renee.

Thanks to the bravery and testimony of George and all the Allied forces and liberators, Renee finally has some clarity. Eighty years after her father vanished on their arrival in Auschwitz-Birkenau, Renee was able to discover the truth.

Documents discovered by the Wiener Holocaust Library's International Tracing Service in February 2024, and confirmed by the Kaufering memorial, reveal that Szaja was not murdered in the gas chambers but was deported out of Auschwitz-Birkenau on 1 September 1944, not long after Renee and her mother. He was sent directly to Kaufering IV, where he was most likely worked to death, or died of disease.

Of the 23,500 Jewish prisoners who passed through the eleven Kaufering sub-camps, approximately 6,500 died of starvation, disease and executions. That figure does not include those who were returned to Auschwitz-Birkenau to be gassed, or died on the death marches.

When Kaufering IV was sealed off in December 1944, becoming a death camp, prisoners were left to perish in freezing underground earth huts with no access to the daily 'bunker soup' served at work sites and no medicine. Prisoners died in their hundreds every day and their naked bodies were hauled to the mass graves in handcarts by death commandoes of prisoners.

Szaja died on 20 January 1945, fourteen weeks before the camp was liberated in April 1945, and he was buried in a mass grave, over a mile from the camp. These graves were situated further away from the camp because the local mayor, when asked by the SS where to dig, didn't want to 'waste' farmland.

The dead from the Kaufering sub-camps were reported to the main camp, Dachau, and recorded in a handwritten list, which still exists today. The cause of Renee's father's death is listed by the camp as '*Allgemeiner Kräfteverfall*' – general decline in strength.

Eight decades on from their terrible separation at Auschwitz-Birkenau, Renee finally knows the truth.

In 1950, the site of the mass graves where Szaja and 3,000 other Jewish prisoners from Kaufering IV are buried was turned into a cemetery and opened to the public. Working with Jewish organisations, the Bavarian government installed a memorial stone to commemorate the deceased. The tortured victims now

EPILOGUE

rest in tranquil grounds surrounded by a nature reserve. Each spring, a blanket of wild flowers, thyme and rare orchids smother the cemetery and surrounding meadows. Renee's father's name now lives on in a slate plaque on the north wall of the cemetery, erected on Father's Day 2024, side by side with the names of many of his fellow prisoners.

It wasn't easy to hear, but at least I know. My question has been answered. Knowing the date of my father's death and what happened to him means I have closure. The Nazis worked hard to cover up the truth about what happened to our loved ones, so it's important that we never stop searching for the truth. At last, I found out what happened to my father.

Remembering matters. The past must never be forgotten.

The plaque Renee and her family commissioned, erected on Father's Day 2024 at the site of her father's grave

Dear Mama, Tatuś and Stenia,

How terrible it was we had to part. Thank you for being such wonderful parents. You both saved my life over and over again during the Holocaust. I survived because of your sacrifices.

My dear Tatuś. After so many years, I know what happened to you after we were forced apart at Birkenau. I never believed I would find out. I have erected a plaque in your name in the place we now know you are buried. It's a reminder that you existed, that you mattered. Thank you for being a wonderful father.

Mama. I love you so much. Thank you for caring for me until the very end and for giving me the best childhood a girl could wish for. It's heartbreaking it didn't last for much longer. Your prayers in the ghetto had an effect on me. I still say the same prayer every night before I go to bed.

I am ninety-five years old now. I hope I've made you proud. You have two wonderful grandchildren, Sharon and Martin, and five beautiful great-grandchildren, Rebecca, Daniela, Shoshana, Adrian and Benjy.

Stenia, my dear, brilliant little sister. It is you I miss most of all. Not a single day goes by when I don't think of you. I miss you more with every passing day. You would have been ninety-four in 2025 if the Nazis had let you live. I love you with all my heart. I hope we will all meet in heaven one day.

May your memories be a blessing.
   Love always,
      Your Renia
      November 2024

Kate and Renee

In Search of Renee's Past

by Kate Thompson

I met Renee Salt on 19 October 2022 at the launch event of an exhibition about Auschwitz-Birkenau in London. Renee, then ninety-three, had come with the Holocaust Educational Trust in order to speak about her experiences. She looked so small in front of the pack of assembled journalists, photographers and camera crews, and something in me folded. Surely this was too much for such an elderly woman? Then she began to speak and I realised how clumsy I had been in my assumptions. Her presence grew in front of my eyes until she filled the space with her light. Far from frail, she was the strongest, most resilient person in that room.

Renee spoke unprompted for thirty minutes and then took questions. I could not believe what I was hearing. Of course, I knew about the Holocaust, but to hear the human lived experience of it from a survivor was incredibly powerful.

Afterwards, I went to thank her for sharing her story and I asked whether she had ever had her own book published. She told me she hadn't, but she would like to share those experiences, 'if I felt there was enough to make a book'!

Three months into the research and writing of Renee's book, I'm ashamed to admit I crumbled. I had spent many hours getting to know this extraordinary woman and the more I got to know her, the more emotionally involved and overwhelmed I became. *Why was I writing this book? How on earth could any words do justice to her survival story?* The weight of the story she had entrusted me to tell felt too big to carry.

Very unprofessionally, I broke down in tears midway through a conversation about Renee. Fortunately, this was in the company of a woman I barely knew but instinctively trusted. Ellie Olmer is an outreach teacher for the Holocaust Educational Trust and she told me this: 'The Holocaust demands and takes every emotion from you.

'It can overwhelm you. It comes with huge and heavy responsibility. If it doesn't sometimes leave you in pieces, you shouldn't be doing it! But being with Renee is like looking into an abyss and finding a glimmer, a beautiful and vulnerable girl who survived against the odds and needs to tell her story. It's her therapy; it's the only way she can honour and mourn her family.

'In Judaism, we believe that there are no coincidences with God. Renee believes that "Almighty God" saved her for a reason. You found Renee and she found you.

'Elie Wiesel said, "Once you hear a witness, you become a witness." You've now taken on that responsibility; you are now part of the story.'

And so it came to be. I found myself a part of Renee's life. She and I would sit in her north-west London home, the walls covered in family photos, and we would talk over endless cups of tea.

Renee's story never came in a linear way. It burst out, an unfiltered gush of history that at times threatened to overwhelm her. Every memory Renee recounted, I could see she was experiencing it physically, her fingers splaying out as if to grab at something, her eyes growing wide with fear as if it were happening right there in the moment, not eighty years ago.

This book is Renee's way of honouring the memory of her family and making sense of the unimaginable. Surviving the

Holocaust was rare. Surviving to her age and raking over memories to share every last detail that can be remembered, rarer still. And yet, Renee did precisely that. 'If I want to say something about the past, I close my eyes and I see everything so clearly,' Renee told me when we first discussed the idea of a book.

There are thousands of words in *A Mother's Promise*, but not one that comes close to expressing my admiration for Renee. That intensified after I travelled to Poland in January 2024 and Germany in May 2024, retracing Renee's footsteps to help tell her story.

~

I started in her home town in Poland and followed the train tracks that took her further into hell, from Zduńska Wola, northeast to the city of Łódź, then south to the Auschwitz-Birkenau Memorial and Museum. From there, I travelled to Bavaria, then north to Hamburg and, finally, Bergen-Belsen. At every stage, I reminded myself of the difference between my own journey and Renee's. I was travelling on comfortable trains, not crammed with hundreds of others into freight wagons designed for cattle. I knew where Renee's journey went and how her story would end up. This was not something she ever benefitted from.

Seeing the places and spaces she had played in as a child, from parks to schools and markets, was bittersweet. In Zduńska Wola, I was guided by Dr Kamila Klauzińska, a Polish historian and genealogist who has spent the last two decades preserving the memory of Jewish life in the city.

I was lucky enough to get to visit the apartment block where Renee lived as a child. I thank Daria, the apartment's current resident, for being open enough to let me visit. She had every reason to be suspicious, but she could not have been more welcoming. She even cleaned her windows so I could take a photo out to the street outside. If only the past was always this transparent.

History is sometimes so close you can touch it and feel it. On other occasions, it's a distant planet. The beautiful red-brick textile factory Renee's father worked in is now an Aldi. The orchard she played in a car park. Then you open the heavy original iron door she would have opened every day to go to school, or see the mark of a mezuzah at the top corner of an old building, and it comes rushing back.

Everywhere, you are reminded of the glaring absence of presence and the presence of absence, as someone far wiser explained to me once.

The journey from Renee's childhood quickly turned chilling as I crossed a few streets, which is all it took to walk from Renee's comfortable childhood home to her new address in the ghetto. Her old home in the ghetto is still a mean-looking old building, down a squat and forbidding dead-end street, the tall shadow of the former Gestapo headquarters looming over it from the street behind.

The square where her little sister Stenia was taken in the dawn selection in August 1942, along with several hundred other children, is a very ordinary space. There was nothing to signal the abject horror of the morning so many children were stolen. My walk with Kamila took us next to the Jewish cemetery, where Renee was forced to sit for three days and nights while hundreds more Jewish men, women and children were slaughtered.

The cemetery was overgrown with trees, their dark twisted branches tangled together. Tips of nineteenth-century headstones (*matzevot*) peeked out from under a thick blanket of snow.

It was so quiet. A deer ran across the cemetery, revealing a flash of its silvery fur, almost invisible against the snow. Then, a heavy compressed silence, so different from those days when the residents of Zduńska Wola heard screams and gunfire. The horror of that day is still drenched deep into the ground and the original red-brick perimeter wall.

Kamila and a dedicated team of volunteers have worked tirelessly over the past twenty years to repair the many crumbling and destroyed graves here, and document the long-lost Jewish community of Zduńska Wola.

In the larger city of Łódź, I was guided by the knowledgeable Marcelina Tomza-Michalska, an official Auschwitz-Birkenau guide. There is little this impressive woman doesn't know about the German occupation of Poland.

Some streets looked little different from the ghetto years, with ramshackle old houses, bleak in the January snow and slush. Eighty-two years on, Fire Brigade Square, where Chaim Mordechai Rumkowski made that notorious speech, is a very different place. No longer a wide open square, it's filled with straggly trees and cars.

Radegast is a moving memorial to the lives of those who were transported in and out of the ghetto via the station. It was poignant to find the records of the Berkowicz family, documenting their arrival, including the falsified date of birth Renee's father gave to make her sixteen instead of thirteen.

Our last stop in Łódź was the Jewish cemetery, the largest in Europe. There were so many beautiful and imposing graves from the golden age of Polish Jewry, a stark contrast to the 45,000 graves of the Ghetto Jews, buried in the specially allocated Ghetto Field. We found the graves of the men, women and children who perished in the transport from Zduńska Wola to Łódź, a journey burnt into Renee's brain. As we were leaving, I noticed a series of pits in the ground.

'What are those?' I asked.

'Those are the graves of the people who escaped death,' Marcelina explained.

After the liquidation of the Łódź ghetto in August 1944, approximately 800 ghetto prisoners were left behind, employed in clearing-up squads, not only to tidy up the area, but also to hunt out hidden belongings, as well as to dig their own graves. Perhaps they even came across Renee's blue-and-white polka-dot dress left to her by her aunt, Esther.

In January 1945, when the Nazis started withdrawing from Łódź, they tried to exterminate these Jews, but almost all of them managed to hide from their would-be executioners. They were saved on 19 January 1945, when the Soviet Army liberated the ghetto.

Today, the pits remained unfilled as a symbol of defiance. There can't be many cemeteries in the world with graves for those who escaped death.

At Auschwitz-Birkenau, Marcelina led me to an empty barrack similar to the one Renee was in (the original one in the area known as 'Mexico' has since been destroyed). I sat on the concrete floor and tried to imagine how it must have felt to sit in a human chain, without moving, for days on end.

'Now imagine it's summer and it's so hot the sweat is dripping off you. There is no water. No circulation of air. No food. No chance to move or speak,' Marcelina said.

The next day I went back to Birkenau alone. It was a cold January morning and the quiet gave me time to walk and reflect on the hell that Renee had found herself in.

The *Sauna* building, where Renee and her mother were processed, is now closed to visitors, but I stood by the door and looked through the windows. The shower room is a large, empty space. I imagined the moment Renee closed her eyes, expecting gas, only to feel cold water.

A single red rose had been left on the windowsill, its petals shrivelled in the cold. I wondered about the story of the person who had left it there. How many life stories are contained in this vast camp complex? How many more life stories never got written?

Visiting a memorial site is in itself a deeply unique experience. Every visitor comes away with a memory that stops them in their tracks. One woman I spoke with was struck by the way the silver birch trees that bordered the camp glowed red-gold in the setting sun. 'Did the prisoners see this and how did it make them feel?' she wondered. For others, perhaps it's the dimly lit display cases full of tangled human hair, or the piles upon piles of broken spectacles and luggage. I could have spent all day in the corridor lined with photographs of prisoners in their striped uniforms, studying their faces and reading their names.

Back at home in London, I visited Rabbi Menachem Junik, Jewish Care's spiritual and pastoral lead, and voiced a concern that was worrying me deeply.

Is it right that I, who am not Jewish, write Renee's story?

He told me, 'There is a word in Yiddish, *bashert*, meaning, it's all for a reason; nothing happens by chance. Renee's survival is this.

'Renee's inner spark, her inner faith, was switched on during the Holocaust, and the more difficult, challenging and horrific the situation, the more she felt she was being looked after. Her faith was her anchor. Amplifying her voice is like the striking of a match.'

Soon after my return from Poland, and prior to my research trip to Germany, came some shocking news. Renee never knew but had always assumed that her father had died in the gas chambers at Auschwitz-Birkenau. Unsurprising, as the railway ramp at Birkenau was the last place she saw him alive. She had contacted the Red Cross many years ago and a search did not reveal any answers.

Eighty years and six months on from that separation, however, an International Tracing Report I had requested from the Wiener Holocaust Library in London filled in some gaps with digitised records that would not have been available at the time of Renee's original search.

It appeared that, like Renee and her mother, Szaja was also a 'deposit' prisoner. He was transported out of Auschwitz-Birkenau on 1 September 1944 and sent to one of the myriad slave labour camps in the Third Reich.

As you have already read, he did not die in the gas chambers, but like 6,500 other Jewish prisoners, he died in Kaufering, a sub-camp of Dachau, on 20 January 1945. Szaja's camp, Kaufering IV, was liberated on 27 and 28 April 1945 by the US Army, which encountered only nine survivors.

Sitting down with Renee's son Martin to share this news with Renee was one of the most unexpected parts of writing this book. But the truth, no matter how hard to swallow, is perhaps better than ignorance.

The Nazis went to great lengths to hide their crimes. Every time the truth is revealed, another missing life is no longer just a question mark. I was reminded of this when I travelled to Germany and saw the many *Stolpersteine* or 'stumbling stones', the concrete cubes embedded in the pavement, bearing a brass plate inscribed with the name and life dates of victims of Nazi extermination or persecution. Each commemorates a victim outside their last-known freely chosen residence.

It's intensely moving to look from the brass plaque to the doorstep and imagine their last steps from their place of safety.

Finding one of the liberating soldiers at Kaufering, Professor George Leitmann, and interviewing him in his home in California via Zoom was a salve to the pain of the discovery. The 99-year-old is a humble hero. A Holocaust survivor himself and a US Army veteran, George lives with atrocities in his head, but actively went on to live a life spent in the pursuit of knowledge and peace.

After he was demobbed, he returned to the US where he worked as a rocket scientist in the 1950s, before obtaining his PhD in engineering science and becoming a Professor of Engineering Science at UC Berkeley. Along the way, he married his sweetheart Nancy and had two children. Among his many accolades and awards is the Croix de Guerre, the highest French military medal, and the French Legion of Honour.

His wartime stories as both a survivor and liberator are illuminating.

George Leitmann

'After the war ended, I was transferred into the Military Intelligence Division as a special agent of the Counter Intelligence Corps, where I interrogated Nazis and SS guards at the Nuremberg trials for about six weeks,' he told me. 'It took a direct order from General Eisenhower to allow that.

'It was essential for me to keep my cool, remain controlled and never lose my temper. I had a job to do. If you resort to shouting or violence, you'll never succeed in what you're trying to do.

'Amongst others, I interrogated Mrs Himmler, the wife of Heinrich Himmler, Reichsführer of the Schutzstaffel (SS), one of the most powerful men in Nazi Germany after Hitler. I had to interrogate her and her daughter, a pathetic pair as I remember.

'"I understand your husband was an important man," I said.

'"Oh yes," she replied. "He was the head of all the police in Germany. He was a bad man."

'Okay, I thought to myself, here it comes.

'"He had many affairs," she grumbled.

'Her husband was responsible for the murder of millions of Jews and she was more concerned with his infidelities.

'One of the last groups of people I interrogated was a group of five female camp guards from Bergen-Belsen. They had cooked up a real story. "Belsen was a recreation camp for sick Jews, we were the nurses!"'

The stories George told me were just a fraction of what he had experienced in that last tumultuous year of war. How extraordinary it felt to speak with someone who had lived through so much history.

'I'm so pleased Renee knows what happened to her father at last,' he told me. 'Most people don't have a clue what war is like. They see it in the movies. They read it in books. You can't imagine it unless you have experienced it. I speak to groups of schoolchildren and I tell them: "War must be avoided at all costs." Kaufering defies description. I can still smell those burning bodies.'

In 2010, George finally discovered what happened to his father Josef, whom he had been forced to leave behind in Europe. Josef was able to flee to Yugoslavia in 1940. A year later, Germany attacked and occupied Yugoslavia. Josef was shot through the head in a Serbian concentration camp along with a thousand other Jewish men.

'Naming me as a Holocaust survivor is not deserved by comparison with the fate of my father.'

~

In May 2024, I travelled to Kaufering in Bavaria, southern Germany, to deliver a memorial plaque Renee and her family had commissioned. The site of the mass graves is now a beautiful cemetery nestled in a nature reserve, carpeted with spring flowers, wild thyme and rare orchids. A mile away from the cemetery is the site of the former concentration camp Kaufering IV, where Renee's father perished in the last bitter winter of the war.

The strange sunken huts and barbed wire are long gone, burnt and torn down by the liberating US forces. The land was returned to its original owner, a farmer.

Kaufering is no Auschwitz-Birkenau or Bergen-Belsen. There are no museums or coachloads of visitors. No tour guides herding tourists about. Nothing, in fact, but bucolic farmland and forests, with distinctive Bavarian church spires peeking over the treetops. In certain conditions, you can see the Alps shimmering in the distance.

It all felt incongruous. How can the mind reconcile this serene land as a site of torture? A place where prisoners were beaten in giant underground bunkers, or forced to stand between

IN SEARCH OF RENEE'S PAST

electrified barbed-wire fences without moving for twenty-four hours. How can the tranquil meadows conceal mass graves, where the corpses' bones were deliberately broken so that they might be more tightly packed into the pit?

Even as butterflies dance past, you are quite suddenly reminded of its dark past. As I walked through the farmer's field where the Kaufering IV huts were located, the place where Renee's father died, with memorial historians Helga Deiler and Gerhard Roletscheck, they told me to look down. There, peeking out through the freshly ploughed brown soil, were fragments of the past. I picked up a rusty old nail and several pieces of shattered crockery.

'Those are pieces of the bowls prisoners would have drunk their soup from,' said Gerhard. 'That nail came from the wooden huts.' Holding concentration camp soup bowls in your hand, found in the middle of a field, was the most chilling connection to the past I've ever felt. I tried to imagine how many hands must have clutched those bowls, desperate for a few precious sips of lifesaving soup.

The same day, we held a simple but beautiful ceremony at Renee's father's newly erected plaque. Having just come out of hospital, Renee was feeling too weak to attend, but we did a live link-up via FaceTime so she could watch as we lit a candle and I read some words about finding his grave. It was a beautiful reminder that no story is ever truly finished, and that resolutions and healing can come when you least expect them.

All of this was made possible thanks to Dr Jascha März, Head of Scientific Services and Archives of the Bavarian Memorial Foundation, Helga Deiler from the Kaufering Memorial and local historian Gerhard Roletscheck.

Helga, her late husband Manfred and a small but dedicated team established the European Holocaust Memorial Foundation in 2009. Thanks to their efforts, the public are able to visit and learn about the concentration camps at Kaufering. Like a lot of Holocaust educators, Helga has a personal reason for digging into the past.

'I was born here in Landsberg in 1958 and we were never taught the history of the camps in the area. I wanted to know the truth, to discover what happened here during the war, but it was so hard to get answers. The only way to discover the truth was by reading the English transcripts from the Dachau trials. I was so shocked. I couldn't believe this had happened in my neighbourhood and we never heard anything about it.'

Helga and her husband Manfred devoted thirty-five years to telling the truth about their town's hidden past and often took survivors and their families to Kaufering VII, which still contains some of the huts. The land was purchased with a generous donation from Polish Holocaust survivor Alexander Moksel. It is the only privately owned concentration camp site in Germany.

'It's so important that something is left from this time,' Helga insists. 'These monuments have their own story. They talk to us.'

Word spread and soon documentary crews and journalists also started coming.

'When Steven Spielberg was searching for a location for his liberation scene for *Band of Brothers*, we got in contact with his crew and met in Munich to show them the photos of Kaufering IV,' Helga explained. 'Spielberg built up the film set in Hatfield Park near London.

'Local people didn't like it when we first opened up the camp and started sharing its story. Nobody wanted to find out their father or grandfather was a Nazi or an SS guard who had worked there. There is a German word, *Nestbeschmutzer*, which translated means, 'someone who fouls their own nest'. That's what we were called. People reacted angrily, but we didn't care. We carried on digging into the past. Fortunately, that has all stopped now.

'This part of our history belongs to us. We can't deny it. We need to share and educate.'

Sadly, Helga does this now without Manfred, who passed away in November 2023.

'Manfred always wanted young people to learn how it is possible that a civilised country can come to have this terrible history. That's our responsibility as German citizens to share that history in order to prevent it happening again. In Bavaria, the Holocaust is on the curriculum and schoolchildren have to visit concentration camps. With the rise of the far right across Europe, this is now of vital importance.'

As I leave, Helga tears up in frustration. 'I feel I haven't done enough. I can do more.'

∼

From there, I took a train north to Hamburg and explored inside the warehouse where Renee and her mother were sent when they were deported from Auschwitz-Birkenau to Germany.

Lagerhaus G on the Dessauer Ufer has been a protected building since the end of 1998. It's a building with a past. It is vast, over 24,000 square metres, built in 1907 from red brick and wooden beams imported from England, originally as a warehouse for tobacco, coffee and tea. By the time of the war, it was used to house forced labourers and prisoners of the Neuengamme concentration camp. These male and female slaves, including Jewish and political prisoners, came from all over Europe. Today, its care rests in the hands of the Lagerhaus G Heritage Foundation, whose representative Güven Polat kindly opened it up so I could look around. I visited with Christine Eckel, historian from the Neuengamme Concentration Camp Memorial.

IN SEARCH OF RENEE'S PAST

We clambered down some rickety wooden steps into the bowels of the building, the creepy basement where the waters of the River Elbe lap and rats scurry through the mud. It was cold, damp, smelly and, despite the size of it, horribly claustrophobic. It's hard to imagine a more frightening place to shelter in a bombing raid. At least 150 prisoners died when the north end of the warehouse received a direct hit.

On the walls you can still see a prisoner's name carved into the concrete with the date, 1942. How important it must have felt for him or her to have made their mark in the world, to want someone to know they existed in this dark underbelly of the Reich.

The Rinderhalle, the beef market, in the Heiligengeistfeld area where Renee's mother was attacked by a bull, is now a gentrified neighbourhood full of bars and cafes. The only reminder of its brutal past is a giant stone statue of a bull thrusting out of the side of the old slaughterhouse.

Half an hour by train from the centre of Hamburg, Christine took me to the district of Poppenbüttel and showed me the one remaining prefabricated house the prisoners of the Sasel camp built for bombed-out German families. As we walked, I looked down, wondering whether I was walking on the road Renee and other slaves were forced to build.

'We had a lady who was raised in this prefab housing. It was a happy childhood for her. Finding out it was built by Jewish slaves forced her to rethink her whole childhood,' Christine explains. The tiny house remains, now dwarfed by the nearby shopping centre.

Two kilometres away at the site of the former concentration camp, on the initiative of local students from Oberalster Secondary School, a memorial stone was erected in the 1980s.

This is the only reminder of the camp where Renee and her mother endured that last bitterly cold winter of the war. Today, it's a leafy upper-middle-class suburb of Hamburg. At Poppenbüttel train station, we paused to reflect on a fifteen-year-old Renee waiting on the platform as her mum was unloaded off the train on a stretcher after the bull attack.

From there, I travelled to the Bergen-Belsen Memorial Museum, built on the site of the concentration camp, which I had deliberately left until last. I was fortunate enough to visit with a guide after hours. There was not a soul in sight. It was so quiet you could hear the wind rushing through the silver birch trees and the calling of a cuckoo. Like Bavaria, its peace and beauty are so at odds with the atrocities committed on the land under the Nazi regime. Then, you come across the mass graves and the peace is shattered. Stone markers indicate the number of bodies buried there. 800. 1,000. 2,000. 5,000 . . .

I walked past a headstone erected in memory of Anne Frank and found a much-needed place to sit called the House of Silence, where I could reflect on what I had seen. I tried so hard to imagine what Renee had witnessed as she staggered from hut to hut searching for her mother. Where were the putrid huts filled with the dead and the barely living located? Or the 'hills' that turned out to be piles of corpses? What must it have felt like to see 'walking skeletons', as Renee described them? And here I failed, because it is simply not possible to imagine. I may have travelled to the sites of Renee's persecution, but only she had travelled deep into the abyss of human darkness.

The next morning, my Bergen-Belsen guide, Susanne Seitz, a good friend of Renee's, had arranged a pass for us to enter the NATO base where Renee's mother is buried in the grounds of the former barracks, which the British Military used after the liberation.

Once we had cleared security and were waved past the checkpoint, I realised how unnerving it must have been for Renee to return here in 1995 and have to confront men in uniforms and scrolls of barbed wire.

In the cemetery, I thought of Renee, standing over the grave as a silent fifteen-year-old. Then to the retired 66-year-old woman who found it in herself to return to Bergen-Belsen with her husband and children fifty years later. And then to the 94-year-old widow, now waiting in London to hear all about my trip. Having visited both of her parents' graves, I was reminded of the enormity of her loss, but also the magnitude of her life.

∼

Writing about the Holocaust comes with a heavy duty of care attached and there has scarcely been a moment in the last year and a half of researching and writing when this book has not been in my thoughts (and occasionally my nightmares).

You might be wondering why the book is written in both the third and first person. Renee was ten when war broke out, fifteen when it ended, and existed largely in a bubble of terror, sickness, exhaustion and starvation. Events happened to her and around her. By telling the detail of the stories that directly affected her, which she cannot possibly have known in that moment, I hope to have provided a more detailed picture, for both Renee and the reader.

On the significant eightieth anniversary of the liberation of the camps, we look to Renee and the dwindling band of survivors for the authenticity that comes from saying, 'I was there.'

Dr Teresa Wontor-Cichy, a historian from the Research Center at Auschwitz-Birkenau Memorial and Museum in Oświęcim, Poland told me: 'Learning about Auschwitz and the Holocaust became a challenge for many. But with the help of survivors like Renee Salt, and her story, everything that happened over eighty years ago is so close and personal. Still difficult to comprehend, but empowered with the need for survival. This publication will be part of the legacy so graciously left for the next generation to come.'

IN SEARCH OF RENEE'S PAST

This is a harrowing and emotionally overwhelming story, but its backbone is faith and love. The love from her mother and father, who kept her alive. The love for a little sister who never got to grow up. On one occasion, Renee looked at an empty chair next to her at the table.

'Stenia would have been ninety-three this year had she lived,' she told me.

And in the moment, I was reminded of all the millions of empty chairs at the table.

Often when I went to hug her goodbye, Renee would say the same thing. 'So, you think there's enough for a book?'

And I would always reply with the same comment. 'The question is, Renee, how will we fit it all in one book!' Then she would shrug and point upwards.

'I hope I'm alive to see it. It's all up to Him.'

Renee Salt, then aged ninety-four, prior to giving a talk for the Holocaust Educational Trust. Photo taken at her home in London in 2024

The Archive of Lost Lives

Elise Bath spends her days uncovering lost lives. She is an International Tracing Service Archive Manager for the Wiener Holocaust Library's International Tracing Service. Elise helps survivors piece together the fragments of their shattered pasts.

As early as 1942, the Allied governments recognised that there was a humanitarian crisis of unprecedented scale on mainland Europe. As Elise explained to me: 'There were millions of people in the concentration camp system, forced labourers, or people just forced out of their homes by circumstances of war. And so very early on, as the war was still ongoing, efforts were undertaken to register and trace the missing.

'As the Allies moved through Europe, they would gather up documentation like prison lists and concentration camp lists, from sites of incarceration and persecution.

'These efforts to register and then trace the missing coalesced around a town called Bad Arolsen in central Germany. It was between the four occupation zones and its infrastructure was intact.

'This small town became the hub of tracing the missing and the dead after the Holocaust. The archive and all its physical documents remain in this town still. It's an amazing sight. The archive contains over 30 million documents connected with the experiences of 17 and a half million people.'

The German Army were punctilious record keepers. Contained in the archive are concentration camp lists, prison lists, records of deaths, as well as post-war documentation, including compensation claims after the war and records from the displaced persons camps.

In the immediate aftermath of war, it wasn't always easy to gain access to the archives.

'The archive hasn't always been totally open and accessible. There have been periods when the academic researchers were denied access to the material, and times when access was severely limited, even to relatives of victims and survivors themselves. Enquirers, families and survivors would sometimes find it took years for their requests to be dealt with.

'In the early 1950s, there were even former members of the SS and Nazi Party working there! Then, by the early 2000s, there was a huge amount of international pressure to open the archive up and to make it more publicly available, which was successful. From there, the archive was digitised and since 2008, the ITS has been run by an international commission. Digital copies of the archive have been given to various countries around the world, including the UK. The Wiener Holocaust Library holds and manages the UK's copy.'

In a new era of transparency, Elise explains how this has led to a flood of requests.

'We use the archive to support our own research, academic research and help set up exhibitions, but the heart of what we do is to trace the experiences of individuals, normally for their families.'

Elise is part of a small team and the important work they do is still largely unknown.

'We started doing free searches in 2013. In the years since then, the ITS team has uncovered thousands of people's personal experiences of the Holocaust. We take the work seriously and try

THE ARCHIVE OF LOST LIVES

to be professional at all times, but sometimes it can be deeply emotional work.'

The most memorable search for Elise was the resurrection of the memory of three murdered children.

'I have had cases recently where in the course of doing the family research for enquirers, I came across three children who were so young when they were killed by the Nazis and their collaborators that their surviving relatives had never known, or had forgotten, that they had been born.

'Facing up to the total obliteration of these children, not only physically but also any memory of them, was quite difficult. But a local synagogue has agreed to take responsibility for remembering the lives of these three children and pray for them, which is as positive an outcome as we can hope for in these cases. This represents the power of the archive, though – the Nazis had succeeded in destroying the physical lives of these children, and for a time, even the memory of them.

'Because of the ITS archive, we can search the documents, and at least pull people's names and memories out from the past. Working with the synagogue to have the memories of these children honoured feels like the most significant thing I've done in my career.'

As so many survivors are now passing away, Elise's work becomes even more important.

'We've had a real jump in the number of enquiries from survivors this last year. That makes our work more urgent and more powerful.

'Not everyone persecuted by the Nazis and their collaborators appears in the ITS archive. It is a huge collection, but there are gaps where documents have been lost, destroyed, or were never kept in the first place. But despite that, it is always worth asking us to check to see if we can find a trace of a lost person.

THE ARCHIVE OF LOST LIVES

Sometimes, the act of searching, even if it is unsuccessful, can be a comfort and a memorialisation of sorts.'

For more information about the archive and to request a search, go to www.wienerholocaustlibrary.org/what-we-do/research/its/

Acknowledgements

During the research for *A Mother's Promise*, I have had the privilege of meeting, interviewing and spending time with survivors, archivists, Holocaust educators, faith leaders, support workers, tour guides and historians. The further into my research I delved, the deeper my respect for these dedicated individuals became. Many of them have personal connections to Renee, but even those who didn't went out of their way to help me. I don't know how they have found the coping mechanisms to work so tirelessly to support survivors and immerse themselves in Holocaust education, but they each have my highest respect. I have been guided by the following people in helping to write Renee's story, but any mistakes are my own.

With thanks to:

In the UK

Martin Winstone, Senior Historical Advisor to the Holocaust Educational Trust and Project Historian for the United Kingdom Holocaust Memorial. He is a member of the UK delegation to the International Holocaust Remembrance Alliance (IHRA) and the author of *The Holocaust Sites of Europe* (2010) and *The Dark Heart of Hitler's Europe* (2014). My profound thanks must go to Martin, who not only read multiple drafts but was always at the end of a Zoom call to answer my many questions.

ACKNOWLEDGEMENTS

Sarah Wetton, Testimony Officer at the National Holocaust Centre and Museum, who works hard to support survivors and preserve their testimony at the place Renee has likened to a second home.
https://www.holocaust.org.uk

Anna Bradford and Annabel Pattle from the Holocaust Educational Trust, both of whom support survivors and help them to share their testimony.
https://www.het.org.uk

Ellie Olmer, outreach worker for the Holocaust Educational Trust. Ellie accompanies survivors to talks and pupils to the Lessons from Auschwitz project and has been a great support during the research and writing of this book.
https://www.het.org.uk/lessons-from-auschwitz-online

Naomi Creeger, Sarah-Jane Burstein and Melanie Gotlieb, from Jewish Care's Holocaust Survivors' Centre (HSC), the group that is like an extension of Renee's family. I thank them all for their support and kindness.
https://jewishcare.org/our-services/social-care-and-other-support-services/services-for-holocaust-survivors

Judith Hassan (OBE) who first founded the Holocaust Survivors' Centre. Judith founded the centre on behalf of the funding agencies, Jewish Care and World Jewish Relief. The recommendation to establish the centre emerged from Judith's contact with survivors from the latter part of the 1970s and 1980s. She presented this to Jewish Care's Executive Committee, who unanimously agreed for her to go ahead with establishing it. Judith kindly spoke to me and proofread selected chapters.

ACKNOWLEDGEMENTS

Rabbi Menachem Junik, Pastoral and Spiritual Lead for Jewish Care, and Ilana Greenblatt, Jewish Culture and Faith Manager for Jewish Care. These two wonderful people offered kindness, support and wisdom in abundance.
https://jewishcare.org

Elise Bath, International Tracing Service Archive Manager for the Wiener Holocaust Library's International Tracing Service. With enormous thanks for her tireless work in helping to establish what happened to Renee's father.
https://wienerholocaustlibrary.org/what-we-do/research/its/

Scott Saunders, founder and Chairman of March of the Living UK. In appreciation of the coffee, stories, wisdom and for sharing his dissertation on how survivors of the Holocaust rebuilt Jewish identity in German DP camps after the war.
https://www.marchoftheliving.org.uk

Dr Stephen Smith, co-founder of the National Holocaust Centre and Museum and former head of the Shoah Foundation.
https://www.holocaust.org.uk

All the staff at the archives and licensing department of the Imperial War Museum in London.
https://www.iwm.org.uk/research/research-facilities

My thanks to Hugh Petrie, Heritage Development Officer, London Borough of Barnet, for his kind assistance.

ACKNOWLEDGEMENTS

In Poland

Dr Kamila Klauzińska, Polish historian and genealogist, who made my visit so informative and rewarding.

Marcelina Tomza-Michalska, an official Auschwitz-Birkenau guide. With thanks for her tireless help and for reading multiple drafts.
https://fsp.krakow.pl/en/przewodnik/marcelina-tomza-michalska-2/

Dr Teresa Wontor-Cichy, historian at the Auschwitz-Birkenau Memorial and Museum. With enormous thanks for reading multiple drafts and her assistance during my research trip.
https://www.auschwitz.org/en/

In Germany

My visit to Hamburg, Bergen-Belsen, Kaufering and the installation of the memorial plaque would not have been possible without the help of the following people who showed me such kindness on my visit:

Helga Deiler from the European Holocaust Memorial Foundation.
https://www.kaufering-memorial.de/en/

Alfred Platschka from the European Holocaust Memorial Foundation.
https://www.kaufering-memorial.de/en/

Dr Jascha März, Head of Scientific Services and Archives of the Bavarian Memorial Foundation.
https://www.stiftung-bayerische-gedenkstaetten.de

ACKNOWLEDGEMENTS

Gerhard Roletscheck. Kaufering historian.

Gabriele Triebel, Deputy Leader of the Bavarian Green Party.
https://gabriele-triebel.de

Christine Eckel, historian from the Neuengamme Concentration Camp Memorial.
https://www.kz-gedenkstaette-neuengamme.de/en/

Güven Polat, representative of the Lagerhaus G Heritage Foundation.
https://lagerhausg.org/impressum/

Susanne Seitz, tour guide for the Bergen-Belsen Memorial Museum.

Klaus Tätzler and Katja Seybold from the Research and Documentation Centre at Bergen-Belsen Memorial Museum.
https://Bergen-Belsen.stiftung-ng.de

I am indebted to Sharon Footerman for being such a careful and thoughtful early reader; Martin Salt for taking the time to share his memories and thoughts with me; Adrian Salt for helping to set up the initial conversations with his grandmother; Shoshi Footerman Assaraf for her help with Yiddish translations; Mervyn Kersh for sharing his testimony with me; Ivor Perl for sharing his testimony with me; George Leitmann for sharing his testimony with me; Amy Condon for being an early reader; and Gloria Spielman for writing advice.

Sources and Bibliography

A Mother's Promise captures the verbal testimony of Renee Salt and her experiences of the Holocaust. The interviews were conducted in approximately thirty sessions over the course of nine months, with additional sessions to read back the text and revise on paper. These interviews were transcribed, and in some places her speech is reported verbatim, especially with moments that are seared into her brain. In other places, I have edited our interviews to make the text more fluent, but these are the memories and experiences of Renee as she recalls them. I cross-referenced these against other testimonial sources, such as Renee's responses to the 1,200 questions she was asked for the Forever Project for the National Holocaust Centre and Museum and her interviews with the Imperial War Museum, Wiener Holocaust Library and Bergen-Belsen Memorial. Renee then read the manuscript out loud chapter by chapter, which often triggered more memories and revisions. I am constantly in awe of her commitment to this book and the bravery it took to revisit her past.

Below I list my main sources for historical background research by chapter. All interviews conducted by Kate Thompson unless otherwise stated.

Zduńska Wola (Chapter One to Chapter Four)

Census records, 1930. Museum archives, Museum of the History

SOURCES AND BIBLIOGRAPHY

of the City of Zduńska Wola, Zduńska Wola, Poland.

Dean, Martin, ed. *The United States Holocaust Memorial Museum: Encyclopedia of Camps and Ghettos, 1933–1945*, Volume II. Bloomington, IN: Indiana University Press, 2012. Chapters on the ghetto in Zduńska Wola. Held at the Wiener Holocaust Library.

Ehrlich, Elchanan, and Leila Kaye-Klin, eds. *The Zduńska Wola Book*. Tel Aviv: Israel Press Ltd, April 1968. Published online by JewishGen. https://www.jewishgen.org/yizkor/Zdunska_Wola/Zdunska_Wola.html

Greenblatt, Ilana. Consultation and guidance via Zoom. Jewish Culture and Faith Manager for Jewish Care, 17 and 24 May 2024.

Junik, Rabbi Menachem. In-person interview. Pastoral and Spiritual Lead for Jewish Care, Jewish Care, Amélie House, Maurice and Vivienne Wohl Campus, Golders Green, London, 2 February 2024.

Klauzińska, Dr Kamila. In-person interview. Museum of the History of the City of Zduńska Wola, Zduńska Wola, Poland, 22–23 January 2024.

Neuman, Isaac, and Michael Palencia-Roth. *The Narrow Bridge: Beyond the Holocaust*. New York, NY: Fordham University Press, 2023.

Online information on Chełmno. Shoah Resource Centre, Yad Vashem. Accessed January 2024. https://www.yadvashem.org/odot_pdf/microsoft%20word%20-%205915.pdf

Source for the translation of the prayer on p.29. Chabad.org; line one, '*Shema Yisrael Hashem Elokeinu Hashem Echad*', provided by Ilana Greenblatt, Jewish Culture and Faith Manager for Jewish Care.

Strzelecki, Andrzej. *The Deportation of Jews from the Łódź Ghetto to KL Auschwitz and Their Extermination*. Oświęcim: Auschwitz-Birkenau Memorial and Museum, 2006.

SOURCES AND BIBLIOGRAPHY

The figure quoted on p.44, 'When dawn rose on day three, only around 1,200 people out of an estimated 9,000 had survived the liquidation.' Some sources suggest the figure was 1,500.

Virtual visit to the Museum of the Former Extermination Camp in Chełmno-on-Ner. Memorial Museums. Accessed 15 January 2024. https://www.memorialmuseums.org/eng/staettens/view/122/Museum-des-ehemaligen-Vernichtungslagers-in-Kulmhof-am-Ner

Visit to the Holocaust Exhibition. Imperial War Museum, London, United Kingdom, 14 and 22 November 2023.

Visit to the Museum of the History of the City of Zduńska Wola. Zduńska Wola, Poland, 22 January 2024.

Walking tour of the city, ghetto and Jewish cemetery, with information panels at the site of the former ghetto and outside the Jewish cemetery. Zduńska Wola, Poland, 22–23 January 2024.

Winstone, Martin. *The Dark Heart of Hitler's Europe*. London: Bloomsbury, 2021.

Łódź Ghetto (Chapters Five and Six)

Adelson, Alan, and Robert Lapides, eds. *Lodz Ghetto: Inside a Community under Siege*. New York, NY: Penguin Books, 1991.

Bath, Elise. *International Tracing Service Report*. Compiled by Elise Bath, Archive Manager. Copies held by Kate Thompson and the Wiener Holocaust Library.

Dean, Martin, ed. *The United States Holocaust Memorial Museum: Encylopedia of Camps and Ghettos, 1933–1945*, Volume II. Bloomington, IN: Indiana University Press, 2012. Chapter on Litzmannstadt ghetto. Held at the Wiener Holocaust Library.

Dobroszycki, Lucjan, ed. *The Chronicle of the Lodz Ghetto, 1941–1944*. New Haven, CT: Yale University Press, 1984.

SOURCES AND BIBLIOGRAPHY

Sierakowiak, Dawid. *The Diary of Dawid Sierakowiak*. Edited by Alan Adelson. Translated by Kamil Turowski. New York, NY: Oxford University Press, 1998.

Strzelecki, Andrzej. *The Deportation of Jews from the Łódź Ghetto to KL Auschwitz and Their Extermination*. Oświęcim: Auschwitz-Birkenau Memorial and Museum, 2006.

Tomza-Michalska, Marcelina. In-person interview. Łódź, Poland, 23–24 January 2024.

Tour of the site of the former Litzmannstadt ghetto, Łódź, Poland, 24 January 2024.

Visit to the Jewish cemetery, Łódź, Poland, 24 January 2024.

Visit to Radegast Museum. Muzeum Tradycji. Accessed 24 January 2024. https://muzeumtradycji.pl/oddzial-stacja-radegast/

Visit to Radegast station. Łódź ghetto in Poland, 24 January 2024. http://www.lodz-ghetto.com/the_radegast_station.html

Winstone, Martin. *The Dark Heart of Hitler's Europe*. London: Bloomsbury, 2021.

Wontor-Cichy, Dr Teresa. In-person interview. Historian at the Auschwitz-Birkenau Memorial and Museum, Oświęcim, Poland, 26 January 2024.

Auschwitz-Birkenau (Chapters Seven and Eight)

Czech, Danuta. *Auschwitz Chronicle, 1939–1945*. New York, NY: H. Holt, 1997. Held at the Wiener Holocaust Library. Accessed 30 January 2024.

Tomza-Michalska, Marcelina. In-person interview. Oświęcim, Poland, 25–26 January 2024.

Tour of Auschwitz-Birkenau. Auschwitz-Birkenau, Oświęcim, Poland, 25–26 January 2024. https://www.auschwitz.org/en/

SOURCES AND BIBLIOGRAPHY

Visit to Imperial War Museum Sound Archives, Research Rooms. Imperial War Museum, London, United Kingdom, 1 and 12 December 2023.

Winstone, Martin. *The Dark Heart of Hitler's Europe*. London: Bloomsbury, 2021.

Wontor-Cichy, Dr Teresa. In-person interview. Historian at the Auschwitz-Birkenau Memorial and Museum, Oświęcim, Poland, 26 January 2024.

Hamburg (Chapters Nine and Ten)

Bergen-Belsen Archives. Testimony of Renee Salt. Interview conducted by Karin Theilen, Bergen-Belsen Memorial, 13 June 2002. Interview number BV 14. Accessed 15 May 2024.

Dean, Martin, ed. *The United States Holocaust Memorial Museum: Encyclopedia of Camps and Ghettos, 1933–1945*, Volume II. Bloomington, IN: Indiana University Press, 2012. Chapter on Hamburg-Sasel. Held at the Wiener Holocaust Library.

Eckel, Christine. Interview. Historian from the Neuengamme Concentration Camp Memorial. Hamburg, Germany, 13 May 2024. https://www.kz-gedenkstaette-neuengamme.de/en/

Hastings, Max. *Bomber Command*. London: Pan Books, 2010.

KZ-Gedenkstätte Neuengamme, ed. *Die Gedenkstätte Plattenhaus Poppenbüttel – Die Verfolgung von Frauen im nationalsozialistischen Hamburg und die Erinnerung an die Opfer*. Edited by Karin Schawe. Translated by Casey Sennett. Hamburg: Neuengamme Concentration Camp Memorial, 2014.

Polat, Güven. Interview. Representative of the Lagerhaus G Heritage Foundation, accompanied walking tour of the warehouse heritage site, 13 May 2024.

Walking tour of Poppenbüttel. Site of Hamburg-Sasel

SOURCES AND BIBLIOGRAPHY

Concentration Camp, site of the slaughterhouse and Hamburg dock, 13 May 2024.

Bergen-Belsen (Chapters Eleven to Thirteen)

Bergen-Belsen Archives. Testimony of Renee Salt. Interview conducted by Karin Theilen, Bergen-Belsen Memorial, June 13, 2002. Accessed May 15, 2024.

Davidson, Ian Reginald. Interview with the Imperial War Museum in London, United Kingdom. Catalogue number 9309. Interview by Conrad Wood. IWM (Production Company), 6 November 1986. Accessed during in-person visit, 1 and 12 December 2023.

Dean, Martin, ed. *The United States Holocaust Memorial Museum: Encyclopedia of Camps and Ghettos, 1933–1945*, Volume II. Bloomington, IN: Indiana University Press, 2012. Chapters on Bergen-Belsen. Held at the Wiener Holocaust Library.

Guided visit to Bergen-Belsen Memorial and Exhibition. Led by official tour guide Susanne Seitz, 14–15 May 2024. https://bergen-belsen.stiftung-ng.de

Hardman, Reverend Leslie. Interview with the Imperial War Museum, London, United Kingdom. Conducted by Lyn Smith on 22 September 1997. Catalogue number 17636. IWM (Production company). Accessed 29 November 2023.

Imperial War Museum, London, United Kingdom. *War Office Second World War Official Collection: Photographic Images of the Liberation*. Catalogue number BU9710. Accessed during in-person visit, 29–30 November 2023.

Kersh, Mervyn. In-person interview at his home in London, United Kingdom. 17 December 2023.

Le Druillenec, Harold. 'Quote from Harold Le Druillenec'. https://www.frankfallaarchive.org/people/harold-le-druillenec/

SOURCES AND BIBLIOGRAPHY

Salt, Charles. Interview with Karin Theilen, Bergen-Belsen Memorial, 13 June 2002. Interview number BV 3. Accessed during in-person visit to Bergen-Belsen Archives, 15 May 2024.

Salt, Charles. Interview with the Imperial War Museum, London, United Kingdom. Conducted by Lyn Smith on 4 July 1995. Catalogue number 15623. IWM (Production company). Accessed 29 November 2023.

Salt, Charles. Interview with the National Holocaust Centre and Museum. Conducted by Stephen Smith in London on 4 December 2001. Accessed via in-person visit to the centre on 7 December 2023.

Seitz, Susanne. Interview. Tour guide for the Bergen-Belsen Memorial Museum, at her home in Celle, Germany, 14–15 May 2024.

Shephard, Ben. *After Daybreak: The Liberation of Belsen, 1945*. London: Pimlico, 2006.

Tätzler, Klaus, and Katja Seybold. Interview. Research and Documentation Centre, Bergen-Belsen Memorial Museum, 15 May 2024.

Visit to the grave of Sala Berkowicz. NATO military training base, Bergen-Hohne camp, site of former displaced persons camp, 15 May 2024.

Return to Poland and Paris (Chapters Fourteen to Sixteen)

Bath, Elise. International Tracing Service Archive Manager, the Wiener Holocaust Library. Information on Gitel and Lejzer. Report provided via email, 16 May 2024.

Imperial War Museum, London, United Kingdom. Kielce Pogrom. Accessed during exhibition visit, 29 November 2023.

Salt, Charles. Interview with the Imperial War Museum, London,

SOURCES AND BIBLIOGRAPHY

United Kingdom. Catalogue number 15623. Interview by Lyn Smith. IWM (Production Company), 4 July 1995. Accessed 29 November 2023.

Yad Vashem. *Kielce Pogrom.* Accessed 10 June 2024. https://www.yadvashem.org.

Dyhouse, Carol. *Glamour: Women, History, Feminism.* London: Zed Books, 2011.

London (Chapters Seventeen to Twenty-Two)

BBC Archive. *Grandchild of the Holocaust.* Originally broadcasted in January 2005.

In-person interview with Sharon Footerman at her home in north London, on 10 January, 13 March and 30 April 2024. Interview with Martin Salt at the Wiener Holocaust Library, London, on 30 January 2024.

Interview with Scott Saunders, founder and Chairman of March of the Living UK, via Zoom, on 8 January and 19 April 2024, and in person in Hendon, London, 7 June 2024.

Petrie, Hugh. Heritage Development Officer, London Borough of Barnet. Assistance with research on Charles and Renee's deli and shared memories from past customers. Research and memories emailed, 9 February 2024.

Phone conversation with Judith Hassan (OBE), 30 August 2024. Discussion of her book, *A House Next Door to Trauma: Learning from Holocaust Survivors How to Respond to Atrocity.* London: Jessica Kingsley, 2003.

Provided by Sarah Wetton, Testimony Officer at the National Holocaust Centre and Museum, 27 April 2024. Salt, Renee. 'Return to Belsen'. *Holocaust Survivors' News*, September 1997.

Thompson, Kate. *The Stepney Doorstep Society.* London: Michael Joseph, 2018.

SOURCES AND BIBLIOGRAPHY

Visit to Jewish Care, Holocaust Survivors' Centre, 9 January 2024. Interviews with staff.

Visit to the National Holocaust Centre and Museum, Nottinghamshire, 7 December 2023. In-person interview with Sarah Wetton, Testimony Officer at the National Holocaust Centre and Museum. Follow-up Zoom conversation with Sarah Wetton, 12 March 2024.

Epilogue

Bath, Elise. Report compiled by the Wiener Holocaust Library's International Tracing Service, London. Received on 18 February 2024. Copy held by Kate Thompson and the Wiener Holocaust Library.

'Chapter on Kaufering'. In *The United States Holocaust Memorial Museum: Encyclopedia of Camps and Ghettos, 1933–1945*, Volume II, edited by Martin Dean. Bloomington, IN: Indiana University Press, 2012. Held at the Wiener Holocaust Library.

Interview with Dr Jascha März, Head of Scientific Services and Archives, Bavarian Memorial Foundation, Munich, Germany, 8 May 2024. https:// www.stiftung-bayerische-gedenkstaetten.de

Interview with Gabriele Triebel, Deputy Leader of the Bavarian Green Party, Kaufering IV Cemetery, Bavaria, Germany, 10 May 2024.

Interview with George Leitmann, via Zoom, at his home in California, United States, 9 and 30 April 2024.

Interview with Gerhard Roletscheck, Kaufering historian, Landsberg am Lech, Bavaria, Germany, 9–10 May 2024.

Interview with Helga Deiler, European Holocaust Memorial Foundation, Landsberg am Lech, Bavaria, Germany, 9–10 May 2024.

SOURCES AND BIBLIOGRAPHY

Interview with Ivor Perl, Kaufering IV survivor, at his home in London, 26 May 2024.

Salt, Renee. Interview with Karin Theilen, Bergen-Belsen Memorial, 13 June 2002. Interview number BV 14. Accessed during in-person visit to Bergen-Belsen Archives, 15 May 2024.

Visit and guided tour of Landsberg am Lech in Bavaria, Kaufering Concentration Camp VII, and Kaufering IV Camp and Cemetery, 9–10 May 2024.

Additional Notes for Sources:

Consultations with and guidance from Martin Winstone, Senior Historical Advisor to the Holocaust Educational Trust, via Zoom, on 1 March, 22 April and 23 May 2024; and via email on 11 September and various dates throughout 2024.

I found the following useful as a source: The Forever Project. The National Holocaust Centre and Museum, Nottinghamshire, United Kingdom. 1,248 questions and answers with Renee Salt about her experiences during the Holocaust, filmed in 2015. A copy is held in their archives, and a transcript was emailed to me in December 2023.

Salt, Ryvka Rachel. Interview with the Imperial War Museum, London, United Kingdom. Catalogue number 15622. Interview by Lyn Smith. IWM (Production Company), 3 July 1995. Accessed 29 November 2023.

Salt, Renee. Interview with Karin Theilen, Bergen-Belsen Memorial, 13 June 2002. Accessed during in-person visit to Bergen-Belsen archives, 15 May 2024.

Salt, Renee. 'The Girls': A Documentary Oral History Project. Interview by Katherine Klinger. Filmed on 15 May 2007. Video held at the Wiener Holocaust Library. Accessed 15 November 2023.

SOURCES AND BIBLIOGRAPHY

I found Yad Vashem – The World Holocaust Remembrance Center online resource to be extremely helpful. https://www.yadvashem.org/index.html

In addition, I have read and can recommend for further reading:

Eger, Edith. *The Choice.* London: Ebury Publishing, 2017.

Eichengreen, Lucille, with Harriet Hyman Chamberlain. *From Ashes to Life: My Memories of the Holocaust.* San Francisco, CA: Mercury House, 1994.

Eisenstein, Bernice, Robert Jan van Pelt, and Eric Beck Rubin. *Memory Unearthed: The Łódź Ghetto Photographs of Henryk Ross.* Edited by Maia-Mari Sutnik. New Haven, CT: Yale University Press, 2015.

Hersh, Arek. *A Detail of History.* Quill Press in association with the National Holocaust Centre and Museum, 1998.

Holden, Wendy. *Born Survivors.* London: Sphere, 2015.

Kraus, Dita. *A Delayed Life.* London: Ebury, 2020.

Lasker-Wallfisch, Anita. *Inherit the Truth. 1939–1945.* London: Giles de la Mare, 1996.

Levi, Primo. *If This Is a Man and The Truce.* London: Penguin Books, 1979.

Perl, Ivor. *Chicken Soup under the Tree: A Journey to Hell and Back.* London: Lemon Soul, 2023.

Saunders, Scott. 'How Did Survivors of the Holocaust Rebuild Jewish Identity in German DP Camps after the War?' PhD dissertation, 2014.

Stone, Dan. *The Holocaust: An Unfinished History.* London: Pelican Books, 2023.

Wiesel, Elie. *Night.* Translated from the French by Marion Wiesel. New York, NY: Hill & Wang, 2006, recorded books.

SOURCES AND BIBLIOGRAPHY

Winstone, Martin. *The Holocaust Sites of Europe.* Third edition. London: Bloomsbury, 2024.

Picture Credits

All images are courtesy of the author, except for those appearing on the following pages:

p.9   © Maidun Collection / Alamy
p.44 © CBW / Alamy
p.82 Photo from 'The Auschwitz Album: The Story of Transport', Yad Vashem, Auschwitz-Birkenau Memorial and Museum 2002 / Alamy
p.92 © Michael Grubka / Alamy
p.100 © Niday Picture Library / Alamy
p.103 © Trinity Mirror / Mirrorpix / Alamy
p.121 © Associated Press / Alamy
p.128 © Associated Press / Alamy
p.139 © Vintage_Space / Alamy
p.146 © piemags / ww2archive / Alamy
p.197 © Martin Salt
p.198 © Martin Salt
p.227 © Martin Salt
p.235 © Toby Melville / Pool / AFP via Getty Images
p.242 © Getty Images
p.245 © Kate Thompson
p.248 © Kate Thompson
p.257 Reproduced by kind permission of George Leitmann
p.266 © Ellie Olmer